CONQUEROR OF THE WORLD

Les grands pays muets longuement s'étendront—A. de Vigny

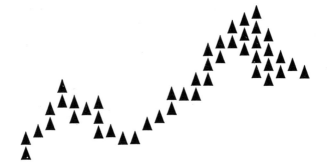

RENÉ GROUSSET

CONQUEROR
OF THE WORLD

THE LIFE OF CHINGIS-KHAN

Translated from the French by Marian McKellar and Denis Sinor
With Introduction, Notes and Bibliography by Denis Sinor

NEW YORK   *THE VIKING PRESS*

To the memory of
ANATOLE LEWITZKY,
attaché at the Musée de l'Homme,
who died for France
at Mont Valérien
23 February 1942,

this book, which owes so much to
his scholarship and friendship, is
dedicated.

R.G.

Contents

Introduction

The aims of this introduction are as follows: First, I should like to introduce René Grousset, as many of those who will pursue this book and will want to read others written by him may wish to know something about this exceptional historian. Second, I will try to assign a place to this biography of Chingis-khan in the whole oeuvre of Grousset. Last, I will elaborate on the principles that guided us in preparing the English edition of this work.

René Grousset (1885-1952) was a Frenchman. No short sentence could characterize him any better, for this one gives the essence of his whole being. He was French by birth, by education, by civilization, by conviction. He was French when in 1915, leading his soldiers to the attack he was grievously wounded. He was French in his lucidity, the elegance of his style, his deeply felt Christianity, which was Catholic, i.e. universal, embracing the whole of humanity. Here lies the solution to the apparent puzzle of a man, deeply embedded in the civilization of his own country, yet who spent his life trying to understand other civilizations—spent his life in the service of international understanding in the narrowest sense of this word. At a time when it was not as fashionable as it is now, in all his works he proclaimed the inherent values of civilizations that differ from our own.[1] His first work, a three-volume history of Asia written before the First World War and published in 1922, was a pioneer work

---

[1] Much interesting and often moving information about Grousset, including a bibliography, can be found in No. 88-89, Septembre-Octobre 1953 of *France-Asie. Revue mensuelle de culture et de synthèse franco-asiatique,* published in Saigon.

in more than one respect. Grousset brought equal understanding to any aspect of any of the non-Western civilizations, to the history of the Far East (1929), or, more specially, to the history of China (1942), to Indian philosophy (1931), to Buddhism (1929), and even to the history of Armenia (1948). Grousset's monumental *Histoire des croisades et du Royaume Franc de Jérusalem* (I-III, 1934-36), and his *L'empire du Levant, Histoire de la question d'Orient* (2nd ed. 1949), both packed with facts, show an unsurpassed mastery of the complicated interaction of various civilizations.

Grousset's approach was not limited to one discipline, his interest was not focused on one aspect rather than another of any civilization. His integration of art history in the greater stream of history is, in itself, an achievement of great importance.

Grousset had extraordinary gifts alike of analysis and synthesis. In a mass of facts he could pick out those that were essential and group them in a synthesis that was basically new. He was no compiler in the conventional meaning of this word. For him "vulgarization"—popularizing shall we say?—did not consist in degrading the results of historical research to the lowest common intellectual denominator of the reading public. For him, it meant the art of presenting the dry facts in a way that even the most fastidious reader, even the expert should find therein food for thought. Grousset differs vastly from most other scholars who attempted great historical syntheses by his almost unbelievable command of facts. To be sure, as all of us, he made mistakes, but as a rule, his facts were accurate. One may disagree with his interpretation but not with the basis on which it rests. Grousset's capacity for work was prodigious but, beyond that, he had a very unusual method of securing accurate information: he interrogated his colleagues. In this he was well served by the circumstances. It is difficult to recall the splendor that was Parisian orientalism in the interwar years. To mention only those who are dead now, there were Maspero, Granet, Sylvain Lévy, Massignon, Masson-Oursel, Przyluski, Hackin and so many others in addition to the towering, almost superhuman figure of Paul Pelliot. Collaboration between him and Grousset had been very close. There was nothing official about it and the pattern was fairly simple: Grousset asked the questions and Pelliot answered them, as he always answered all the questions asked him. But Grousset was more assiduous, he asked them more often, with greater perspicacity, and he diligently noted down the answers in a tiny note-book with a microscopic hand. This note-book—all knew it. There was no way of avoiding it. At any meeting, any party, any lecture Grousset extracted it from his pocket. Even the younger generation, like myself, could not escape. I will never forget Grousset in his black jacket which he wore with striped trousers appearing, as he invariably did, at all the parties, cocktails and other social occasions, smiling, saying kind words to everyone and then steering straight to some specialist, with a direct, precise question. The answer was immediately noted down and Grousset sailed away in search of other facts. . . . He never denied his indebtedness to others. In Grousset's *L'empire mongol,* published in 1941 during the German occupation of France, there are scores of references to the opinions of a mysterious G.B. These were those of Willi Baruch, then in hiding, whom Grousset, for very good reasons, did not wish to name. But he just could not bring himself to omit credit where credit was due.

It seems to have been Grousset's method first to give a general birds-eye view of the history of an area and leave the examination of limited subjects for later. I have mentioned how he started on his career with a history of Asia. *L'empire des steppes* is not only more mature and better documented, but also a work more limited in scope. But once it had been written, Grousset embarked on a number of monographs designed to give more detailed treatment to some of the subjects covered therein. Thus in 1941 he published his *L'empire mongol, Ière phase,* and in 1944, *Le conquerant du monde,—Vie de Gengis-Khan,* the English translation of which is here presented.

Grousset was fascinated by "great men." No hero-worshiper, he firmly believed—as did many other eminent historians—that individuals could have decisive influence on the course of history. His book *Figures de proue* (1949) is a product of this belief. It is thus not surprising that having traced the lines of the history of Central Eurasia in general and later of the Mongols in particular, Grousset should have concentrated on the life of the man who transformed a little-known, hungry, persecuted tribe of Central Asia into one of the greatest powers the world has ever known.

As I have said, Grousset's *L'empire des steppes* is a work of exceptional scope and value. No other work encompasses as accurately as much of the multifaceted history of Central Eurasia. But for considerations of proportion, Mongol history could not receive full treatment within the framework of this book. Thus Grousset produced *L'empire mongol, 1ère phase,* one of his weakest works, written in 1939 and printed in very difficult circumstances. Grousset was in Paris, occupied by the Germans; the book was printed in Toulouse, then still "free-zone," with correspondence between the two limited to open postcards of a special type. I vividly remember Grousset's anxiety with proofs not forthcoming and author's corrections impossible. These and other circumstances may explain the fact that the *remarques et références* are relegated to pp. 395-559 with no reference to them in the text—an arrangement which makes the reading of this book an agonizing experience. The footnotes in the body of the book together with *remarques et références* constitute about one third of the text.[2] In addition for his *L'empire mongol,* Grousset had to rely on the old (1866) Russian translation made by Palladius of the Chinese version of the *Secret History of the Mongols.* Grousset knew no Russian, so the original Mongol text reached him through three translations. Grousset was very unsatisfied with this work.

For his life of Chingis, Grousset could avail himself of welcome if not unexpected help from Erich Haenisch who, in 1941, published his complete translation of the *Secret History.* Herein lies one of the principal merits of *Conqueror of the World.* None of the previous biographers of Chingis—and there are many—had access to the *Secret History* which remains by far the most authoritative source on the subject. With his customary generosity, Grousset wrote an "historical introduction" to the French translation of Vladimirtsov's biography of Chingis,[3] published four years after *Conqueror.* This introduction, basically a rehash of an article *État actuel des études sur l'histoire gengiskhanide* (1941),[4] is worth reading as it sheds valuable light on Grousset's sources for his own biography and on his method of work.

---

[2] It should be noted that the "Appendice" pp. 359-390 was not written by Grousset, but by Eugene Cavaignac, editor of the *Histoire du monde* of which this work was vol. VIII.3.

[3] No. 39. (Numbers refer to Bibliography).

[4] Bulletin du Comité international des Sciences historiques. No. 46, Juin 1941, pp. 22-40.

Conqueror of the World was written for a wide public by an expert in Mongol history: herein lies its uniqueness. Whatever the merits of a great popularizer, such as Harold Lamb, who did more than anyone else to make Chingis's name known to a wider public, his facts cannot be trusted. This is not the case of Grousset. Behind each of his sentences, however "literary," however evocative, lie years of hard work and a thorough knowledge of the smallest details of Mongol history. As his biography of Chingis-khan was intended for the non-expert, educated public, he did not include in the form of footnotes the whole apparatus that would have burdened the text. Even so, here and there, he could not resist introducing some remarks for the specialist.

In his introduction to Vladimirtsov's biography of Chingis, Grousset laments the inaccessibility of Juwaini's work—the most important Persian source of Mongol history. Grousset did not live to see the publication of Boyle's excellent translation,[5] nor could he make use of the material included in the *Cheng-wu ts'in-tcheng lu*.[6] But it can be said that all this material, known to Grousset only in a fragmentary way, does not alter in any substantial way the picture we have of Chingis-khan— a picture which, in all probability, is almost definitive. This is why, twenty years after its publication and for many years to come, *Conqueror of the World* is and will remain the standard work on Chingis.

The task of the translators was far from easy. Perhaps as much as a quarter of the text consists of almost verbatim quotations from the sources: *Secret History, Juvaini,* etc. Instead of translating into English quotations embedded in Grousset's text, we rather adopted, where they existed, up-to-date, scholarly translations of the sources made directly into English by scholars such as Waley, Boyle and Krueger. Such quotations are always acknowledged but this does not mean that all the paraphrases of Grousset were always traced back to their sources. As Grousset did not give references, the tracing of all his quotations would have involved months of research, with very little benefit to the reader. For, as long as they do not lead to the distortion of historical facts, these quotations by Grousset are intended to evoke the times rather than to give accurate translations of the original. Thus, very often, we simply

[5] No. 7.
[6] No. 9.

translated into English Grousset's French—eliminating the quotation marks where it seemed to us that Grousset's text was more a paraphrase than a translation of the text as it is known to us today. In a great number of instances Grousset's quotations from the *Secret History of the Mongols* were brought closer to the original, but no claim is made for strict philological accuracy. The quotation marks in Grousset's original text (with no reference given to the original of the passage quoted) are simply meant to make the reader aware of the fact that he is reading contemporary evidence and not Grousset's own words.

All the proper names are given in a transcription that is in conformity with English usage. It must, however, be remembered that in a very great number of cases we simply do not know what the pronunciation of the original was. In spite of vigilant care some inconsistencies may have remained in the transcriptions. They are of no consequence, as often one is almost tempted to toss a coin to decide on which transcription to adopt. As a rule, a conventional anglicized transcription was used throughout. The transcription of Chinese names is based on the conventional Wade system, but many names familiar to the average reader were left in the customary form used in newspapers, etc.—*e.g.,* Peking.

The problem was more difficult with names pertaining to the Islamic world, but, here again, the reader will have no difficulty in finding, on a good map, the place-names mentioned in our text.

The transcription of the Mongol proper names and other words used in the text was anglicized so far as it could be done without completely distorting the originals.

We adopted the form *Chingis* to transcribe the name of the hero of this book. There is a very simple reason for doing so: this is the correct form. It has been used quite consistently by experts, past and present, writing in English. In recent years, via Hollywood, the spelling *Gengis,* the traditional French form, gained some popularity. We feel it would be a pity if it ousted the correct English spelling adopted in this book.

Many of Grousset's original footnotes have not only lost their usefulness but have become misleading. In some of them he referred to problems since solved, in others he quoted publications, or even papers read at the Société asiatique, which since then have been respectively superseded by more detailed works or published in articles. Thus we simply deleted those of the footnotes that have become obsolete, brought others up to date and, finally, added a few new ones—these being marked with square brackets.

It must, however, be said most emphatically, that we have not re-written Grousset's work. We assume no responsibility for his views, or for the facts he quotes. They are his alone, and so are this work's great merits.

A word of the division of labor between the two of us may not be superfluous. The translation as such was done entirely by Marian Mc-Kellar; my own contribution was limited to the re-reading of the translation, transcription of proper names, etc. For any alterations in Grousset's text such as referred to (changes in footnotes, comparison of Grousset's translations with the originals, etc.) I am solely responsible.

Extraordinary misfortune presided over the preparation of this English version. We accepted the assignment when I was still in Cambridge. My move to Indiana University not only caused the disruption normally connected with a change of residence, but also entailed our having to rely on correspondence for the solving of many problems presented by the translation. A series of singularly inept typists spoiled two manuscripts, and my very heavy administrative responsibilities prevented me from devoting as much time to this work as was needed for a speedy publication. All these difficulties were met with an exceptional understanding and patience by the British publishers Oliver and Boyd. The reader will judge the quality of Marian McKellar's translation; I would simply say that it has been a very real pleasure to work with her. My wife Irene made a heroic effort to eradicate most of the mistakes made by the typists. Finally, thanks are due to those authors and publishers who allowed verbatim quotations to be made from the works on which they have the copyright.

Denis Sinor

Indiana University
April 1965

Part

The Ancestors

The Sons of the Grey Wolf
and the Tawny Doe

The setting of this wild story is country flaunting some of the most striking contrasts in all Upper Asia. In the north, great mountain chains—Altay, Sayan, Khangay, Yablonovy, Khingan—rear their 6,000 feet and
more: wooded massifs in essence extensions of the immense, impenetrable Siberian *tayga,* and still for the most part turning the same front of
sturdy larches, "patient under the cold," to the flaying north wind, with
pines on their southern faces. This subalpine flora climbs to 6,300, even
to 7,300 feet. Below it, cedars carpet humid slopes and valley hollows.
Below these again come poplars, birches, willows, that then push out
down along the river courses into the heart of the steppe.

There is pasture—particularly lush pasture—way up in the alpine
zone, at the very foot of the mountains. Then as one moves south, in the
face of the wind from the Gobi, subalpine meadowland gives way to a
steppe-type vegetation—mainly clematis, liliaceae, *absinth,* or couch
grass (this last much appreciated by livestock) according to soil. In
spring, the steppe stretches as far as the eye can see, one vast carpet of
green, hymned by every Mongol bard. In June, it is a rash of many-
colored flowers. Till, come mid-July, a furnace heat shrivels all this vegetation, scorches the plains to a drear, unrelieved yellow.

So the "smile of the steppe" is short-lived. "Already by October it is
winter, with swirling snow. By November ice has the water courses prisoner, in a grip not to be released till April." Through these months Mongol territory is an annex of Siberia. The second fortnight in July, torrid
heat turns it into an annex of the Asiatic Saharas. "The steppe shimmers

in the sun; noon each day breaks into frenzied storm." [1] Temperature oscillations are truly formidable: at Ulan Bator, the present Mongolian capital, the range is from a winter —45° Fahrenheit to +101° Fahrenheit in summer. As if that were not enough, mountain and steppe are swept regardless of season by winds that can almost lift a rider from his saddle. If the Mongols became the iron race of the Ancient World, it was because they were forged in the harshest of existences, hammered out by their brutal climate on the anvil of their land of sharp excesses, of extremes adaptable to only those organisms tough and resilient enough not to succumb to them forthwith. Of such caliber were these forest-living hunters, these pastoral nomads—hunters at the edge of the *tayga,* herdsmen on the approaches of the steppe. You can see it to look at them— men of "basic faces," flat with jutting cheekbones, weathered-complexioned and eagle-eyed, seemingly iron-chested, massive of torso, knotty of trunk, bowlegged from a life constantly in the saddle. The same goes for their little shaggy, stunted horses, rough-hewn and resistant as themselves. Here were horse and rider custom-built to brave storms of snow or of burning sand, scale the alpine massifs of the north with their impenetrable forests, endure in the south through the waterless wastes of the Gobi, pit their speed anywhere against the totem animals of steppe and forests, the maral and the wolf.

The stag and the wolf! They figure in the hundreds, these two, in the curious animal-motif bronze plaques or statuettes that from the Minussinsk region, in the heart of Siberia, to the loop of the Ordos, on the Chinese frontier, from perhaps the seventh century B.C. right through into the Middle Ages, represent *par excellence* the art of the peoples of Upper Asia. The Mongol legend (like the Turkish, whence it doubtless hails) sees in them, indeed, the very ancestors of the race. Forth from the legendary cave of Erkene-qon (to be thought of as lying to the north, toward the forest-covered mountain chains, since there the Mongols originally dwelt, only later moving down out on to the steppe) comes the Grey, or rather Grey-Blue Wolf (Börtechino). The great ancestral wolf meets his future consort, the Tawny Doe (Qo'a-maral), and the course they take together brings them into the heart of what is to be Mongol country. From the shores of Lake Baykal—for the bard of the Chingis-

---

[1] Mongolian summer and winter rainfall are violently disproportionate: of the annual total, 75% falls in summer; the winter figure is 2% to 3%, or even less.

khan era, "the sea" (*tenggis*)—they come to settle at the source of the river Onon, by the sacred mountain of Burqan-qaldun, by the massif that is known today as that of the Kentey. Holy places if ever there were any. From out of the thick pine forests at its base the Kentey rears to 9,300 feet the gneiss and granite blocks of its flat summits and bare cupolas, home of the god of the blue sky—Kökö Tengri—supreme deity of the Mongols. Here it was, indeed, that Chingis-khan was to come, at crucial moments in his career, climbing the sacred mountain to place himself under the protection of the heavenly powers.

The Kentey does indeed seem to preside over the destinies of the Mongol country, whose two zones it demarcates: to the north of it, as we have seen, the forest zone, simply an extension of the *tayga,* and, south, the steppes, heralding the bare expanses of the Gobi. The Onon, by the headwaters of which the Wolf and the Doe called a halt, is a river of transition, running in its uppermost reaches through the *tayga,* then turning into a typical river of the dry steppe; moving sluggishly over clay and sand, now a trickle, now full to overflowing, each bank a border of rich pasture. Here in this predestined country the Grey Wolf and the Tawny Doe lay together. From their son Batachiqan was to spring the family of the Chingisids.

The genealogy that follows, dry as any in the Bible, yields only names, though they are ones that gleam for us sometimes with strangely reflected light. There is Yeke-nidü, or "Big-Eye," a sort of Cyclops—his story otherwise shrouded in obscurity. A few generations down we seem to mesh again with reality. Torgholjin the Rich (*bayan*) sires Dua the Blind (*soqor*), that is, the One-Eyed and Dobun the Sagacious (*mergen*). It was the latter who was to perpetuate the line. One day when the two brothers had climbed Burqan-qaldun—Mount Kentey—they saw, over toward the Tönggelik, a small right-bank tributary of the Orkhon, marked on our maps as the Qara, "the black river," a band of people on the move. The One-Eyed told his younger brother: "Among these people, going before a black chariot, I see a very pretty young woman. If she is not already bound over to a husband, I shall ask for her, brother Dobun, for you." The young woman was called Alan-qo'a, "Alan the fair." She was of good stock, belonging to the forest-dwelling tribe of the Qori-Tümet who lived by fur-hunting on the western shore of Lake Baykal. Her father, Qorilartay-Mergen, had quarreled with his family, and had left his native forests, with their thickets full of martens and sables, to seek his fortune, also, in the protective shade of Mount Burqan-qaldun. This request for his daughter must have come for him as a fine opportunity to get himself accepted by the people of this country. He gave his consent, and Dobun the Sagacious married Alan the Fair.

2

The Heavenly Visitor

These traditions are interesting because they confirm that, like the great
ancestral wolf, the early Mongols were in fact forest-dwelling hunters,
or, at most, a people of the forest-pasture borderland. Significantly, the
Mongol bard when he treats of mythical times speaks only of hunting,
never of stock-raising. So it was with Dobun the Sagacious. After his
marriage with Alan the Fair, one day when he was out hunting on Mount
Toghochaq he came on a man of the Uriyangqay tribe who had just
brought down a three-year-old stag. The man was roasting the entrails
when Dobun called to him: "Friend," he cried bluntly, "give me some of
that meat." So commanded, the man obeyed. Life for these savages must
have been made up of such unwelcome encounters, in which the law of
the steppe prescribed submission, especially when the newcomer appeared to have the advantage in both weapons and strength. Keeping for
himself only breast and hide, the hunter relinquished to Dobun all the
rest of his kill.[1]

Dobun set off with the bag he had got on such easy terms, and on the
way met a poor man of the Baya'ut tribe, who was leading his small son
by the hand. The poor creature could scarcely stand for hunger. "Give
me some of your game," he beseeched Dobun, "and I will give you my
son." The bargain seemed a good one. The Sagacious One handed the
suppliant a haunch of venison, and took the child off to his *yurt* to be his
servant.

---

[1] The first episode in this chapter bears a relation to the Mongol custom known as
that of the *shiralgha,* according to which any man, meeting a hunter who had just
made a kill, might claim a portion, provided the animal had not yet been carved.
The law of the steppe thus took on the aspect of a gesture of comradeship in a community of hunters. Cf. Paul Pelliot, Sirolγa-širalγa, (T'oung-pao, XXXVII, 1944,
pp. 102-113).

It is not impossible that this young man, bought for a portion of venison, was the ancestor of Chingis-khan. Disturbing things were now in fact to happen in the house of Dobun. He had had two children by the Fair Alan when he died. Then, after his death, behold the Fair one bore three sons more. Seeing which, runs on the Mongol bard ingenuously, the two elder sons—Dobun's—began to murmur: "See, our mother, being without a husband, has yet brought into the world these three further sons. But in her *yurt* has been no other man than the Baya'ut. The three children might well be his. . . ."

Such indeed was the very human explanation of these surprising facts. But there was a factor such hasty conclusions left out of account: the intervention of heaven—of the *Tengri,* in person—anxious, as we know today, to ensure the ascendancy of the hero. This the dowager Alan herself disclosed to her elder sons. One autumn day, she brought them together with their three younger brothers at a family festivity (she had roasted a yearling lamb). And she explained the mystery she had till then kept secret: "Each night, a resplendent being, the color of gold, came down through the air hole of my *yurt,* and he caressed my belly and a ray of light from him entered my womb. Then he would depart on a moonbeam or a ray of sunlight. He was like a yellow dog. Let us have an end, then, my two firstborn, to ill-judged talk. For beyond doubt your three brothers are the sons of *Tengri* himself. Would you speak of them as of ordinary mortals?" And, in a cloudy phrase, the great dowager prophesied, it seemed, that the children of these children, sons of miracle, would be one day conquerors of the world. . . .

At the same time Alan-qo'a had given to each of her sons an arrow, and invited him to break it, which all of them did without difficulty. She handed them then another five arrows, tied up in a bundle, and the bundle none of them could break. Now she pointed the moral: "Oh my five sons, let division come between you, and you will be broken one after another as you broke each separate arrow. Stay but bound together as the arrows in the bundle, and who will ever be able to break you?"

△
△△
———————

3

The Gest of Bodonchar

After the death of the great dowager, her five sons portioned out among themselves her herds—the nomad's principal wealth. Or rather, the four eldest took almost all for themselves, leaving the youngest, Bodonchar the Simple (*mungqaq*), nothing, "because of his simpleness and weakness."

Here begins, in the recital of the Mongol bard, the Gest of Bodonchar —curious sequel to the tale of the Wolf and the Doe, and that of the divine bastardy, bringing us from heaven down to earth to follow the wretched life of a marauder of the steppe. Bodonchar the Simple finally realized that in the eyes of his family he was of no account. He decided to leave them, to strike out for himself. He took a poor horse, "a white one with a black blaze, with most of its tail missing, and a scarred back," and launched into open country. He did not delude himself that with such a nag, miles from anywhere in the steppe, his fate was anything but precarious: "If my horse holds out, I shall survive. If not, I perish." He traveled down the valley of the Onon. Opposite the island of Baljun-Aral ("the miry island"), he built himself a wretched thatch hut. Nearby, he saw a female goshawk—of the kind that hunts flying almost at ground level—busy devouring a black chicken of the steppe. "With hairs from the mane of his horse he made a noose and captured the goshawk." He tamed the bird of prey and trained it to kill small game. In the spring, when the wild geese and duck came down in the thousands on the waters of the Onon, he starved his goshawk, then sent it among them, and for long weeks at a time both of them had meat in abundance. When the game did run short, Bodonchar, like Mowgli, joined the packs of wolves that drove roe deer, stags, antelopes, or *dziggetais* to the Onon

bank. "He watched the prey that the wolves had driven back and surrounded on the incline; he shot it with his arrows, and shared it with
them. What the wolves left made a meal for himself and his goshawk."

The harsh existence of the Mongol Mowgli was disturbed by fresh
incomers. A band from the basin of the Tönggelik (undoubtedly, as we
have seen, the present Qara, tributary of the Orkhon, north of Ulan
Bator), arrived and halted in the region. The Simple One got on at first
well enough with them. Each day, after hunting with his goshawk, he
would come to them to beg mare's milk, which was not withheld. But the
way of all these folk was withdrawn and wary. Neither Bodonchar nor his
neighbors asked indiscreet questions about the other's race or origins, and
at evening he withdrew prudently to his hut.

Meantime, however, the eldest of Bodonchar's brothers, Buqu-qatagi
("the powerful stag"), began to make inquiries as to what had become
of him. From the description given, the people of the neighbor tribe recognized their man. "He whom you seek," they said to Buqu, "lives
beside us. Each day he comes to us to drink mare's milk, but where he
goes at night we do not know. When the wind blows from the northwest,
the feathers of the wild geese brought down by his goshawk fly over to
here like flakes from a snowstorm. But you will not have to wait to see
him: this is his time." And indeed Bodonchar was even then approaching. He and Buqu recognized each other, and they went away together
along the Onon. As they rode, Bodonchar thrice remarked enigmati-
cally: "It is good that the body should have a head and the suit a collar."
When his brother asked the meaning of this riddle, he explained: the
tribe alongside which he had been living made do without chiefs, in a
state of anarchy: "They make no distinction between head and shoe, all
are equal." And regardless of the fact that these people, by giving him
daily milk, had saved his life, Bodonchar, pure steppe brigand, added:
"Things being thus, it would not be difficult to surprise them and lay hold
of their goods." Buqu, delighted with this windfall, took the exile back
with him to the family camp, where the three other brothers likewise
applauded the idea. All jumped to their horses, and set off at a gallop to
Bodonchar's hut, Bodonchar in the lead to guide them. On the way, they
captured a pregnant young woman, whom they forced to tell them more
about the tribe in question, generically a section of the Jarchi'ut. The
surprise was complete. "They fell on them," the Mongol bard tells glee-

fully, "they seized their herds and their provisions, they took their families into slavery."

The episode shows up these savage mores in their true raw light. Bodonchar the Simple, but recently humiliated by his brothers, forced to go into exile because of his weakness, is now rehabilitated and honored by them, precisely because he has repaid with blackest treachery the too trusting hospitality of the Jarchi'ut. More: in the story as the Chingiskhanid bard tells it, this deed, at bottom felony, constitutes his main claim to glory. A phrase of Bodonchar's own, indeed, focuses for us the ineluctable laws of the life of the steppe, so close to the law of the jungle: "The tribe of the Jarchi'ut is easy to strike down because it has no chiefs." Chieftains in war, leaders of men, organizers born—this was what Bodonchar's descendants were to prove themselves, in amazing measure; this was to earn them their conquest of the world. To that end, however, they had first to do as the dowager Alan had counseled, make one sheaf of the Mongol arrows, unite the tribes.

▲
▲▲

4

Misery and Grandeur of the Nomads

This reuniting of the tribes, one day to be achieved by Chingis-khan, was several times embarked on by his forebears. Several times, it seemed indeed to have been acomplished, only shortly after to break up again, with a reversion to the old clan fragmentation, the bitter feuds, the anarchy and impotence. There could then be no more unhappy situation than that of the descendants of the Wolf and the Doe.

Bodonchar's grandson, Menen-tudun, died while still a comparatively young man, leaving his wife Nomolun with seven sons, whom the genealogists are at pains to list for us, from the eldest, Qachi-kulug ("Qachi the Hero"), to the youngest, Nachin-ba'atur ("Nachin the Brave").[1] The forceful Nomolun remained the head of the tribe, personification of these *qatuns,* the Mongol princesses who in times of interregnum laid such able, virile hold of the tribal *tuq,* the flag made of a pole decked with stallion or yak tails. About this time, Mongolia experienced a sudden jostling of tribes, caused by an incursion of the Jurchets, a Tunguz people from the Manchurian forest, then in another quarter in process of making themselves masters of Northern China. The Jurchets attacked the Jalair tribe, a group, possibly of Turkish extraction, settled on the banks of the Kerülen, and wrought great carnage among them. Seventy Jalair families fled in the direction of the upper Onon, toward the grazing grounds of the Mongols, then ruled by the dowager Nomolun. Driven by hunger, the emigrants came seeking roots in the grassland where the Mongols exercised their horses. This Nomolun determined to prevent.

[1] According to the Persian historian Rashid-ed-Din, the Lady Nomolun (whom he calls Monolun) is Qachi-külüg's mother. In the *Secret History of the Mongols,* ¶ 46, she is Qachi-külüg's wife.

She drove her chariot against the Jalairs, and, in her anger, wounded several. They retaliated by driving off her herds of horses. This was war. The sons of Nomolun rushed into the fray without so much as putting on their armor of boiled leather. The dowager, anxious now at the turn things were taking, commanded her daughters-in-law to take their armor to them forthwith, but by the time they reached them with it six of them had been slain. Then the Jalairs killed Nomolun herself. Of all the family there remained only the seventh son, Nachin the Brave, who had married a girl of the country of Barghuchin, and settled there, and a child, Qaydu, son of Qachi-külüg, offshoot, that is, of the senior branch of the family.

The land of Barghu, "Barghuchin," where Nachin had married, lay along the eastern shore of Lake Baykal, and more specifically the longitudinal valley of the river of the same name, separated from the lake by a coastal range 4,000 to 4,600 feet high, thickly forested. When news reached him of the massacre of his family, Nachin set out posthaste from Barghu for the familiar territory along the upper Onon. But there was nothing to be done. He found only a few aged women the Jalairs had not bothered with, and his nephew, the child Qaydu, whom they managed to save by hiding him in time behind a pile of firewood or under a milk jar.

Nachin the Brave, man of feeling, burned to avenge his family; good Mongol, to snatch back the horses—the nomads' primary wealth—which the aggressors had seized. But he had no horse. Luckily one chestnut had escaped from the Jalair camp and made its way back to its native ground. Nachin bestrode it and headed toward the enemy *yurts,* by the river Kerülen. "First he met two horsemen, riding a certain space apart, each with a falcon or a goshawk at his wrist. The birds of prey he recognized at once as having formerly belonged to his brothers." He accosted the younger of the riders and inquired if he had not seen a brown stallion moving eastward at the head of a herd of horses. They entered into conversation. Then Nachin, on a bend of a winding path along the Kerülen, suddenly stabbed this traveling companion. With astonishing coolness, he tied horse and falcon to the corpse, then went calmly toward the remaining huntsman. The latter, who from a distance had not been able to make out clearly what was happening, asked why the first rider stayed lying on the ground so long. Nachin beguiled him with some explanation or other; then, picking his time, killed this man also. Further on, he saw several hundred horses grazing in a valley, watched over by a few youths. No doubt about it: it was his family's herd! He climbed a rise, scanned the horizon carefully: not an armed body of any kind. The enemy, sure of their victory, had turned attention to their normal affairs elsewhere. Nachin swooped down on the young herdsmen, killed them, and drove the horses back to the family grazing grounds, making a joyful entry with his brothers' falcons at his wrist. But fearing that the Jalairs might return to the attack, he gathered his nephew Qaydu and the old people, and took them, with stallions, mares, and geldings, back with him to his wife's country, to the glades of eastern Baykal, the land of Barghu.

Qaydu, as we have seen, came of the senior line of the family. When he reached man's estate, his uncle Nachin loyally acknowledged him chief of the tribes. Qaydu then led his people in a war of revenge on the Jalairs, whom he defeated utterly and forced to pay tribute to him. There is reason to believe he set up camp then in the old fatherland, southeast of Mount Kentey, by the sacred springs of the Onon and the Kerülen.

"Families of divers tribes," Chinese annals inform us, "came one after another to place themselves under his protection, and the number of his subjects mounted daily." This was a paradigm of the nomad ascendancy: the prestige of a leader served as rallying point for broken and hungry clans, isolated families in search of a protector, adventurers after good swordplay, archers anxious to turn bowmanship to account in booty and venison. The kingdom founded by Qaydu—the first historic Mongol kingdom—prefigures the Chingiskhanid kingdom to come. Mongol bards, Chinese annalists and historians made no mistake. Qaydu is the first of his race to whom they accord the title of *qan*—that is, king. Certain of them go so far as to dub him *qaghan*—emperor—but this is quite obviously consecration after the event, as if the titles of the Chingiskhanid conquerors must at all costs go back to their far-off ancestor.

In another aspect, this sudden rise to power of Qaydu, survivor from the slaughter of all his family, affords striking illustration of the fragility of these nomad empires, and of how a tribe, reduced to nothing by loss of its grazing grounds, massacre of its young manhood, and seizure of its mares, yet bursts suddenly into new demographic expansion the moment hunting and breeding space is not denied it.

As to dating of these events, this is of course something there can be no precision about. Indications are, however, that the happenings just outlined bring us into the second third of the twelfth century.

Rude Chieftain at the Court
of the King of Gold

After Qaydu, the first Mongol khan, the tribes seem to have been apportioned among his three sons, a measure that cannot but have weakened
the young royal house. And indeed we hear next to nothing of his successor, his eldest son Bay-shingqor-doqshin, "the Dread Falcon." But
Bay-shingqor's grandson, the khan Qabul, was a great chief. With him the
Mongols, whose horizons hitherto have scarcely extended beyond the
environs of Mount Kentey, make their entry into world politics. They are
sufficiently a power already for the court of Peking to take notice.

Peking and Northern China were in the hands at that time of the Jurchets, come down from Manchuria and of Tunguz extraction, near relatives, that is, of the present-day Manchus. The Jurchet princes, bearing
the Chinese title of *Kin* or "Kings of Gold," held sway from the forests
of the Amur to the approaches of the Yangtze-kiang. They were pressing
forward toward the Yangtze at the expense of the Chinese empire, reduced by them now to the provinces of Southern China. Wanting to have
their hands free for this southern activity, they were anxious not to be
harassed in their rear by the nomads from Mongolia. Did this mustering
of the Kentey tribes around khan Qabul represent a threat? To satisfy
himself, the King of Gold invited the Mongol leader to his court, either
at Peking itself or in one of the royal hunting lodges in Manchuria.

Qabul conducted himself there like a barbarian indeed. The Jurchets
themselves, still only at one remove from Manchurian barbarism, with
the barest veneer of Chinese civilization rubbed off on them, scarcely
represented refinement. But the manners of this Mongol guest dumbfounded them—and in particular his gargantuan appetite. Persian histo-

rians, it is true, have a curious explanation for this appetite. The barbarian, a guest among all these fine lords, ill at ease amid all the affluence, and suspicious especially of the cunningly concocted dishes, the mysterious sweetmeats that might conceal poison, went out at intervals to make himself vomit; after which he returned to table and began cheerfully to eat and drink once more as if nothing had happened. But the dishes must have been particularly tasty, the rice-spirit have flowed particularly abundantly, for Qabul, getting drunker than was usual with him, so far forgot himself as to clutch at the King of Gold's beard. Told when he had sobered up of the crime of *lèse-majesté* he had committed, he asked what his punishment should be. The king, however, only laughed—either he thought a savage could not be expected to know better, or he preferred not to incur Mongol hostility at a time when the Jurchets still had the Chinese to cope with on the Yangtze. He over-looked Qabul's misdemeanor, and sent him back to Mongolia with rich presents, gold, precious stones, robes of honor.

Then, all the same, on reflection, the Jurchets decided that beneath the bonhomie, this barbarian they had entertained so lavishly might well be a neighbor to be feared. Scarcely had Qabul departed than the King of Gold, on the advice of mistrustful counselors, had second thoughts. He sent messengers to invite the Mongol to return. The Mongol smelt danger, and declined. The envoys then seized him, but "mounted on a grey colt" he managed to give them the slip, and, furious at the trap, had a bloody end put to the court of Peking's ambassadors.

These colorful episodes, which found their way through the Mongol bards into Persian sources, are corroborated by Chinese annalists; we know, in fact, that in 1139 and again in 1147, the Kings of Gold were at war on their northern frontiers against the Mongols, to whom they had finally to cede several frontier districts. Every year from 1148 on, moreover, the Peking court sent the tribes an ostensible gift of cattle, sheep, and grain—in fact a tribute designed to secure peace along the Great Khingan marches. More, in a typically Chinese maneuver, the King of Gold made appropriate acknowledgment of the enemy leader, dignifying him by the imposing title of King of the Mongols, with the reservation merely that he affected to treat him as a protégé and subordinate.

Mongol sources tell us nothing about this bargaining. They do, however, go on to trace out the line of obscure clan chieftains whose privilege it was to be near ancestors of Chingis-khan. Thus we learn that khan Qabul left seven sons whose strength and bravery earned them the name of *Kiyat,* which signifies "torrents," and which passed from them on to their descendants, who formed a special subdivision of the royal clan of the Borjigins. These seven sons recur often in the recitals of the Mongol bards, for all these nomads, no matter what state of beggary they might be reduced to, clung jealously to their genealogy. They were Ökin-barqaq, Bartan-ba'atur ("the Brave"), Qutuqtu-munggur, Qutula, Qulan (*"Dziggetai"*), Qada'an, and Tödöyen. Yet to none of these was it that Qabul transmitted his kingship; it was to his cousin Ambaqay, also a grandson of khan Qaydu, and chief of the clan of Taychi'ut.

Unquenchable Hatreds:
The Death Throes of Ambaqay

The Mongol kingdom was to all appearances at its apogee when deadly enmity sprang up suddenly between it and the Tatar people.

The Mongols, as we have seen, lived their nomadic existence at the foot of the Kentey chain, near the springs of the Onon and the Kerülen, the twin rivers that flow almost parallel, one north, one south, toward the east. The two river valleys, however, soon take on different aspects. The Onon, at least on its left bank, which continues skirting the edge of the *tayga,* remains a tumbling mountain forest watercourse. The Kerülen, on the other hand, becomes almost at once a river of the steppe, making its way with scarcely a gradient to speed it through country flat to the horizon, dried up for part of the year, like a ribbon crossing the desert. When it reaches Lake Kölen, it is six feet deep at most at midstream, and 65 to 130 feet across. "A foreigner in transit," it has been called, with no relation with the country it passes through. Its valley, six to nine miles across, forms a solitary strip of meadow and willow clumps, with at either side of it steppe vegetation taking over, just grass and bushes, *artemisia, derissus* and *karagans.* Lake Kölen itself, into which the Kerülen flows—a shrinking lake, marshy-shored—is linked only at times of high water with the Argun River, by a canal otherwise dry. Another river also feeds it, however: the Urshi'un (or Urshun), which serves as outlet from another lake, further south, Lake Buyur, itself fed by the Khalkha River, which runs down from the wooded slopes of the Great Khingan. For the most part it is semi-desert country, with its sprinkling of salty marshes and pools. Toward the longitudinal chain of the Khingan, however, vegetation makes its appearance again, with, shortly, great grasses rising shoulder-high, and still green in August. Groves of elms, birches, poplars stud the grassland. As for the Great Khingan, with its peaks of six thousand feet and more, it is predominantly covered with thick forest, as in the Mongol *tayga,* of larch.

All this region, from where the Kerülen flows into Lake Kölen to the Khingan across the river Urshi'un, was the habitat of the Tatars, a people long thought to be of Tunguz extraction, like the Manchus, but in fact of purely Mongol stock. An ancient people, even, since mention is made of them in the eighth century Turkish inscriptions of the Orkhon. Their sorcerers apparently had a reputation, for when the brother-in-law of khan Qabul fell ill, a Tatar shaman was called in to treat him. All his incantations, however, failed to prevent the sick man's dying, upon which the relatives of the deceased accused the shaman of evil intent, went after him as he was on his way home and killed him. The Tatars were in arms at once to avenge their shaman, while the sons of Qabul ranged themselves against them.

This clash of two peoples of common stock has its special interest. What was at issue was who was to take pride of place among the Mongol nations: the tribes of Mount Kentey and the upper Onon, or those of the lower Kerülen and Lake Buyur—a point still unsettled two generations later in the time of Chingis-khan, and which it took that leader to decide conclusively. For the moment, the dispute merely served the ends of the court of Peking and the King of Gold, who saw in it his opportunity to set nomad against nomad, and so check their advance. The Mongols seeming for the moment the more formidable, the Peking government decided in the circumstances to help the Tatars. Tatar and Jurchet, joining forces, were to put the young Mongol power to cruel testing.

Did the Mongol khan Ambaqay sense the hatred against his people the murder of the shaman had engendered? He may have thought it had all died down and the affair been forgotten. He may have thought to break up the bundle of the Tatar tribes by contracting an alliance with one of them. At all events, he betrothed his daughter to a chief of the Tatar group of the Ayri'uts and Buyru'uts, nomads of the river Urshi'un, between Lakes Kölen and Buyur. But the hatred had in no whit abated. As unsuspecting Ambaqay made his way with his daughter to the country of her betrothed, another Tatar tribe, the Jüyins, seized his person, and carried him off under heavy guard to hand over to the King of Gold. The court of Peking must for its part have been nursing real wrath at the depredations of the Mongols, for it put the prisoner to a hideous death: khan Ambaqay was impaled on a wooden ass. The oldest son of the dead khan Qabul, Ökin-barqaq, also taken prisoner by the Tatars, was likewise handed over to the King of Gold, and underwent at his command the same torture.

These were atrocities not to be forgotten. Before he died, Ambaqay had contrived to send a messenger—Balaqachi, of the clan Besüt, the bard tells us—to Qutula, most forceful of the sons of the dead khan Qabul, as well as to his own sons. "I, supreme leader of the Mongol people, have been seized by the Tatars even as I took my daughter to them. Let my example be a lesson to you. And now, avenge me, if you have to wear down your every fingernail straining your bow, nay if you have to shoot your ten fingers themselves." And before he died he warned the King of Gold that his vengeance would be fearful. And indeed, an unquenchable hatred was building up in the hearts of the Mongols—a hatred that Chingis-khan and his sons were to assuage one day in the blood, first of the last Tatar, then of the last of the Kings of Gold.

The Mongol Hercules

After the tortured death of Ambaqay, the Mongols proper and their brothers, the Taychi'uts, proceeded to the election of a new khan at an assembly at Qorqonaq-jubur, a forest on the banks of the Onon. Qutula was chosen, the third son of the dead khan Qabul. The election was the occasion for a great celebration, with dancing and feasting. "Beneath the thickly leaved trees of Qorqonaq-jubur they danced till their thighs were in the ditches, their knees in the dust." And the new khan was foremost in this sacred dance, in the totemic disguise, perhaps, still donned by some of the *tayga* peoples.

By all accounts of the legends, he was a terrifying creature, this last khan before Chingis, a sort of Mongol Hercules, half bestial, half divine. Long after his death, bards still sang, awed, of the mighty voice, rolling like thunder through the mountain gorges, and the fearsome hands, like great bear paws, that could snap a man in half as if he were an arrow. "They told how at night in winter he would lie down naked by a fire of great trees, and how he would feel neither the sparks nor the brands that fell on his body, and take the marks in the morning for insect bites. He ate a whole sheep every day and downed an enormous jar of *qumiz,* or fermented mare's milk."

Scarcely elevated to the felt carpet of royalty, Qutula set out with his brother, Qada'an, to make war on the Tatars, to avenge Ambaqay. Thirteen times they did battle with the Tatar chiefs Koton-baraqa and Jali-buqa (the Bull). But despite all their efforts, the Mongol bard has sadly to record, they were unable to wreak vengeance on the criminals, to deal them the punishment they deserved. From which it is to be understood, presumably, that they were unable to bring off any decisive victory. We have no details of these encounters, save that Qutula's nephew, Yesügei-ba'atur—Yesügei the Brave—took prisoner several Tatar chiefs, among them Temüjin-üge and Qori-buqa. We shall see that it was to this circumstance that the future Chingis-khan was to owe his name. The same fact also enables us to set a rough date for Yesügei's victory over the two Tatar chiefs, in or about 1166. The first date in this history.

Qutula it would seem pushed his raids not merely into Tatar country, but right to the territory of the King of Gold, in all likelihood, that is, virtually to present-day Mongolo-Manchurian country. Tradition recounts how once, when on one of his campaigns he had relaxed and given himself over to hunting, he was attacked out of the blue by people of the tribe of Dörben, in fact a Mongol tribe—demonstration of how scant was the respect the royal house commanded outside the circle of groups with whom the khan was directly connected. Deserted by his followers, Qutula plunged into a marsh, where his horse sank in up to its neck. "Standing up on his saddle, he jumped clear of the swampy ground. The Dörbens, arriving on the opposite bank, did not trouble to pursue him, saying: 'What is a Mongol without his horse?' " Meantime, Qutula's servants had spread word that he was dead, and his nephew Yesügei had done as was customary and brought meats to the family to eat with them the funeral repast. But Qutula's wife, one of the Mongol Amazons who play so recurrent a part in this epic, refused to believe he was dead. "How should a warrior whose voice shakes the vault of heaven, whose hands are like the hands of a three-year-old bear, fall into the clutches of the Dörbens? Believe what I say. I know he will soon stand before us." And indeed Qutula, once the Dörbens had made off, had calmly retrieved his horse from the swamp by hoisting it up by the mane. In the saddle once more, he saw a herd of mares grazing on Dörben grassland with a stallion. He jumped astride the stallion, mastered it, drove the mares on before him, and arrived so before his *yurt* just as the tears commenced to flow for him.

But a harsh end was put to such exploits. Mongol tradition tells of disaster overtaking the Mongols in a battle near Lake Buyur against the combined forces of the Tatars and the King of Gold. Chinese sources confirm that in 1161 the latter monarch, determined to put an end once and for all to the ravages of the nomads, dispatched an army to Mongolia. Peking strategy and Tatar arms would seem together to have been too much for the first Mongol kingdom. And indeed, in the next generation, Tatars had supplanted Mongols as masters of the eastern Gobi. Tatar power was to assume such proportions, in fact, as finally to make the *Kin* sovereign of Peking, the King of Gold himself, uneasy; and it was to the consequent about-turn of alliances that Chingis-khan was really to owe his first successes.

We know nothing of the end of khan Qutula, save that he had no successor. Of his three sons—Jöchi, Girma'u, Altan—none assumed a throne. Nor did Qutula's nephew, Yesügei-ba'atur, on whom Mongol epic did not fail to confer the title of khan, however slight the possibility that he ever bore it, since he was the father of Chingis-khan. Clearly the first Mongol kingdom, broken, how exactly we do not know, by the Tatars and the court of Peking, had lapsed again into tribal fragments.

With the collapse of the first Mongol kingdom there seems to have set in, to judge by all the evidence we possess, utter anarchy, with the dissolution not only of political ties, but only too often of family ones as well. The milieu of the first part of the *Secret History* is that of the Red Indians—vendettas between tribe and tribe, clan and clan, brigandage a way of life, horse stealing, rape, fratricide. "Before your birth," Kököchü was to tell the sons of Chingis-khan, "Mongolia was full of trouble. Everywhere tribe was at war with tribe. There was safety nowhere."

Part  2

Conqueror of the World

△
▲▲

———

1

Yesügei the Brave and Prester John

Few men have had bestowed on them by history greater posthumous renown than Yesügei the Brave (ba'atur): he was the father of Chingiskhan, and his son's fame was reflected back on him. But his life was a hard one. He was born into the dark days of Mongol history, when the first kingdom founded by his family was disintegrating in face of concerted attack from the Tatars and the court of Peking. It seems never to have occurred to him to assert his claim to the title of khan borne by his uncle Qutula. He remained simply a chieftain of a subclan, the subclan (*yasun*) of the Kiyats, subdivision in turn of the clan (*oboq*) of the Borjigins. For all that, it would be wrong to dismiss him as playing an insignificant role. In the war his people waged with the Tatars, and in which they were for the most part the losers, he scored apparently his measure of personal success, defeating, as we have seen, two enemy chieftains; a victory gratifying enough for him to commemorate it by calling his eldest son after one of the losers: Temüjin.

It was Yesügei moreover—and this is a fact too often lost sight of—who laid the foundations of Chingiskhanid political ascendancy by securing for his house the Kereit alliance, without which, as we shall see later, the career of Chingis-khan could never have been.

The Kereits are one of the most mysterious peoples in history. They were by origin Turco-Mongol—so much is sure: but how far predominantly one or the other we have no means of telling. They make to all intents and purposes their first appearance in the chronicles only in the generation before Chingis-khan, and step forthwith into a leading role. It is the endlessly recurring pattern of these empires of the steppe, raised in a matter of a year or two to crumble as precipitately.

Even the extent of the territory they were wont to range is in doubt. A number of passages in the *Secret History* do tell us, however, that their kinds camped frequently along the River Tula, in the vicinity of the Black Forest (Qara-tun), a wooded massif which may be that of Bogdo-ula, lying south of that river and what is today the town of Ulan Bator. Another reference in the same text gives as their western frontier a River Nekün, which has been taken as the present-day Narün which runs down from the Khangay mountains toward the Gobi, southwest of Qaraqorum. The Persian historian Rashid ed-Din also seems to set them a limit about here, at the mountains of Qaraqorum; that is, at the Khangay massif, by the headwaters of the Orkhon. Elsewhere, Rashid ed-Din speaks of them as pursuing their nomad paths eastward right to the sources of the Onon and Kerülen, into the country, that is, of the Mongols proper, and southeast across the Gobi, as far as the Great Wall of China.

The Kereit country, in so far as we may thus delineate it, was dominated to the northwest by the last eastern escarpments of the Khangay mountains, whose peaks, near the source of the Orkhon, went up to 11,000 feet. Mount Bogdo-ula, "the Holy Mountain," similarly dominated the next section, the left bank of the Tula. "First sight of the mountains," writes Grenard, "tells the traveler here is the demarcation line between two quite distinct zones: northward, mountain forest and meadow; to the south, steppe and the Gobi; no gradual modulation blurs the contrast—southern flank, bare rock, northern, from 5,600 feet all the way to the 8,300 feet summit, dense forest, pine, birch, aspen, to this day religion-protected in its profusion."

To the south, the Kereit country extended into the Gobi. Southwest, there lies in between the last eastern outposts of the Khangay and their Altay counterparts a "desert gulf," a projection of the Gobi, alive only where six rivers flow north to south, fed by the Khangay. "They flow swiftly, over stony beds grooved in flat valleys, from the Baydarik to the Onghin. They finish up in salt lakes, lodged in the depression that follows the northern foot of the Altay, bordered by reeds and sand-growing *saksauls* and tamarisks. In autumn and winter the most easterly, the Onghin, peters out in the plain before it ever gets to Lake Ulan, leaving the latter's red clay basin dry. Lake Orok, into which the Tuin flows, can in some years be forded. The Boum-tsaghan, further west, is stabler, but its waters are almost saturated with salt and sulphur." It is the same in the east, south of Ulan Bator and the Tula, where the desert is broken only by one or two short-lived streams.

After that comes the Gobi proper, the flat expanse where "gravel, sand and clay make a surface hard and even as that of a race track, with the occasional variation of small dunes or rocky patches." Travelers have often been moved to try their hand at describing these lone desert wastes, stretching as far as the eye can see, their only vegetation one or two greyish dwarf irises, *kharmyk* or *budargan,* or rare clumps of *derissus* "dull-leaved, with twigs hard as wire." Only the *saksaul,* "a shrub with leafless branches, and a trunk sometimes a foot wide, standing up to ten or thirteen feet high," breaks with the occasional thicket the expanse of sand. Inhospitable country if ever there was such, with animals glad to come where they may find wretched grass, "yellow by July and scarcely distinguishable from the brownish waste." Yet these desert grazing places are usually frequent enough to keep caravans alive.

Such was the domain of the Kereits. Poor as it might seem, it yet gave them control of a great part of the Gobi, this "dry sea," as the Chinese called it, that was so important politically since its tracks were the link between the Mongol steppe and China. The upper Tula basin, moreover, with its rich grasslands, constituted not only· a summering place where the Kereits could recuperate, but a natural geographical center, well placed for control of western Mongolia, inhabited, as we shall see, by the Nayman Turks, and eastern Mongolia, where the Mongols proper, the ancestors of Chingis-khan, were struggling for supremacy with the Tatars.

In virtue, doubtless, of this situation, the Kereits seem to have aspired to authority over both the Gobi and the Mongol steppe. And indeed in our view they had not inconsiderable claims to such a role. While they cannot be said to have been more civilized than their neighbors (the lives of their sovereigns will betray some singularly murky passages), it is noteworthy that through their role of warders of the Gobi they received the Christian message. If we are to believe the Syrian chronicler Bar Hebraeus, they were converted shortly after the year 1000. One of their kings had got lost in the desert. At his last gasp, he was saved by the miraculous appearance of Saint Sergius. Touched by grace, and at the instigation of Christian merchants then passing through his kingdom, he sent to the Nestorian Metropolitan of Merv, in Khorassan, Ebed-jesu, with a request that priests should come to baptize himself and his people. A letter from Ebed-jesu to the Nestorian Patriarch of Baghdad, John VI dated 1009 and quoted by Bar Hebraeus, states that nomads were then baptized with their king to the number of 200,000.

All hinges here on whether the name Kereit was not interpolated by Bar Hebraeus after the event to please the Chingiskhanid princes, who, as we shall see, counted Kereit princes among their ancestors. Even if this were so, however, the fact remains that in the twelfth century the Kereits had embraced Christianity, specifically the Nestorian Christianity which had its Patriarch in Iraq, at Seleucia-Baghdad, and numbered prosperous communities in the east Iranian province of Khorassan or in Transoxania, toward Samarkand. And the test in question is certainly accurate when it assigns origins in that region to the Khorassani or Soghdian caravaneers who, on one of their trading trips across the Gobi, converted the Kereit king. No less certain is it that at the end of the twelfth century the Kereit khans were Nestorian Christians by father-to-son transmission. Whence the legend, propagated by Marco Polo, of "Prester John," although this personage has been subsequently identified (arbitrarily) with the Negus of Ethiopia. At all events, Kereit Nestorianism is destined to play a considerable part in this story: it was through it, as we shall see, that Christianity was to become one of the official religions of the Chingiskhanid empire.

Kereit aspirations to hegemony in Mongolia are plain from the texts. Two generations before the time of Chingis-khan, we learn of their khan making war on the Tatars of the eastern Gobi, who, as we have seen, received support from the King of Gold in Peking. This khan had the double name of Marghuz Buyruq, the first part of which is none other than the Christian name Mark, quite common among the Nestorians of Upper Asia. He was taken prisoner by the Tatars, and handed over by them to the representatives of the King of Gold. The latter put him to the same ignominious torture as they had earlier the other Mongol princes: they had him nailed or impaled on a wooden ass. His widow, the fair Qutuqtay-Irikchi, resolved to avenge him. She pretended to come to terms with circumstance, and presented herself gallantly to do her homage to the chief of the Tatars, bringing with her as her gift one hundred leather jars, ostensibly containing *qumiz,* the fermented mare's milk that was the nomads' favorite drink. In fact, each jar contained a warrior. In the midst of the feast given by the Tatar chief for his visitor, the hundred Kereit soldiers burst from their concealment and slew the enemy prince and a great number of his followers. *Arabian Nights,* Mongol style.

Marghuz left two sons: Qurjaquz, that is to say Cyriac (again a Christian name), and Gur-khan, of whom the first succeeded him. Qurjaquz seems to have been another to have a troubled reign: he came very near to being dethroned by the Tatars, and was only saved by the intervention of his neighbors to the west, the Naymans.[1] His eldest son Toghril— "the Goshawk"—plays a major part in this story. He was Marco Polo's "Prester John," protector of Chingis-khan in his early days. In fact, it must be admitted this representative of Upper Asian Nestorian Christianity made his way to the throne by methods that could scarcely have been less Christian. At their father's death, he put to death two of his brothers who might have disputed his accession to power. A third brother, Erke-qara, whom he aimed to dispose of likewise, escaped to the Naymans.

The Naymans, who thus make their second appearance in this story, dwelt, as we shall see more fully later, in western Mongolia west of the Khangay, namely in the Kobdo lakes region, the Mongol Altay, and the valleys of the Black Irtysh and the Imil, in Tarbagatay.[2] Their khan Inanch-bilge—a redoubtable man of whom it was said no enemy had seen his back, or his horse's croup—gave hospitality to the exiled Kereit princes, Toghril's brothers. He apparently extended aid also to Toghril's uncle, Gur-khan, likewise in revolt against Toghril, who headed the insurrection. Gur-khan drove Toghril from the Kereit throne and forced him to flee with the last hundred still loyal to him to the river Selenga, towards the gorges of the Qara'un mountains. Masters here were the

[1] The Persian historian Rashid ed-Din reports that Qurjaquz had married the sister of the Nayman king. It was because of this relationship that the Naymans intervened to save him from the Tatars (probably around 1140). At their victory, the Tatars had taken prisoner Qurjaquz's son, the young Toghril, then a boy of thirteen, and they put him to herding camels. Toghril managed to escape, not without his quota of camels. Cf. Pelliot, No. 40, p. 68.

[2] We know from the Persian historian Rashid ed-Din that in the first half of the twelfth century the Naymans were headed by the clan Betekin (M. Pelliot's reconstruction). It was a Betekin prince who had, about 1140, saved the Kereit king Qurjaquz. Then the Betekins lost their pre-eminence among the Naymans, and the royal title passed to another house, that of the Kuchugurs. Cf. Pelliot, *ibid.,* p. 41.

Merkits, Mongol forest-dwelling tribes. To establish good relations, Toghril offered his daughter Huja'ur to their king Toqto'a. But he does not seem to have received from them any effective aid.

As a last resort, he went to Yesügei (re-enter the hero of our chapter) and beseeched his assistance: "Help me to wrest my people from the clutches of my uncle Gur-khan." "Since you thus implore me," Yesügei answered, "I will take my two Taychi'ut warriors, Qunan and Bagaji, and together we will give you back your people." So saying, he mustered his men, set out to attack Gur-khan over toward Qurban-telesüt, and forced him to flee to the Tanguts, in what is today the Chinese province of Kansu.

Yesügei the Brave's decisive intervention had thus re-established Toghril on the Kereit throne. In the Black Forest of the Tula they swore eternal friendship. "In memory of the service you have rendered me," Toghril declared, "my gratitude shall be manifested to your children and to your children's children, may the high heavens (de'ere tenggeri) and the earth be my witness." Weighty words, by which Toghril and Yesügei became brothers by oath, and which would in the future assure to Yesügei's son Toghril's protection.

The whole of the first part of the reign of Chingis-khan, up to 1203, was to be dominated by the memory of the "oath of the Black Forest."

△
△△

2

Yesügei's Conquest
of the Lady Hö'elün

Yesügei's union with the woman who was to be the mother of Chingis-khan is told by the Mongol bard pithily and extraordinarily baldly. No episode conveys more vividly the primitiveness of life at this period.

Yesügei was hunting with falcons on the banks of the Onon when he saw coming from the direction of the river a noble Mongol of the Merkit tribe called Yeke-Chiledü. The latter had just taken to wife a girl of the clan of the Olqunu'ut, a division of the Onggirat tribe, nomads from near where the River Khalkha joined Lake Buyur, in eastern Mongolia. Yeke-Chiledü was bringing back his young bride, who was called Hö'elün—a name we are to meet many times in the course of this story. To the couple's great misfortune, they were seen by Yesügei. Yesügei certainly had good eyes: he saw that the young woman was very beautiful. He hastened to his *yurt* and came back reinforced by his two brothers, Nekün-tayshi and Daritay. Seeing them coming towards him, Chiledü took fright. Whipping up his horse—a chestnut charger, the bard notes conscientiously—he fled toward a nearby hill, the three brothers after him at a gallop. As, having rounded an abutment of the mountain, he turned back to his wife Hö'elün in her chariot, she, being a woman of sense, said practically: "Have you taken a look at these men? They seem to me scarcely to bode us good. Apparently they are out to kill you. If you can get away alive, you will not want for maidens perched on wagon seats, or women even in the black wagons . . . She whom you choose you give my name, call her Hö'elün in memory of me. Save your life! Escape! Yet take this, that you may have my perfume also to remember me by. . . ." With which she pulled off her shift and threw it at him. He jumped from his horse and seized it. Already the three brothers were coming around the mountain and were almost upon him. He brought his whip down on his charger, and made off at full gallop up the Onon valley. The three brothers hurled themselves in pursuit. They crossed seven hills without being able to catch him; then they returned to the wagon. Yesügei claimed the fair Hö'elün and brought her triumphantly home. The bard shows him rejoicing in his conquest and driving the wagon himself, while his brother Nekün-tayshi went before to show the way and the third member of the party, Daritay, rode by the shafts.

But poor Hö'elün in the wagon moaned and lamented: "My husband who till now had never exposed a hair of his head to the wind! He who in the steppe had never known hunger! Now as he fled galloping his two plaits were beating in the wind, on his back, then on his chest. That he should be brought to that!" "So she spoke," the bard goes on, "and the echo of her lament troubled the waves of the Onon and set the trees of the forest agroan." But the youngest brother of her ravisher, Daritay, who was riding alongside the wagon, told the poor young woman mockingly: "The man you want to hold again in your arms is already far off, and in his flight he must have already crossed not a few rivers. You do no good weeping, he will not turn round, and you will not see him again. You would not even be able to pick up his traces. Come, be quiet." So he advised her to make the best of circumstances. And indeed she followed Yesügei to his *yurt,* and from that day forward, as a woman of sense, devoted herself entirely to him.

This famous episode is highly informative. It tells us that the exogamy the Mongols made a family rule only too often drove them, when they wanted a wife, to resort to kidnaping, which perpetuated war among the tribes. Between the Merkits and the Mongols of the upper Onon, woman-snatching was to go on endlessly, till an unassuageable hatred built up and, transmitted from generation to generation, led eventually to one of the two groups being exterminated. Here also is one more proof of the anarchy the tribes had relapsed into, following the collapse of the first Mongol royalty, an anarchy affecting not merely the political framework but all social relationships. And indeed, we shall see that when the order of Chingis-khan was established in Mongolia, the exogamy rule whereby a Mongol must find a wife outside his own tribe proved observable by way of peaceable negotiation, with no need to resort to kidnaping.

Lastly, this quaint little drama the Mongol bard has staged for us acquaints us forthwith with the character of the lady Hö'elün: a dutiful woman, surely, loving her first husband and even in love with him, as she shows by her touching sorrow as he disappears over the horizon, and the spontaneous gesture of the very personal souvenir she bequeaths him; but at the same time a realist with feet on the ground, knowing when circumstances have the whip hand, and unprevaricating, as when, out of tenderness for her husband, she consoles him for what he is losing and urges him to save his life. Once she has entered the house of Yesügei she will attach herself to him with the same unswerving loyalty; and likewise to her new family, who later, when they fall on evil days, when Yesügei is no longer there, will look to her for, and find, virile direction. Who can say, even, whether without a mother of such simple rectitude, of such energy, of such realism and practicality, the career of Chingis-khan could have been what it was?

3

Childhood Days of Chingis-khan

According to the findings of M. Pelliot (1939), the eldest son of Yesügei
and the lady Hö'elün, the future Chingis-khan, was born in the Year of
the Pig, 1167.[1] His family were encamped at the time at Deli'ün-boldaq,
close, that is, to the lone hill (*boldaq*) of Deli'ün, on the right bank of
the Onon. The infant came into the world clutching in his right hand a
clot of blood the size of a knucklebone. His father named him Temüjin,
to commemorate his capture, about the time of the child's birth, of the
Tatar chief Temüjin-üge. As to the etymology of this name, it seems that
the interpretation of it as "Blacksmith," from the Turco-Mongol root
temür, "iron," is phonetically correct. Chance, through triumphs of his
father's, dictated that the future "Conqueror of the World" should be
marked out as it were by name as the man of iron whose work it was to
be to forge a new Asia. After him, Yesügei and Hö'elün had three more
sons: Jöchi-Qasar, Qachi'un, and Temüge, the last designated *otchigin,*
literally "prince of the hearth," that is, the youngest. They had also a
daughter, Temülün. By another woman—called, perhaps, according to
Pelliot's last researches (1941), Söchigil—Yesügei had two other sons,
Bekter and Belgütei.

The chronicles are not as informative as they might be about the phy-
sique of Chingis-khan. They do say the child had eyes of fire and a singular light in his face, perhaps a reminder of the Spirit of Light that had
once overshadowed his mythical ancestor Alan-qo'a. As an adult, he was
notable for his height, the sturdiness of his frame, his wide forehead, a
relatively long beard (long at least by Mongol standards), and finally his
"cat's eyes." These cat's eyes, which have been taken to be grey-green,

---

[1] Concerning the exact date of Chingis-khan's birth, see pp. 281-88 of No. 18.

have greatly intrigued commentators. Could the future Chingis-khan be "of Turkized Aryan race," like the peasants of Kashgaria? But the author for one has personally numbered among his close feline acquaintances cats whose eyes were brownish-yellow, and in any case the Mongol bards have too carefully recorded the genealogy of their hero for there to be any doubt about his Altaic origins.

Betrothal must have been customary at a very early age in Mongolia. Temüjin was only nine (bringing us to 1176) when his father Yesügei set forth with him to find a fiancée. Yesügei intended to go first to the relatives of his wife Hö'elün, the Onggirats of the Olqunu'ut clan, whom he expected to find roaming, as we have seen, in eastern Mongolia, near Lake Buyur. On the way, father and son made a halt at the camp of another Onggirat chief, named Deisechen (the Wise), between Mounts Chekcher and Chiqurqu, identified respectively by Professor Haenisch as the modern Altan-nomor and Dulan-khora, on the west bank of the River Urchun, between Lake Kölen and Lake Buyur. Deisechen inquired the reason for·their journey. Yesügei told him he was seeking a betrothed for his son in the Onggirat country. The questioner was interested. "Your son," Deisechen told him, "has fire in his glance and a glowing countenance. Now, friend Yesügei, last night I had a strange dream. A white falcon, with the sun and the moon in its claws, came down from heaven and perched on my hand. It was a fine omen, as I understand now that you come to us with your son with you. My dream was to announce that you came, you of the clan Kiyat, as bearers of good fortune."

Deisechen was not called "the Wise" for nothing. The Onggirats were famous for the beauty of their daughters, but politically, they were a minor tribe: they were not in the same class as the Kiyats, the royal clan *par excellence*. They were flattered, then, when, by what seems to have been a tradition, the men of the royal clan came to them for their wives. Or so Deisechen gives to understand in his words to Yesügei: "We are celebrated for the beauty of our daughters and our nieces, but we have never sought to turn this to the advantage of our people. When there has come over from you a new khan, we have hastened to set in one of our big *qasaq* wagons one of our fine-faced girls, with a dark grey camel in the shafts, which we put to a spanking pace, and she has gone to you to take her place as a wife on the royal throne beside your khans." The whole passage seems to indicate that in the Mongol practice of exogamy there was particular *jus connubii* between the clan of the Borjigin and the Onggirats.

The verse leads up to Deisechen's final suggestion: "Friend Yesügei, let us go to my *yurt.* I have a daughter, already growing up. Come and see her!" Yesügei followed his host into his thick felt tent. He must have sat in the seat of honor, beside the master of the house, in the center of the tent, or rather, near the fire that took up the center. At the back, to the right, the lady of the house would be sitting, with the children. Among these would be—thoroughly alive already, it may be imagined, to what was happening—the young Börte, whose name, we have already learned, also means grey-blue. Yesügei looked at the little girl, and his heart was satisfied. She was indeed very pretty. The bard even takes care to say of her what he has just said of Temüjin: she, also, had fire in her glance and a face that shone. Incidentally, she was ten, one year older than Temüjin.

Next morning, Yesügei made the formal request for her in marriage. His host was a sagacious man who knew that one must neither be too coy nor give consent too soon. And Börte, even though the Mongols married young, was only a little girl. Deisechen, after a generality or two ("it is the lot of girls to be born in the paternal *yurt,* but not their destiny to grow old there"), made a waiting-period suggestion: "It is agreed, I shall give you my daughter. But, when you go, leave your son with me as a son-in-law" (more precisely, as a son-in-law-to-be; one might almost say, as an "apprentice son-in-law"). Yesügei agreed to do this, but adding a rider to his consent that, referring to the future Chingis-khan, comes as something of a surprise: "So be it, I will leave my son with you. But you should know he is afraid of dogs. Friend, see that dogs are not allowed to frighten him!" In fairness to the young Temüjin (and, affianced as he was, he was after all only nine), it should be added that the great Mongol dogs, black and bristly, are particularly formidable. The Roerich mission reports that only a few decades ago, in the town of Urga, now Ulan-Bator, strays attacked people on foot, and even on horseback, and one night made a meal of a sentry.

These recommendations made, Yesügei, leaving his son to serve his apprenticeship with Deisechen, mounted and set off for home. On the way, he met a group of Tatars gathered for a banquet on the Yellow Steppe (Shira-ke'er) near the Mount Chekcher that Haenisch, as already mentioned, identifies with Mount Dulan-khora, between Lake Buyur and the inflow of the Kerülen into Lake Kölen. Thirsty, he sat down beside them, and asked them for a drink. He had rashly forgotten the old hate of the Tatars for his house. Now, they had recognized him: "But it is Yesügei the Kiyat coming to us"—Yesügei, who in former warring had led so many raids on their encampments. The time of vengeance had come, fate had delivered him into their hands. They mixed poison in his food, a poison of the slow-acting kind. It was only when he was once more on his way that Yesügei felt the first effects. Three days later, when he reached his *yurt,* his condition was so much worse as to leave him in no doubt what had happened to him. Yesügei the Brave was going to die, "Yesügei the Brave was entering the death throes." He called out: "Who is beside me?" Mönglik, son of the old man Charaqa, of the Qongqotat tribe, answered: "I am here, oh Yesügei." Then the dying man made his last dispositions: "Mönglik, my child, listen: my children are still young. When I had left my son Temüjin over there as betrothed, and while I was returning here, I was poisoned by the Tatars. I feel my strength ebb. . . . What is to become of my children and all those I leave behind, my young brothers, my widow, my sisters-in-law? This is anguish. . . . Mönglik, my child, go at once quickly and bring back my son Temüjin!" And with these words, he died.[2]

The dramatic death of Yesügei, the anguished fears and recommendations of the dying man for his family—this is the opening chapter of the personal history of Temüjin, of the future Chingis-khan. Something of the Mongol chronicler's indrawn breath still communicates itself to the reader here. They were grim conditions indeed attached to the future world conqueror's apprenticeship to life! We know the savagely fierce ways of the Mongolian forest and steppe, the life of ambush, treason, abduction, and killing, with the manhunt as frequent as hunting for the maral or the *dziggetai*—a milieu we have already compared to the American prairie in the days of the scalp hunters. Into this iron society the young Temüjin was cast, bereft of paternal protection, a fatherless boy of nine.

By Pelliot's calculations, this was in 1176.

---

[2] Mönglik, whom we shall meet again later, must have been young enough himself, since a little further on (¶ 204) the *Secret History* assures us, doubtless with some literary license, that he was born about the same time as Chingis-khan and that they grew up together.

4

Orphans Driven from the Clan

Mönglik did at once as he was charged by the dying Yesügei. He went into the Onggirat country, to Deisechen, to bring back the young Temüjin. But with the prudence of the prairie hunter, he was careful not to tell his host of the catastrophe that had befallen his tribe. Who knew whether Deisechen, if he learned that the Kiyat chief was dead, might not seize the child as a slave? So Mönglik used subterfuge. "Your brother Yesügei," he told the Onggirat, "cannot get used to being without Temüjin. His heart is wrung when he thinks of him." Deisechen found this quite natural. "If Yesügei's heart is sore for Temüjin, take him to him; then, when he has seen him, bring him back soon."

And Mönglik took the young Temüjin from Buyurnor to the upper Onon, to the *yurt* where Yesügei had just died, and his widow, the lady Hö'elün, had assumed control.

But it was not long before the situation worsened for Hö'elün and her children. Yesügei, toward the end of his life, had contrived by his prestige to bring together under his authority, grouped around the subclan of the Kiyats, a certain number of consanguineous clans. The Taychi'ut princes, notably, his cousins, had, as we have seen, accepted him as leader in war and in the hunt. It was a typical instance of the duration-of-life grouping that would take place around the man of strength and capacity, it being in the clan's interests, for raiding as for larger-scale battle, to place themselves under an experienced leader. When the leader died, however, the grouping broke up. This is what happened at the death of Yesügei. The Taychi'ut chiefs now wanted to assume again the authority that had once briefly been theirs with Ambaqay, last but one of the khans of the Mongols. In the face of their pretensions, what could the family of

Yesügei do, decapitated by the death of its chief and with for representative a child of nine? Brutally, matters were brought to a head.

It was in spring. The widows of khan Ambaqay, the two Taychi'ut princesses Örbey and Soqatay, had come to the place of consecration to make the ritual offerings to the ancestral spirits. The ceremony over, those present shared among themselves the proffered meats. Now Örbey and Soqatay had deliberately omitted to invite the widow of Yesügei, the dowager Hö'elün. Hö'elün came nevertheless, but she arrived late for the sacrifice, and sat down a latecomer also to the ceremonial meal. This, as we know, was a strong woman, positive, possessed of singular drive, in spirit a chief. Chief of the subclan of the Kiyats was what she now was, in the stead and place of her husband, in the name of her still minor sons, and it was not her intention to have her rights laid down for her. With the two Taychi'ut dowagers, she took a tone of great hauteur, and went in forthwith to the attack, threatening them: "Now Yesügei the Brave is dead, you think all is permitted you. Do you then imagine his children will not grow up? And that you will not when that time comes have to cower to their anger? Sharing the meat and drink of the sacrifice, would you leave me out? When you had eaten, would you prepare to strike camp without awakening me?"

It is quite clear that in the framework of the shamanist beliefs of the time, exclusion of Hö'elün from the sacrificial communion, from the consuming of the meats offered to the ancestors, would have had social results of a most serious order. Apart from the personal insult an act of such discourtesy was in itself, its effect would have been practically to banish the heirs of Yesügei from the community of the clan Borjigin, to make the widow and her children veritable outcasts.

Hö'elün had thought she could intimidate the two other dowagers. But the young widow had miscalculated. Whatever her assertions, a dead Yesügei and the young children impressed no one any more. The two old women rounded on her in a wave of unleashed smarting feminine spite: "So you were not invited to the feast? Is it not a habit of yours to invite yourself, and to serve yourself liberally? And then when you—oh yes, you give invitations; only at your table one does not get a bite to eat!" Venomous barbs of malevolent old women in the smoke-thick atmosphere of a Mongol *yurt,* clustered around the best-looking part of mutton

—nothing could convey more vividly the beggared life of all these monarchs of the steppe.

Then the Taychi'ut princesses held long council together. When they broke up, the order was given: "Strike camp and let the widow and her children look after themselves! Away, let us leave them to their fate." And so it was. Next morning, the two Taychi'ut chiefs, Tarqutay-Qiriltuq and Tödöen-Girte, made off with their people down the Onon valley. "Mother Hö'elün" was left helpless with her fatherless children. One former faithful follower of Yesügei alone tried to help her. He was of the Qongqotat tribe, the old man (*ebügen*) Charaqa, father of that Mönglik whom Yesügei had charged with his wishes as he lay dying. Running after the Taychi'uts, Charaqa tried to persuade them to change their minds, to stay with the great widow. But Tödöen-Girte told him the break was final: "The deep water is dry, the brilliant stone is split." Did the old man, in his loyalty, insist too much? Anyway the Taychi'uts booed him out, and as he turned to go he got a lance wound deep in his spine. He came home dying to his *yurt*. Temüjin came to his couchside. The old man had still strength enough to tell his master's son the outcome of his gesture: "They want to lead away out of your reach all these people your noble father once united under his command. I tried to stop them, and see what they have done to me!" Tears were hot on the boy's cheeks as he left the *yurt* where this man—the last defender of his cause—lay dying for him. This visit to the deathbed of his old retainer was, for this child of nine, his first action as a chief. He served his apprenticeship in a society of iron, and his every political act was to bear the mark of the harshness of the lessons he there received. But let us not forget these tears Temüjin shed by the deathbed of Charaqa; that, disconcertingly, our first glimpse of the personality of the future Chingis-khan is a reaction of affection and human tenderness.

Meanwhile Hö'elün his mother did not give way to despair. Abandoned with her children, betrayed by all those she might have counted on, this courageous woman took magnificent action. She seized the *tuq,* the yak or stallion-tail standard that was the banner of the clan, mounted a horse, galloped after the departed tribes, and brought half of them to a halt. For a moment it seemed her courage, and the memory of Yesügei, might prevail over Taychi'ut enmity. Picture the tribes on the march with their wagons, horsemen, beasts, and the great widow overhauling them at the gallop, waving her *tuq,* and haranguing the "deserters," reminding them of the oath they swore in former days to Yesügei the Brave. Imagine the waverings in the column of marchers, the uncertainty in minds confronted with the call to duty, the objurgations of Hö'elün, and commitments made the night before to the new Taychi'ut chiefs. In the end it was they who triumphed. Those of the clans Hö'elün had managed momentarily to move or intimidate turned from her once more to follow Tarqutay-Qiriltuq and Tödöen-Girte. And all this people, once the people of Yesügei the Brave, disappeared along the Onon, and Hö'elün and her family were left alone in the deserted camp. Besides her four sons —Temüjin, Jöchi-Qasar, Qachi'un, and Temüge—and her daughter Temülün, there were Bekter and Belgütei, the two sons Yesügei had had by a second wife.

She was to look after all alike. It is now that "Mother Hö'elün," as the Mongol bard henceforth calls her, shows herself at her true stature. Think for one moment of the situation of this widow and seven children, abandoned by all their followers, cast down overnight from the life of horde chieftains to the existence of the shunned and outlawed, lost between forest and steppe, in this harsh country of the upper Onon. Far from despairing, this valiant woman, summoning all her resources, showed her right to that other title the bard bestows on her, Hö'elün the Wise (*mergen*). First she had to see the children did not die of hunger. For that she resorted to the harvesting of the primitive, simply gathering. "Her hat pulled firmly on and tied tight on her head, she worked from top to bottom the banks of the Onon, plucking wild sorb apples and berries." In Transbaykalia there are in fact to be found in the woods and up to the alpine zone sorbs, bilberry and whortleberry bushes, bearing fruit with which, at the right season, the outcasts could cheat their hunger. Juniper branch in hand, Hö'elün prised up edible roots. These she gave her sons to eat, and garlic and onions. They themselves, as soon as they were a little older, began to help. They made hooks with points and fished from the bank of the Onon, bringing in sometimes only paltry small fish, but sometimes also shadows, fish not unlike salmon, which are quite numerous in the rivers of Transbaykalia. They also used nets, and brought the catch to their mother.

So life for the outcast family went on. The clans who had abandoned them on the shores of the upper Onon counted apparently on their perishing, left to their own devices, of poverty and hunger. In that unrelenting climate, in that society of iron ruthlessness, how should the widow and children do otherwise? Yet they survived because they were themselves of iron race.

The very games of these children were games of hunting or of war. Temüjin made friends with a young boy of the region, Jamuqa, of the Mongol tribe of the Jajirats. "He was eleven when Jamuqa gave him as a present," the Chingiskhanid epic carefully recounts, "a roe deer's knucklebone. Temüjin for his part gave Jamuqa a similar toy in copper, and with these they played together on the ice of the Onon." When it was spring, they practiced archery together with little wooden bows. Jamuqa had made himself sounding arrows with the ends of a young bullock's horns, while Temüjin sharpened arrows in cypress or juniper, and the two children would take turns with each other with these "toys."

Suddenly among the outcasts there broke out a savage family drama.

▲
▲▲

5

The Young Chingis-khan
Kills His Brother

The young men of the wild that Temüjin and his brothers had become
had the brusque reactions to be expected of youths reared as they had
been. They had also the domestic jealousies, the sly fraternal rancors,
nourished in isolation and poverty. The jealousies had an extra edge in
that Yesügei's children came, as we have seen, of two different mothers:
on the one hand the four sons of the Lady Hö'elün, of whom the eldest
was Temüjin, and on the other the two sons of the second wife Söchigil,
namely Bekter and Belgütei. Between these two groups of adolescents
rivalry was not slow to manifest itself. The Mongol epic's bald telling of
the tale, and the backdrop of the action's desolate setting, makes it all
read for us like one of those scenes from life in Siberia in certain Russian
novels.

One day when Temüjin, his younger brother Qasar, and their two half
brothers Bekter and Belgütei were sitting on the bank of the river fishing,
they caught a little fish—a little beauty, shining all over—and, suddenly,
quarreled over who should have it, Temüjin and Qasar against Bekter
and Belgütei. The two latter were stronger and they appropriated the fish.
Back at the *yurt,* Temüjin and Qasar came complaining to their mother:
"A shining fish bit at the hook, but Bekter and Belgütei have taken it
away from us!" Greatly to their surprise, no doubt, the lady Hö'elün, far
from taking their part, defended against her own sons those of the second wife. She was the woman-leader, who thought only of the interest
of the clan: "Let matters be! How can you fight like this, between
brothers?" She reminded them of their isolation as outlaws: "Your only

companions are your shadows!" She recalled the duty of vendetta that lay upon them: "You must have one thought only: how to avenge the injury done to you by the brothers Taychi'ut. Would you show yourselves as disunited as were once the five sons of the fair Alan?"

But Temüjin and Qasar were unconvinced. For Bekter was making a habit of this. Already, a little while back, he had snatched a lark from them, a lark that their arrows had brought down. "Yesterday it was a lark, now it is a fish. We cannot go on living with him!" And with this, angry, full of hate, they flung aside the carpet that served as the *yurt* door, and rushed out.

And the drama moved fast to climax among these adolescents in whom their life of hardship had developed all the passions of grown men. Bekter was sitting on a knoll, whence he guarded his family's horses, nine beasts, among them a fine gelding, silver-grey. Like two redskins in a tale of the Far West, Temüjin and Qasar made their plan. Temüjin came up behind, Qasar in front. Both crept through the grass on all fours, as hunters do who do not want to alert game too soon. The game was their half brother Bekter, still sitting on his knoll, unsuspecting. He became aware of them only when they were drawing their bows, taking aim. He tried to calm them by recalling, as their mother Hö'elün had done a moment ago, their solidarity in face of a common enemy, the Taychi'uts: "Instead of killing each other, we should be carrying out our vendetta on them. The humiliation they put us to is still not avenged. . . . Why do you treat me like an eyelash in the eye, a splinter in the mouth?" Then, as they stood inexorable, arrows at the ready, he made a last plea: "Do not put out my hearth's flame, do not kill my little brother Belgütei!" Then he awaited death, seated cross-legged on top of the hill. Temüjin and Qasar, adjusting their arrows, took aim, "as at a target," one from the front, one from behind. They shot him down and went away, their deed done.

When the two young murderers returned to the *yurt,* their mother Hö'elün, simply from their sinister expressions, understood what had happened. Furiously, she raged at them. "Murderers! One of you [Temüjin] came into the world clutching a clot of black blood! The other is like the savage Qasar dog whose name he bears. You are like the *qablan*-tiger that jumps down from a rock, like the lion that cannot control its fury, like a giant snake that wants to swallow its prey alive, like the falcon that swoops on its own shadow, like the pike that, silently, swallows up the other fish, like a male camel that bites its own colt in the heel, like a wolf that attacks under cover of the storm, like a wild duck that devours its own brood when it cannot follow it, like a jackal that, as soon as it can move, fights for its lair, like a tiger that carries off its victim, like a wild beast that charges blindly. Yet save for your shadow you have no companions, save for your horses' tails you have no whip. The outrage the Taychi'ut committed against us, you cannot even avenge it!"

"Thus the great dowager upbraided her sons, quoting them maxims of time past and the words of the ancients." Meantime Temüjin, having killed the only one of his brothers who dared stand up to him, was now, young as he was, chief of his clan.

Chingis-khan Pilloried

Mother Hö'elün holding up before her sons the threat of the Taychi'uts was indulging in no mere empty rhetoric. That sword indeed hung continually over them, as events were not to be slow to bring home.

The Taychi'ut chief Tarqutay-Qiriltuq, the same, it will be remembered, who had caused the widow and children of Yesügei to be abandoned to their fate, was anxious to find out now what had happened to the outcast family. Doubtless he regretted not having made an end of them while they were so young. "The evil brood must be able to fly by now. They were children, still dribbling. They must have grown up. . . ." Obscurely, he sensed a threat. Grown men, the sons of Yesügei the Brave and the indomitable dowager would not fail to avenge with Taychi'ut blood the injuries done them. Possible revenge must be nipped in the bud by seizing—while there was still time—the whole brood. The Taychi'ut chief set out then at the head of his horsemen for the pastures where Mother Hö'elün and her children led their wretched lives.

At the sight of them, the great widow and the youths at once grasped their peril. They fled in terror to the thickest part of the nearby forest, and took refuge behind a hastily built barricade of trunks and branches. Belgütei cut trees to strengthen the entrenchment, while Qasar, who was showing himself already the skillful archer we are to know later, engaged the assailants in an exchange of arrows. The two younger brothers, Qachi'un and Temüge, and their little sister Temülün, had hidden in a crevice in the rock.

While arrows sped from both sides, the Taychi'ut chiefs shouted what they wanted: "It is your eldest brother, it is Temüjin we want. We wish the rest of you no harm!" By taking Temüjin, they thought they would decapitate the clan. Hearing this, Temüjin's mother and brothers put him on a horse and told him to flee.

Temüjin fled into the forest that covered this corner of the upper Onon, among the cedars of the humid slopes, the larch trees and pines of the higher reaches. But the Taychi'uts saw him and the manhunt began. He plunged into the thickest part of the forest, at the top of Mount Tergüne. The Taychi'uts did not attempt to penetrate so far, but threw a net of sentries around the forest, sure that fatigue and hunger would deliver the fugitive to them. For three days and three nights Temüjin lay low among the thickets. Then finally he decided to try a breakout. As he was going down toward the edge of the forest, leading his horse, the animal's saddle slipped around. He turned, examined the straps: chest harness and girth were both well done up, yet the saddle had worked loose and fallen. Finding no explanation, the hero decided this must be a sign from heaven: the *Kökö Möngke Tengri,* the Eternal Blue Sky, which watched over his race, forbade him to go further. He turned about, went back into the wood, and stayed there another three days and three nights. At the end of that time, driven no doubt by hunger, he made another move to come out, but at the moment he was about to leave the underwood an enormous rock, white—a rock as big as a *yurt,* the bard tells us—came loose from the mountain and rolled to his feet where it blocked the way. This time, there could be no doubt: the Eternal Sky had forbidden him to go farther. A second time he retraced his steps, and held out another three days and nights in the forest.

But the ninth day his strength was exhausted, for during all this time he had had nothing to eat, save probably a few wild berries. Death without glory awaited him, and he chose rather to make his bid. Resolutely, he worked around the white rock that blocked his way, cutting away the branches around it with his archer's knife—the knife he used to sharpen arrows. The moment, leading his horse, he had stepped past the rock, Taychi'uts men stationed there surged up on all sides and threw themselves on him. On the instant he was a prisoner.

Yet, perhaps out of a last feeling of respect to the memory of Yesügei the Brave, the Taychi'ut chief Tarqutay-Qiriltuq did not have Temüjin executed. He was to confess later that he had thought of doing so, but an invincible force had held him back.[1] He contented himself with putting a

---

[1] Undoubtedly there were also between them memories of the former life of the tribe together, when Yesügei was alive. "When Temüjin, was little, as he had been

cangue around his neck and placing him in turn in charge of the guards of different *ayil,* the encampments of *yurts* constituting the nomads' various tribal villages.

---

left alone in the camp (perhaps while Yesügei was away fighting), I would go to look for him, and as he had eyes of fire and a face of light, and as he was attentive, I became fond of teaching him, like a horse of two or three years." So Tarqutay-Qiriltuq was to say later. And even if these are simple euphemisms to recount how later he led the child captive with a cangue around his neck—in truth a somewhat rude education—it must be said that when all was said and done, he spared his life. (*Secret History,* para. 149, No. 25, p. 50.)

Chingis-khan Escapes

How long did the young Temüjin live thus a prisoner, trailing his weary days, with a cangue around his neck, from *yurt* to *yurt,* forever under guard as the heir, the possible avenger, of an enemy clan? His captors were certainly not contemplating freeing him, when he had an opportunity to attempt an escape.

It was the beginning of summer. The Taychi'uts were holding a ceremonial feast on the banks of the Onon. They were to hold festival all day, then break up at sunset. The prisoner had been placed in the charge of a young man who was something of a weakling. Temüjin noticed it. He had soon taken the measure of his escort's strength. Like the youth of the wilds he was, full of cunning and quick decision, he made his plans. He waited till at nightfall the Taychi'uts, full of *qumiz,* had retired to their *yurts.* Then he turned on his guard, and using his cangue as a weapon, brought it down so heavily on his head that it laid the young man out on the floor. Then he took to his heels. But where was he to go? Try to hide in the woods along the Onon banks? They would surely track him down. Resolutely, he plunged into the river, probably among the reeds at the edge, letting only his face show above water. The wooden cangue, still fastened to his neck, now served as a buoy.

Meantime his guard, coming to, had sounded the alarm. The Taychi'uts mustered and organized a systematic beating of the woods and the riverbank. The trees stood out in the moonlight, one could see between them as if it were day. Suddenly one of the pursuers caught sight of Temüjin where he lay absolutely still in the river. By good fortune, this man, a certain Sorqan-shira, did not belong to the Taychi'ut tribe, but to that of the Suldus, mere payers of tribute to the Taychi'uts. He bore the

fugitive none of the bitter hatred of the people of Tarqutay-Qiriltuq.
When, moving along, he saw Temüjin's desperate young face at the
water's surface, he whispered, in pity, and low enough for Temüjin alone
to hear him: "It is for your far-seeing intelligence, for the fire in your
eyes, for the light in your countenance, that the brothers of Taychi'ut
hound you. Do not move. I shall not denounce you." And he kept on his
way.

Meantime the Taychi'uts went stubbornly on beating the riverbank.
Sorqan-shira persuaded them first to work the parts around the tracks that
led to the *yurts*. As soon as they had moved off a little, he warned
Temüjin: "They will come back, with fangs sharpened. Not a movement!
Careful!" And, sure enough, the patrol returned, ready to embark again
on a systematic search of the whole area. Not without courage, though
without overstepping the limits of prudence, Sorqan-shira continued to
dissuade them. "You let him escape in full daylight. And now you think
you are going to recapture him in the middle of the night! Come back as
soon as it is light, and we shall not fail to catch him. Where can a boy get
to, after all, with a cangue around his neck?" Once he was alone, the
excellent man, leaning over the bank, told Temüjin what was happening:
"They are gone now till tomorrow morning! Now, quickly, make your
way back to your mother. Whatever happens, above all never tell anyone
you have seen me!"

An ordinary youth would have done as he was bid, without ado.
Temüjin decided there was more to be made of this stroke of fortune. The
Taychi'uts had gone away. He considered: in his time as a prisoner, he
had been handed over for guard to many heads of *yurts*. In none had he
been treated with so much kindness as in that of Sorqan-shira. Taking
pity on him, Sorqan-shira's two sons, Chimbay and Chila'un, had loosed
him at night from the terrible cangue, to let him sleep. And, today,
Sorqan-shira had discovered him and had not given him up. Perhaps they
would get him away? His mind made up, he went downriver along the
Onon, looking for the *yurt* of Sorqan-shira. He recognized it by a familiar sound: the beating of the churns, which went on into the early hours of
the morning, churning cream for butter. With this to guide him, he found
the *yurt,* and, resolutely, presented himself.

Sorqan-shira might have just saved the young fugitive; he was furious,
for all that, at this uncalled-for appearance, which, if it were to be dis-

covered, could mean his execution as an accomplice. His welcome was accordingly chilly: "Did I not tell you to return to your mother? What are you doing here?" But his two sons, Chimbay and Chila'un, intervened for the wanted man: "When a bird escapes from its cage and takes refuge in a bush, the bush saves its life. How can you treat thus one who seeks refuge with us?" And without waiting for their father's answer, they set Temüjin free from his cangue, and, to be rid of it without trace, threw it on the fire. Behind their *yurt* was a wagon full of wool. They hid him in it, bidding their younger sister, Qada'an, watch over him, without breathing a word to anyone.

For the danger was not over; far from it! After searching in vain for three days, the Taychi'uts, convinced someone must have hidden the fugitive, turned to visiting the *yurts*. At Sorqan-shira's, they searched the whole place, in the wagons, under the beds. Seeing the wagon where Temüjin crouched, they began systematically unloading the wool that concealed him. They were nearly to the bottom when Sorqan-shira, who stood looking on, to all appearances quite calm (his life was in the balance, and he knew it), contrived once again to stop an operation in time. In a tone of total unconcern, he pointed out that the search was ridiculous: "In this heat, who could hide for any length of time at all in a cartful of wool and not suffocate?" The argument had its effect, the Taychi'uts left, but Sorqan-shira, who had given himself up for lost, made haste to get rid of Temüjin: "You have all but had me swept away in the storm like a handful of ashes! Now, away, this minute, back to your mother!" He gave the young man a sterile mare, straw-yellow with a white muzzle, had a lamb roasted for him, filled him two leather bottles, or rather two gourds, of mare's milk. He gave him also a bow with two arrows, but, notes the epic, neither saddle nor flint. Thus equipped, he dispatched him, and must only have breathed freely again when the mare's gallop faded over the horizon.

Temüjin was lucky to meet no enemy. He came without incident to the place where he and his brothers had withdrawn when the Taychi'uts came behind their branch barricade. His family had left the place, naturally, but he could make out their tracks in the grass, going down toward the Onon. He followed them to the junction of the River Kimurqa. Thence they led downstream. Finally, he came on those he sought not far from there, near the hill of Qorchuqi.

The Mongol epic passes over what must have been the joy of these outcasts at the return of the young chief they had believed lost. Shortly after, the whole family moved off for a camp near the Blue Lake (Kökö-na'ur), at the site of the Qara-Jirügen, in the upper Sangghur River valley, within the Gürelgü mountains which project from the Burqan-qaldun massif, that is to say, from the Kentey. In other words, they left the basin of the upper Onon for that of the upper Kerülen, of which the Sangghur is one of the first left-bank tributaries. But the life of the banished family continued to be one of dire hardship; they were reduced to eating the rodents of the steppe, like the *tarbaqan* or *tarbuq,* the meadow marmot, still hunted with dogs in the burrows of the region.[1]

[1] Bouillane de Lacoste, *Au pays sacré des anciens Turcs et Mongols,* p. 159.

The Theft of the Horses

The ray of light in Temüjin's fortunes was his horses. One day when eight of them, among them a silver-grey gelding, of celebrated role in this history, were grazing in front of the *yurt,* they were swept off by raiders from the steppe. Temüjin and his brothers had to stand by, powerless, and watch the theft, for the only remaining horse, a brown charger, had been taken by Belgütei, out hunting marmots in the steppe. They made a vain dash in pursuit on foot: it was of course hopeless to overtake the marauders. Toward evening, at sunset, Belgütei came home at last, leading the brown horse, the animal so laden with marmots that its burden swayed.

When Belgütei heard of the disaster—for such it was: eight out of nine horses gone, for these unhappy people, was quite simply ruin, irreparable —he was going on forthwith himself in pursuit, but Qasar protested: "You will not succeed, let me go!" But it was Temüjin who as young chief took the decision: "Neither of you will succeed. It is I who am going after them!" He jumped astride the brown charger and sped into the grasslands following the tracks of the stolen herd.

He rode for two days and two nights. At the end of the third night, in the light of dawn, he saw a young boy with a group of horses, milking the mares. He asked him about the stolen chargers. The boy answered that he had indeed seen during the night, shortly before sunrise, people passing who drove before them eight horses, one of them a silver-grey gelding.

The boy's name was Bo'orchu. He was the only son of the Mongol Naqu bayan—Naqu the Rich—of the tribe of the Arulats. He was frank and full of liveliness and he was at once attracted to Temüjin: "Friend (*nökör*)," he declared, "I see you are in trouble. I offer you my friendship and help." He suggested, indeed, that he should guide Temüjin in the direction the robbers had taken with the horses. The brown horse Temüjin was riding was exhausted. Bo'orchu gave him instead of it a fresh mount—a white charger with a black stripe on its back. He himself took a particularly fast cream-colored horse. Clearly, if he had consulted his father the latter would have prevented him getting drawn into such an enterprise out of mere chivalry for a stranger. But Bo'orchu took care not to reappear at his *yurt*. He did not even take back the milk, but left the leather pails, full as they were, in mid-pasture. The two jumped into the saddle and made off after the thieves.

For two days, they scanned the horizon of the steppe in vain. On the evening of the third day, as the sun went down behind a hill, they descried a small herd grouped around a camp, doubtless with wagons disposed Mongol-fashion to form an enclosure. There were the eight stolen horses—among them the silver-grey gelding—not on the move, but grazing! Temüjin at once instructed his young companion: "Do not move from here, friend! I am going to drive the horses out of the park." But the excellent Bo'orchu intended to share the risks of his friend: "I came to help you. Why should I stay here doing nothing?" They went together into the park, rounded up the eight chargers, and made off with them into the plain. The robbers, naturally, as soon as they realized what was happening, hurled themselves full gallop after them. One warrior, on a white horse, drew ahead of the group and was already brandishing a lasso: "Friend," cried Bo'orchu to Temüjin, "quick, pass me a bow and arrow. I want to draw on that man!" "I do not want you to be wounded because of me," the young hero replied. "It is for me to challenge him!" He turned and, bow taut, took aim at the man on the white horse. The latter halted, and, on his side, threatened Temüjin with his lasso. Meantime the others of the pursuing party had come up with their comrade, and things might well perhaps have taken a critical turn for Temüjin, if darkness falling had not prevented combat. Not daring to risk a manhunt in the growing obscurity, over the immensity of the steppe, the pursuers turned about. Temüjin and Bo'orchu, who for their part knew their way, galloped three days and three nights till they arrived at Bo'orchu's *yurt*.

There, Temüjin thanked Bo'orchu with great warmth: "Friend, how, without your help, should I ever have found my horses again? We shall share them: how many do you want?" The magnanimous Bo'orchu would have none of them; what he had done, he had done out of sympathy with the young chief: "If I joined in your quest, it was because I saw you in trouble and wished to help you recover what was yours. How should I now take a part of your herd? My father is called Naqu the Rich and I am his only son. That patrimony is enough for me. I will accept nothing from you!" Together they made toward the *yurt* of Naqu. He was weeping over the disappearance of his son. At the sight of him he had thought lost, he wept again, but tears of joy. After which he had for Bo'orchu, for the anxiety he had caused him, a sharp reprimand. But he did not forget his guest: he had roasted a suckling lamb, which he gave Temüjin as provision for the last part of his journey. And for the rest before Temüjin set out again, he gave his blessing to the friendship his son and the young chief had formed: "Keep always the same faith with one another," he said to Bo'orchu and Temüjin. "Let no angry word ever come between you!" The friendship was to endure, indeed, as long as the two men lived.

Taking farewell of his two friends, Temüjin, driving his horses before him, took once more the road to the family encampment. Another ride of three days and three nights brought him at last to his own people on the banks of the River Sangghur. Uneasy as his absence first drew out, his mother Hö'elün and his brothers, beginning with Qasar, had by now reached a state little short of anguish. And here now he came, safe and sound, and bringing with him the eight horses his valor had recovered. Joy and confidence reigned again in the little band.

These were the modest debuts, similar to those of every young man of the steppe, of one who was one day to be Conqueror of the World: an adventure that almost turned out badly, or at least almost ended in perpetual captivity, but from which he escaped by audacity and *sang-froid;* then a theft of horses that he succeeded in recapturing, by dint, again, of decisiveness and determination. What is striking in the two cases is the attraction he has for all who come in contact with him, the respect accorded him, young as he still is, as the natural due of a powerful personality. Remember the words of Sorqan-shira, when he saw him surfacing between eddies in the moonlit waters of the Onon: it was because he had been as if fascinated by the power in the eyes of this youth, bespeaking already the soul of a chief, that Sorqan-shira, at the risk of his own life, saved the hunted boy. And then we have the young Bo'orchu, at the first meeting making himself over to Temüjin, linking their fortunes for all time. He also found irresistible "the unwithstandable light of those falcon's eyes."

And we shall see successively, and in mounting tempo, clans and tribes, peoples and kingdoms, pledge themselves to him, won by his gifts of command, his senses of equity, his gratitude for services rendered. His affection for his friends of the early days, like Bo'orchu, was to be proverbial. A code of great tenets, where loyalty to friends was matched only by the ferocity shown to enemies.

 ▲
▲▲

9

Chingis-khan's Marriage

Temüjin had sufficiently redeemed his fortunes to think of marriage. He did not forget that at the age of nine he had been bethrothed by his father to Börte, daughter of the Onggirat chief Deisechen. The girl, even at that time, already stood out among the "fine-cheeked" Onggirat girls with the dazzling faces, sought after in marriage by the chiefs of the Mongol clans. She must now be grown up, and the time was come for marriage, provided Deisechen was still of the same mind. Temüjin, anxious to have things settled, took his young brother Belgütei and with him made his way down the valley of the Kerülen towards the Onggirat country.

Deisechen was camping still in the same region as formerly, between the Chekcher and the Chiqurqu mountains; that is, between the inflow of the Kerülen to Lake Kölen and the River Urshi'un that runs into the same lake. He gave the young man the warmest of welcomes: "I knew the Taychi'uts were out against you, and I was greatly anxious for you. But you have come back!" Perhaps he had felt remorse for having let him depart on that earlier occasion, alone and so young amid so many dangers. Perhaps also he was thinking to himself that, considering he was his son-in-law-to-be, he had done little enough to help him through the years of hardship. At all events, seeing him now grown and strong, he hesitated not at all in giving him in marriage the beautiful Börte. He then accompanied the young couple up as far as Uraq-chöl, on the lower Kerülen. And his wife, Shotan, Börte's mother, came with her daughter all the way to the encampment of Temüjin's family, by the River Sangghur and Mount Gürelgü. Before she left, she made a present to Temüjin's mother, the lady Hö'elün, of a magnificent coat of black sables. We shall see that the young chief was not long in turning this to sound diplomatic account.

Temüjin, now wed, turned to increasing his military strength. As a start he called on his friend Bo'orchu: he sent Belgütei to fetch him. Bo'orchu once again did not stop to tell his father. He jumped on a horse—a brown horse with a slightly arched back—made a roll on the saddle of his cloak of grey felt, and came in immediate response to his young chief's summons.

He was one day to be first "marshal" of the "great army" that was to take shape up there, on the *tayga*-grassland border.

In this epic, Börte, Temüjin's new wife, was to have her part to play. She was to be for him a pillar of strength. First and foremost—for a Mongol the essential—she bore him four sturdy sons: Jöchi, Jaghatay, Ögödei, and Toluy. But she also proved for the hero a sagacious counselor, whose advice he heeded. At the decisive moments, when the future Chingis-khan hesitated over which path to take, it was Börte's ideas that prevailed. And behind these ideas lay both drive and foresight. Börte, for the rest, always enjoyed great prestige in the eyes of her redoubtable husband. To be sure, like all Mongol chiefs, he had no hesitation, later, in taking secondary wives, whom as occasion arose he would take with him on his far-flung campaigns, while Börte stayed in Mongolia. But only the children of Börte were to share in the paternal inheritance. Börte alone ranked above all others, men or women. The respect her husband invariably showed her was unaffected even when she was carried off by Merkit bands and, nine months after, returned pregnant and bore a son. This unfortunate episode Chingis-khan chose not even to inquire into. Börte remained after it, as before, the highly esteemed "lady" (*qatun*), the conqueror's partner in the triumph of this prodigious epic.[1]

[1] [Concerning a fifth son of Chingis by a secondary wife (a Nayman woman), named Jürchedei, who apparently died about 1213-14, Cf. Pelliot, No. 10, p. 923.]

The Coat of Black Sables

Temüjin's marriage marked for him the end of the years of trial. He had eluded the Taychi'uts; he had established himself as the up and coming younger man beginning to be feared or sought after in the region; he could think now of renewing old alliances.

Yesügei, Temüjin's father, had formerly, it will be remembered, helped to re-establish on the throne one of the most powerful kings of the steppe, Toghril, king of the Kereits, that people of uncertain origins who led a nomadic existence around the upper Tula. Temüjin was now firmly enough in a saddle to be able, without importuning Toghril, to remind him of these earlier events. He did so, naturally, with all the modesty befitting one whose position was but briefly re-established, but also with a dignity befitting one of his lineage. With his two brothers Qasar and Belgütei, he set out on horseback for the Black Forest (Qara-tun) on the banks of the River Tula, where Toghril lived. Their road, from the source of the Kerülen, where the hero's family was then encamped, to the upper Tula, is one of those the most often described in Mongol itineraries. A grass landscape, particularly picturesque in the spring, "when the lush grass is bespangled with the bright yellow of crucifers and buttercup, the mauve of the tufts of thyme, the violet of iris, the pure white of stellaria or the pale velvet of edelweiss." Winding through this steppe runs the Tula, its course marked by a double row of poplars and willows. Northward, on the horizon, rise the tormented granite contours of the Kentey. To the south, the rounded breasts of the foothills stretch in a chain toward the Gobi. To the west, the range of Bogdo-ula, dividing the Kerülen basin from that of the Tula, is covered, from 5,800 to 8,300 feet, with a dense forest of conifers, birches, and aspen, safeguarded by religion as the dwelling of the spirits. Lower and middle slopes bear the Transbaykalian pines after which this forest is named, whose clearings served as royal residence for the sovereign of the Kereits.

It was indeed at the verge of one of these forests of the Ulan Bator region—the Black Forest, of frequent mention in this story—that the Kereit king Toghril was encamped. Introducing himself, Temüjin with his first words renewed the links of the past: "Formerly you and my father made yourselves brothers in oath [*anda*]. Now, therefore, you are as my father." And in support of his sentiments the young chief proffered to the Kereit king a singularly acceptable gift: the coat of black sables that had been his wife's family's wedding present.

Toghril, flattered by this tribute, assured him of his support in re-establishing his father's kingdom. "Your people, who have left you, I will bring them back to you. Your people, who are scattered, I will bring them together again for you." This was a solemn pact by which the Kereit sovereign took under his protection the son of his former *anda,* and by which Temüjin formally acknowledged himself client and even vassal of Toghril, a most important pact, which was to hold until 1203. Over all that period Kereit support was to enable the future Chingis-khan, as their chief had promised, to triumph over the greater part of the ancient Mongol tribes. Reciprocally, the loyalty of Temüjin to his suzerain was to guarantee the latter against all revolt or aggression.

Indeed, this pact concluded, Temüjin found his position remarkably strengthened. It was not necessary for him to make the overtures to strike up or renew invaluable friendships. He had scarcely returned from Kereit country to his Bürgi encampments near the source of the Kerülen before his nascent reputation began to bring him adherents. Thus there arrived from the region of the Burqan-qaldun—that is, from the Kentey mountains—a member of the Uriyangqay tribe, the old man Jarchi'uday, "with his smith's bellows on his shoulders." The detail is interesting, since from earliest times these populations of the Altay, whether of the Mongolian side or the Siberian, have been reputed experts in metallurgy. In prehistoric days, it was probably the ancient metallurgists of the region of Minussinsk, in Siberia, who taught China the use of bronze, and later, in the sixth century A.D., the ancient Turks of the Orkhon were equally celebrated as smiths.[1] Jarchi'uday, the aged smith, came down

[1] [Denis Sinor, "The Historical Rôle of the Türk Empire," *Journal of World History,* Vol. I, 1953, pp. 423-34.]

from the sacred mountain of Burqan-qaldun armed with the ancient secrets that made sword edge and arrow point sure instruments to their purpose. Furthermore, he brought leading him by the hand to Chingis-khan his young son Jelme. And the good old man said: "When you were born near the Deli'ün hill (Deli'ün-boldaq), on the banks of the Onon, I was there, O Temüjin. I offered you then a couch of sable fur. I offered you also my son Jelme as servant, but he himself was then too small, and I took him away with me. But now here he is. It is he who will saddle your horse and who will open the door of your *yurt*."

We shall see with what magnificent fidelity Jelme was henceforth to serve his master, and with what affectionate gratitude the future Chingis-khan rewarded him.

The Abduction of the Beautiful Börte

Temüjin had re-formed his clan. He had obtained the protection of the powerful king of the Kereits. After so many years of hardship, the future seemed to smile upon him. But these empires of the steppe were curiously unstable. Just when the young chief thought his fortunes assured, all was suddenly thrown once more into jeopardy.

Temüjin was still camped by the Bürgi, near the source of the Kerülen, with his young wife, the beautiful Börte. They cannot long have been married. One morning, in the first glimmerings of dawn, a woman in the service of Mother Hö'elün, old Qo'aqchin, heard, putting her ear to the ground, the sound of a band of galloping horsemen approaching. She jumped to her feet, calling Hö'elün, wakening all the *yurt:* "Mother, Mother, quickly, up! The ground shakes. It is like thunder. It is perhaps the terrible Taychi'uts!" Hö'elün commanded her sons to be roused, and herself rose in haste. In an instant the whole clan was up. Only just in time. The enemy came on like a whirlwind. It was not this time the Taychi'uts, as old Qo'aqchin had thought, but the Merkits, a Mongol tribe of the southern Baykal region, three hundred of whose horsemen hoped to take the sons of Yesügei by surprise. There were bitter enmities between them, an old vendetta to settle: had not Yesügei, in former times, once snatched from a Merkit the lady Hö'elün? The Merkits thought to avenge themselves by carrying off their enemies' women, and first and foremost the young wife of Temüjin.

The latter—and this is beautifully illustrative of milieu and time— seems there and then to have resigned himself quite coolly to his misfortune. Or so the Mongol epic makes no bones about giving us to understand. Despite his increased resources, Temüjin still possessed only nine horses. He, his mother Hö'elün, his brothers Qasar, Qachi'un, Temüge and Belgütei, his two followers, Bo'orchu and Jelme, each bestrode one. Hö'elün took the little Temülün, Temüjin's young sister, up before her. The group took a led horse in case of emergency, and there was no mount for the beautiful Börte, for Temüjin's own wife, whom he abandoned without a qualm. Left behind likewise was the second wife of Yesügei, Belgütei's mother.

While Temüjin and his family fled galloping on their chargers towards the massif of Burqan-qaldun, the present-day Kentey, poor Börte made her efforts to escape the enemy. Her old servant, the valiant Qo'aqchin, hid her in a black wagon, to which she harnessed a speckled ox, and drove her as far as she could, up the bank of the little River Tenggeli. But dawn began to light the valley. To the wagon came a Merkit party who questioned Qo'aqchin. She told them that she had come to work at Temüjin's camp for the sheepshearing, and was now on her way home. The Merkits for their part asked if Temüjin was still at his *yurt,* and how far they were from this. She simply gave the direction of the *yurt* from which Temüjin and his followers had fled. The Merkits went on their way, and the old woman, desperately, flogged the oxen to get away as fast as she could. But now the wagon axle broke. There was nothing for Qo'aqchin and Börte but to go on on foot, under cover of the woods that bordered the Tenggeli. But before they had set out, the Merkits returned. They had found in the *yurt,* naturally, none of the chiefs of the clan, only women and children, among them the mother of Belgütei whom they had seized and whom one of them now had across his saddle bow. More suspicious than at the first encounter, they wanted to know what was in the wagon. In vain Qo'aqchin, with her fine *sang-froid,* assured them it was only a load of wool. They were not satisfied. The oldest of the Merkit horsemen ordered the younger men to dismount and search the vehicle: it did not take them long to find poor Börte. They seized her and Qo'aqchin, hoisted them on their horses, and set off again at a gallop in pursuit of Temüjin, whose tracks, clearly visible in the grass now that it was daylight, led them toward Mount Burqan-qaldun. Coming to the foot of the mountain, they circled it three times without finding where Temüjin had plunged into the underwood. The approaches to the mountain were indeed barred by marshes and dense thickets. The Merkits tried in vain for a way through, then became discouraged and gave up.

But out of a curious spirit of revenge they gave Börte to one of their number, Chilger-bökö—Chilger the Athlete—because this warrior was the young brother of Yeke-Chiledü, from whom Yesügei had once snatched his wife, the lady Hö'elün. So the vendettas were perpetuated, tribe to tribe, with their train, for every generation, of abductions and brutal amours.

Meantime Temüjin, in the mountain thickets where he had made himself a hut of elm and willow branches, waited on events. Had the Merkits gone home or had they mounted some kind of ambush in the vicinity? He sent out Belgütei, Bo'orchu, and Jelme to reconnoiter, and they searched the country over a wide area for three days without coming on an enemy. Reassured, he came down then from Burqan-qaldun, not forgetting to give thanks first to the divinity of the mountains. Striking his breast, he cried to the sky: "Thanks to the weasel's ear and fox's eye of old Qo'aqchin, I have escaped with my life, I have been able to slip with my horse along the paths of deer and elk. I have been greatly afraid. But Burqan-qaldun has saved me: each morning henceforth, therefore, will I honor him with offerings, each day address prayers to him; and, after me, my children and my grandchildren shall remember and do likewise." So he spoke, and, following Mongol custom, turned to face the sun, took his belt up to hang around his neck, uncovered his head, struck his breast, genuflected nine times, and poured a libation.

Here is one of the characteristic ceremonies of primitive Mongol religion. The homage paid Burqan-qaldun was part of the cult the Altaic peoples addressed to the divinities of the mountain tops by which the ancient Turks of the seventh century, for instance, had worshiped the forest-covered mountain of Ötüken, apparently identifiable with a peak of the Khangay. The offerings to the sun (naran) are part of the more general cult of the Tengri, or, to keep the ritual Mongol formula, the Kökö Möngke Tengri, the "Eternal Blue Sky," the Mongol's supreme deity. The offerings in question consisted basically in libations of qumiz, the fermented mare's milk that was the pastoral nomad's favorite drink. The genuflections or prostrations, finally, in series of nine, form part of Mongol ritual, and also protocol, figuring in both the cult of the gods and in monarchic ceremonial.

If we are to go by the very shocking account in the Mongol epic, Temüjin appears to have accommodated himself with some equanimity to the abduction of his young wife. He had preferred to see her carried off rather than jeopardize his personal safety by giving up his led horse. And in fact his calculations had been sound, Börte's capture having undoubtedly delayed the aggressors and given the Mongol chief time to reach the shelter of Burqan-qaldun. The words of his mother Hö'elün in analogous circumstances come to mind: "If you can get away alive, you will not want for maidens perched on wagon seats, or women even in the black wagons."

Notwithstanding this scarcely chivalrous philosophy, Temüjin had not forgotten the beautiful Börte. He was in no sense resigned to losing her for ever. So as soon as he took reassurance from the departure of the Merkits, he drew up his plan of campaign to get her back. Did he know that, as we have seen, his young wife had been handed over to one of the Merkit chiefs, to Chilger the Athlete, and shared his *yurt*? If he learned of it, the sting of the news can but have revived his desire. It should be remembered that Börte was still a very young woman, that she had not yet borne him a child, and that the loving of these two had been too brutally cut short for Temüjin to feel anything now but bitter regret at losing her. Possibly also he reproached himself with having so readily sacrificed her instead of taking her with the rest of his family, on the led horse.

▲
▲▲

12

Chingis-khan Wins Back the Beautiful Börte

To win back the beautiful Börte, Temüjin thought at once to beg the assistance of the Kereit king Toghril, of whom he had but lately acknowledged himself the client and adoptive son. With his brothers Qasar and Belgütei he set out then for the Black Forest country, on the Tula, where Toghril lived.

The request he made in his circumstances is precisely the one a young baron of twelfth-century Western Europe would in similar plight have brought to the feet of his suzerain: "Behold three Merkit tribes fell on us suddenly and carried off our wives and children. O khan, my father, help us, we beseech you, to deliver them!" And Toghril on his side answered as would have one of our feudal kings: "I have not forgotten the services rendered me by Yesügei your father. Moreover, the aid you ask of me today, did I not already promise it to you the day you came with your offering of black sable furs? Remember my words. Your wife Börte shall be restored to you, come all the Merkit tribes at once against us!"

War on the Merkits was in fact a considerable undertaking. They were a group of tribes of Mongol stock who dwelt on the border of the steppe and the Siberian *tayga,* in the northern basin of the Selenga. There were three principal tribes: the Uduyit-Merkits, the Uwas-Merkits, and the Qa'at-Merkits. The first, under their chief Toqto'a-beki, were camping at that time at Bu'ura-ke'er, that is, in the "steppe of male camels," which Haenisch locates toward the lower Uda, east of Verkhne-udinsk. The Uwas-Merkits, under chief Dayir-usun, were camping at Talqun Island, at the forked confluence of the Orkhon and the Selenga. The Qa'at-

Merkits, lastly, under the command of Qa'atay-darmala, were over toward Qaraji-ke'er, another steppe of the region. These were the wooded
steppes of Transbaykalia, with alternating grassland and pine, the latter
thickly undergrown with rhododendrons and orchids. Then, moving
north, the forests stretched ever denser, birches and larches predominat-
ing, to the chains of mountains separating this region from the southern
shores of Lake Baykal, mountains with peaks rising to 6,600 feet, marking the start of the true Siberian *tayga*.

Before embarking on war with the Merkits, the Kereit khan called on
a third ally, Jamuqa, chief of the Mongol tribe of the Jajirats, or Jadarans. Jamuqa, it will be remembered, was the former childhood friend
of Temüjin, and both continued to think of themselves as brothers. The
title "brothers by oath" (*anda*) had in Mongol society real validity, imposing duties on the two warriors who had thus designated themselves,
just as did the title of "father" (*echige*) Temüjin gave the Kereit khan.

While Temüjin was setting about rebuilding the strength of his clan,
Jamuqa also had become a chief, and even probably a more powerful
one, since he commanded a whole tribe. Toghril had good reasons, therefore, when he suggested Temüjin ask his childhood friend to take part
in their enterprise. "Send a message to your young brother Jamuqa."
Jamuqa was encamped at that time near the river Qorqonaq, one of the
tributaries of the Onon, probably the present-day Kurkhu, or, less probably, the Kirkun, farther to the northeast. Toghril promised Temüjin to
start off with 20,000 Kereits, who would form the right wing of the
army. "Little brother" Jamuqa should bring a like number of warriors to
form the left wing—which shows that the young Jajirat khan had under
him, as already suggested, a quite considerable grouping of clans. Toghril left it to Jamuqa to decide where they should join forces.

Acting on Toghril's advice, Temüjin sent his brothers Qasar and
Belgütei to Jamuqa to tell him: "The Merkits have cast me into afflic-
tion. They have carried off my wife: my bed is now deserted. The half of
my breast has been snatched from me. Are we not, you and I, of the same
lineage? Shall we not avenge this injury?" To which message Jamuqa
returned the reply of the chivalrous knight: "I had learned that the bed
of my friend Temüjin was deserted, that the half of his breast had been
snatched from him, and my heart [literally: my liver] has been grieved.
We shall therefore crush the three Merkit tribes, and set free our lady

Börte!" And the Mongol epic, in best Homeric vein, here has Jamuqa (and also Toghril) breathe out fiery threats against the two enemy chiefs, Toqto'a "who will take fright simply at the beating of the felt saddles, thinking he hears already the sound of our drums," Dayir-usun, "who will panic merely at the sound of our quivers."

Jamuqa outlined to Temüjin's two envoys the plan of operation. He had been finding out how things stood. The three Merkit tribes, come together briefly for the carrying off of Börte, had gone their separate ways again. Leaving aside for the present the Uwas-Merkits, encamped, as stated, at the confluence of the Orkhon and Selenga rivers, the allies would concentrate their attentions on the Uduyit-Merkits, the principal tribe, then under their chief Toqto'a in the lower Uda valley. Toghril, Temüjin, and Jamuqa himself, marching south to north, would make a raft crossing of the River Kilko, the Khilok of our modern atlases; then they would fall on Toqto'a "as through the airhole of his *yurt;* they would throw down his *yurt's* master pole." [1]

Before Qasar and Belgütei remounted, Jamuqa charged them again to assure "his friend Temüjin" and "his elder brother Toghril" of his complete dedication to their enterprise: "I have consecrated [to the Spirits] my standard of yak tails seen from afar. I have had sounded my drum of black bull hide. I have put on my leather armor, mounted my black charger, seized my lance and my curved saber, notched my arrows of peachwood. With the Merkits it is now war to the death!"

The plan of campaign drawn up by Jamuqa, as set forth by the Mongol bard, was precisely mapped out. Toghril, with the Kereit army, setting out from his Black Forest camping ground, near the present-day Ulan Bator, was to join Temüjin below Mount Burqan-qaldun—the present-day Kentey—and both were to move on to the steppe of Botoqan-bo'ordji, to the headwaters of the Onon; while Jamuqa himself made his way up the actual Onon valley to meet them there and join forces. This was by any standard a major operation, if what was involved was indeed, as the Mongol bard says, the assembling, without alerting the enemy, of some 40,000 horsemen, maneuvering through a series of cols, in this high "region of springs" on the northeast slopes of the Kentey. In

---

[1] The supporting beam that among the Mongols had a sacred character, or, if the Mongol *yurt* of the twelfth century was like those of today, the internal framework of wooden shafts over which the felt carpets were spread.

accordance with Jamuqa's directions, khan Toghril advanced with 10,000 Kereits to Mount Burqan-qaldun, toward the settlement of the Bürgi-ergi, near the source of the Kerülen. Temüjin, who was camped at Bürgi-ergi, made way for him and moved up toward the Tana, a tributary stream of the Kerülen, at the foot of the pine- and larch-covered Kentey. The two forces (Toghril's reinforced by 10,000 more mounted Kereits under his young brother Jaqa-gambu) actually joined up at Ayil-qara-qana, near the stream Kimurqa, apparently one of the sources of the Onon, in the mountain still known today as Kümür, a northeast spur of the Kentey.

Temüjin, Toghril, and Jaqa-gambu came then to Botoqan-bo'ordji, the appointed general assembly point, which lay quite close, also by the headwaters of the Onon. There they found Jamuqa, who had been wait-ing there three days and whose patience had worn thin. He greeted them tartly: "Did we not agree that through the unleashed elements, through the worst of snowstorms even, we should be punctual at the rendezvous? Is the word of a Mongol, or is it not, his bond? He who failed to keep a pact used to be driven out from among us. Yet this is what we have just done ourselves!" Toghril agreed civilly that he and Temüjin deserved a reproof. Jamuqa in fact, at this point, from the role he plays in the cam-paign and from the tone he takes, not only is dominant partner in the "brother" relationship with Temüjin, but with his Jajirats commands suf-ficient force to assert authority over the khan of the Kereits himself.

From Botoqan-bo'orji the allies moved north across what is now the Russian frontier. Crossing the Kümür mountain chain, they made their way probably down the Menja valley into the basin of the River Chikoyi, whence, via the cols of the Malkhan mountains, they pushed on into the heart of Merkit territory, into the valley of the Kilko River, now known as the Khilok, which they crossed on rafts, east of Kiakhta and Troicko-cawsk. Spilling like a waterspout onto the steppe of Bu'ura (Bu'ura-ke'er), which has been sited in the Uda basin—wooded steppe, in that case—they fell at dead of night on the camp of Toqto'a-beki, chief of the Uduyit-Merkits, and seized the women and the children. They had even hoped to surprise Toqto'a asleep, but fishers on the Kilko and sable hunters who had been out setting their traps had had time to give the alarm at the last minute in the darkness. Toqto'a-beki and the chief of the Uwas-Merkits, Dayir-usun, were thus just able to get away in time, making off, with a handful of their followers, down the valley of the Selenga into Barghuchin country, to the eastern shore, that is, of Lake Baykal. They escaped, but only by abandoning everything, *yurts,* families, domestic tools, provisions. They made their way through the Siberian *tayga* into the valley of the Barghuchin, which runs down parallel toward the lake—"toward the sea," as the Mongols say—level with the bay of the same name.

Meantime, in the turmoil of the night attack, the Mongol horsemen galloped on the heels of fugitives, grabbed left and right captives and booty. But Temüjin, heedless of the battle, thought only of the wife he loved. Amid the cries of terror and death, he called desperately for Börte. At that moment, he came on a pack of fugitives, and one of them was Börte—and Börte, caught up in the rout of her kidnapers suddenly recognized her husband's voice. Quivering, she jumped from the wagon that was carrying her away, and with old Qo'aqchin ran in the direction of his voice. A moment and she was there before him. "She seized the rein of his horse. The moon shone full. Temüjin recognized her. They threw themselves into each other's arms." Temüjin sent word at once to khan Toghril and his "brother" Jamuqa: "She whom I sought, she whom I grieved for, I have found. We wish to go no further tonight, but to camp here."

Clearly, the future Chingis-khan did not hold against Börte her forced cohabitation with a Merkit chief; nor does this seem to have caused Börte herself any embarrassment. And she could scarcely feel her place insecure in the heart and passions of a hero who, to win her back, had turned Mongolia upside down, formed a coalition of kings, and mobilized over 40,000 men. But from her time among the Merkits, Börte returned on the verge of becoming a mother: almost immediately on her return to the Chingiskhanid *yurt,* she gave birth there to a boy—Jöchi. The child was to rank officially as Temüjin's eldest son, but the gossip could never be killed that said he was, rather, the work of Chilger-bökö.[2]

It will be remembered, indeed, that during her captivity the beautiful Börte was assigned to Chilger-bökö—Chilger the Athlete—younger

---

[2] Whatever the case, the conqueror seems never to have shown ill-will toward Börte over this delicate matter. There is the point, of course, that any ill temper on his part would have been somewhat illogical, since on the day of the Merkit incursion he had flatly abandoned the young woman.

brother of the Uduyit-Merkit chief Toqto'a-beki. The Chingiskhanid epic tells of the terror of the Mongol Paris at the return of the outraged husband. "The black crow should eat bits of skin. Nevertheless it covets wild geese, swans and herons. So I, Chilger, despite my inferior station, I desired the noble, the holy Börte, and I have brought misfortune on my people!" And to save his life, "which was not worth a sheep's dropping," he went into hiding "in the obscure gorges of the mountain," probably in the chain of the Ulan-burgassu, which looks down from 5,600 feet on the valley of the Uda and the eastern shore of Lake Baykal.

In revenge, Temüjin and his allies seized Qa'atay-darmala, chief of the Qa'at-Merkit tribe. He was put in a cangue, and forced to act as guide for the army back to Burqan-qaldun.

Börte, however, was not the only princess of Temüjin's family the Merkits had carried off. They had seized also the former second wife of Yesügei, Söchigil, mother of Belgütei. Learning that his mother was in one of the *yurts* of what had been the Merkit camp, Belgütei set out to find her. But the former second wife had a noble soul. As Belgütei entered by the right-hand door of her *yurt,* she made a precipitous exit by the left, clad in a tattered sheepskin tunic. "Did I not have it predicted to me our sons should one day become great princes? How should I, who have had here to lie with a common Merkit, dare to show myself again before my sons?" With these words she fled into the thickest part of the forest, and all attempts to find her failed. Belgütei vented his grief on the Merkit prisoners or fugitives: he brought down with arrows all of them he saw, crying: "Bring me back my mother!" As for those of the Merkits who had lately taken part in the kidnaping of Börte and the pursuit of Temüjin to Mount Burqan-qaldun—there were 300 of them, we are told —the Mongol epic declares they were all ruthlessly exterminated "with their children and their children's children," and that no more remained of them than of "dust scattered in the wind." The wives and daughters of the vanquished the victors took as concubines, as many as they wanted; boys and small girls became servants, "to open and shut the door of the *yurt.*"

We shall see, however, that, whatever the Mongol epic claims, the Merkit people were far from being exterminated. Toqto'a-beki and his followers, when they had recuperated in the inaccessible forests of Barghuchin, in the Transbaykalian *tayga,* were to make many comebacks to dispute the Mongol steppe with Chingis-khan, and take part in coalitions against him. But of these seizings of women, repeated generation by generation, was born a hatred nothing could extinguish and nothing end, short of the utter extermination of one of the two tribal groupings.

The Mongol empire was established only by dint of prior massacre of half the Mongol tribes.

The massacres had their delightful incidentals. Found in the Uduyit-Merkit camp was a child of five named Güchü, shining-eyed, wide awake, in a sable bonnet, with doeskin boots and a garment of otterskin. They made a present of him to Temüjin's mother, the dowager Hö'elün, who adopted him.

Temüjin, who owed to "the khan his father" Toghril and his "brother" Jamuqa the deliverance of Börte, gave them magnificent thanks. He rendered thanks too to the *Tengri,* the sky-god of the Turco-Mongols, and to the "earth mother" (*eke-ötüken*) who had helped him to take revenge on the Merkits, "to empty their heart and pull apart their liver." Then the allies split up. If the steppe of Bu'ura-ke'er, where they had thus taken Toqto'a by surprise in the night, was in fact, as Haenisch maintains, the region east of the present-day Verkhne-udinsk,[3] Temüjin, Toghril, and Jamuqa presumably went on to drive the third Merkit tribe, the Uwas-Merkits, from the peninsula formed by the confluence of the Orkhon and the Selenga ("Talqun island, Talqun-aral"), since this was where the army disbanded.

[3] [Today the town is called Ulan-Ude. It is the capital city of the Buryat ASSR.]

▲
▲▲

13

Convoy in the Night and the
Separation of the Hordes

So the allies, having achieved their purpose, separated. That is to say, the Kereit khan Toghril returned to his normal camping grounds in the Black Forest, on the upper Tula, but Temüjin and Jamuqa stayed together. They set up camp in Qorqonaq-jubur, a wooded part near the Onon.

The warfare waged together against the Merkit people had renewed between these two men the ties of their childhood friendship. They enjoyed themselves talking over their memories, how they played with knucklebones on the banks of the Onon and exchanged their little arrows. Now both were chiefs. It was Temüjin who was of nobler blood, as a descendant of the former royal family, but undoubtedly at this time Jamuqa wielded the greater power, as is evident from his role of commander in chief in the campaign against the Merkits. But their relationship was at all events one of complete, unreserved friendship: were they not *anda,* brothers by oath, called on by this sworn fraternal obligation to help each other in all things? They exchanged their booty. Temüjin gave Jamuqa a belt of gold taken from Toqto'a, and Toqto'a's horse, a mare with black mane and tail, and Jamuqa gave Temüjin the gold belt of the other Merkit chief, Dayir-usun, and the latter's mare, a steed white as a sheep. In Qorqonaq-jubur, under a bushy tree—perhaps the same age-old sacred tree in whose shade the last Mongol khan Qutula had been proclaimed—under the steep rock of Quldaqar, they sealed their pact of alliance with a great feast. They danced under the tree as the khan Qutula had danced, and at night they slept under the same covering. This close union lasted a year and a half.

Temüjin and Jamuqa in fact—and the setting of Qorqonaq-jubur is significant in this respect, since it was there the last khan of the former Mongol royal house had celebrated his accession—Temüjin and Jamuqa, after their victory over the Merkits, were resuscitating the monarchy. But they were resuscitating it in the guise of a dyarchy, the title *anda* by which they called one another conferring on their alliance the sacred character of a fraternal bond. But dyarchies, by definition, are unstable. When Temüjin and Jamuqa danced under the sacred tree of Qorqonaq the dance of the earlier king, were they not mindful of the magic significance of such a rite, the consecration, as it were, it undoubtedly implied? If Temüjin had forgotten, one of his followers, Muqali, was to take it upon himself to remind him of it one day. We are shortly to see the two allies who danced there that day both striving to recreate the empire of the steppe, but as rivals.

How did the break come about between Temüjin and Jamuqa? We have to do our own interpreting here of the strange account in the epic. It was the first month of spring. The two sworn brothers had just broken camp to move off, as all nomads do at this transhumance season, in search of fresh grazing for their herds. They rode together side by side at the head of the wagons carrying the dismantled *yurts* and the women and children. The herds came on behind, kept in line by the files of horsemen. On the way, Jamuqa voiced thoughts of his, of how "camp pitched on the slopes of the mountain gave the herders of horses what they wanted, while halt called on the banks of the river meant the herders of sheep were better off." The Mongols, like all primitives, fell readily into expression by image and enigma. Temüjin, not seeing the drift of Jamuqa's words, stayed silent. Then he stopped, letting the wagons pass, to ask the advice of his mother, Hö'elün, whose long experience might be able to guide him in the circumstances. But before Hö'elün had time to answer, Temüjin's wife, the lady Börte, came out with her opinion. "*Anda* Jamuqa has always been reputed fickle. Now here he is tiring of us. The words he has just uttered are certainly intended to apply to us. Let us not camp with him this evening; let us divide from his convoy and put a distance between us during the night."

We come here on one of the curious sides of the future Chingis-khan's character. At the principal junctures of his life, when a major decision must be taken—today in his relations with his ally Jamuqa, tomorrow in his relations with the grand shaman—he is to show himself hesitant, almost timorous, and it is his wife Börte who makes the decision in his place. For when Börte advises, he acts on her advice forthwith, there and then committing his fortunes to the path she directs. The Mongol tribes, as we have seen, were groping confusedly after unity. Jamuqa and Temüjin were both intent on making the most of this trend. The question was which of them should be the real beneficiary. This without doubt the perspicacious Börte had grasped, and she intended her husband should have his hands free again as soon as possible for uninhibited pushing of his own chances.

At nightfall, then, Temüjin's convoy, instead of camping as usual, continued on its way. He came in this way on a third tribe on the move, none other than that of the Taychi'uts, his old enemies. Wakened suddenly in alarm, and thinking this was a nocturnal attack, the Taychi'uts, in the general confusion, struck camp in haste and, in the darkness, made to join Jamuqa. They left behind a little boy, Kököchü, whom mother Hö'elün (of the decidedly strongly developed maternal instinct) adopted on the spot.

All night, Temüjin pushed on. When day broke, the count could be taken of who had followed the young chief and who remained with Jamuqa. From the lists given in the Chingiskhanid epic—as full as those of the *Iliad*—it emerges that the division of the followers between the two rivals, effected as it was in darkness and somewhat hastily, had produced unexpected schisms within a tribe, even sometimes within a clan. Omens, of course, abounded in favor of one or the other party. We are in full shaman milieu, where nothing is ever done without the sorcerer having his say, even if it comes after the event. Thus Qorchi, of the Mongol tribe of the Ba'arins, came to declare to Temüjin that a revelation from heaven had prevented him from following Jamuqa: he had seen in a dream a cow white as snow striking at Jamuqa's *yurt*-wagon till it broke one of its horns: "and it bellowed till Jamuqa had to give it back its lost horn and it struck the ground with its hoof." Then came a white bull, without horns, which bore a great tent stake and followed in the path of Temüjin's wagon bellowing: "Heaven and Earth have decided that the empire [*ulus*] should be Temüjin's; see, I bring it to him!"

But the holy man, even as he declared he had with his very eyes seen this brilliant augury, also, like a true shaman, demanded his reward: "If

you become master of the empire, what will you give me?" And as Temüjin promised to make him chief (*noyan*) over 10,000 men, Qorchi,
aside from his magic powers a gay dog, apparently, put in a request as
well for thirty concubines, with the right to select them from among the
prettiest girls in the country. He also tried, lastly, to get Temüjin to appoint him shaman-counselor, which would have assured him a prominent
seat at the councils of the future Mongol empire. We shall meet other
holy men coveting the same position, with a like eye to the advantages of
a "spiritual ascendancy" over the new monarchy.

The clans who had opted for Temüjin, in the disorder and uncertainty
of the nocturnal break with Jamuqa, were now joined by others, rallying
to his banner after careful weighing of the situation. Particularly valuable was the allegiance of Mongol princes of royal blood, and so closely
related to Temüjin: his paternal uncle Daritay, his first cousin Quchar,
son of his other uncle Nekün-tayshi; then of other more distant relatives,
on the one hand Seche-beki and Taychu, chiefs of the Jürkin or Yürkin
clan, on the other Altan, a most important ally, because he was the son
of the last Mongol khan Qutula. All had left Jamuqa after the initial
break and come to join Temüjin, who was encamped for the moment at
Ayil-qaraqana ("the camp of brushwood"), near the stream Kimurqa
which we look for near what is now Mount Kümür, at the sources of the
Onon. So reinforced, Temüjin moved camp into the upper Kerülen valley. He installed himself there at the site of Qara-Jirügen, on the little
River Sangghur, first left-bank tributary of the Kerülen, on the slopes of
Mount Gürelgü, near a pool here called the Blue Lake (Kökö-na'ur).

Here came to pass the decisive event in his career: his peers proposed
to nominate him king.

Chingis-khan, King of the Mongols

Since the disasters that had ended the reign of khan Qutula, there had been no Mongol monarchy. Altan, Qutula's son, had claimed no royal prerogative. But toward the end of the twelfth century it was apparent that the Mongol tribes, regathering strength despite the fratricidal dispute between Temüjin and the Taychi'uts, were feeling unity again. The question was, as we have already seen, around whom the unity should re-form. First in line of potential pretenders was Prince Altan, son of the last khan, Qutula. After him, other grandsons of one of the previous khans might enter the lists, and among these was Temüjin, but also on a par with him were his cousins, the Jürkin princes Seche-beki and Taychu. Lastly there was Temüjin's own paternal uncle Daritay.

Now it was precisely these same princes, Altan, Seche-beki, Taychu, and Daritay, who decided to elect Temüjin to kingship, to revive for him the title of khan, in abeyance since the death of Qutula. Did they really intend to set a master over themselves? Definitely not, as events were to prove. But feeling the necessity of a war leader, at least for the duration of a common expedition, they thought the son of Yesügei would fill the role. Doubtless they had hesitated a moment between him and Jamuqa, whom, indeed, they had at first followed, at the time of the dividing of the tribes, in preference to Temüjin. But Jamuqa was not of royal line: the genealogies, always so well kept up in the princely *yurts,* traced the origin of his house to a concubine of the Mongol ancestor Bodonchar, but a concubine already pregnant by a foreigner. And indeed Jamuqa, despite his brilliant qualities, was to prove himself inconstant, false, pointlessly cruel, dangerous even to his friends. Temüjin, on the other hand, apart from his princely origins, was always to display sound common sense, a remarkable balance, an innate instinct for government, and, in relations with his allies, a courtesy that, even in a lord clad in animal hides, proclaimed the man of breeding. It was to him then that his cousins the other Mongol princes, disenchanted doubtless with Jamuqa, turned for a king.

The terms in which they made their proposal to him are characteristic: "We wish to elect you khan. When you are khan we will ride in the forefront for you against the enemy. The most beautiful women we capture, we will bring to the royal tent [ordo-ger]. The fine-legged horses, we will lead to you at the trot. When we hunt wild beasts in a half-circle on the steppe, it will be toward you that we shall drive them. If on the day of battle we obey not your commands, strip us of possessions and families, strike off our black heads to the ground. If in the day of peace we fail to keep faith, drive us out far from our kin into the desert!" Pronouncing these oaths and imprecations, they raised Temüjin on the carpet of felt and proclaimed him king under the name, or rather the title, of Chingis-khan.

The title has had etymological connections advanced for it with an idea of strength, whence it would convey the notion of a monarch who is "unshakable," or, as another version has it, "inflexible"; and also with the concept of a universal sovereignty implicit in, literally, "oceanic." Certainly, the name now for the first time hailed out there in some remote grazing ground of the upper Kerülen, sometime in the closing years of the twelfth century, was soon to be common currency, the subject of Mongol acclaim and non-Mongol malediction throughout the ancient world, and subsequently to come down to us across the centuries.

The text of the Mongol princes' electoral address to Chingis-khan makes it clear they thought only to choose themselves a leader in war and the hunt, for raiding and rounding up game, not in the least to appoint themselves a master. The seriousness with which the new sovereign at once set about organizing his nomad kingdom should have been a warning to them. First he created a certain number of dignitaries, the "bearers of quivers" (qorchin), all chosen from warriors devoted to him body and soul. Over them, he set his two faithful adjutants par excellence, Bo'orchu and Jelme: "When I had no companion," he told them, "but my shadow, you made yourselves like my shadow, you gave me peace of mind. You who have been at my side from the beginning, be now above all others." Another of his lieutenants, Sübötei, who was later to prove himself the greatest strategist of the Mongol epic, promised Chingis-khan "to watch over his possessions with the vigilance of the rat, to increase them with the diligence of the crow, to protect his master like a blanket or a felt door-curtain." To all, Chingis-khan declared: "Oh you who have left Jamuqa to join me, you shall be, if Heaven and Earth confirm me in my power, the seniors of my followers, the elders of my empire, my happy companions in good fortune." And he invested each of them with the office he planned for him in the government of the world.

How would the other nomad kings receive the Chingis-khan's elevation? The main thing was for him to secure the allegiance of the Kereit king Toghril he had formerly acknowledged his suzerain. Chingis-khan sent Daqay and Sükegei as ambassadors to him. If the Kereit khan had taken amiss his vassal's increase in power, in all probability the new Mongol royalty's lease of life would have been short. Happily, Toghril, although they had waited till after the fact to consult him, declared himself greatly pleased. "You have raised to the khanate my son Temüjin? Excellent! How have the Mongols lived till now without khans?" And he adjured them always to be faithful to him they had elected.

A more delicate problem was posed by relations with Jamuqa. Toward his former *anda,* it must be admitted the Chingis-khan had at bottom behaved somewhat ill. On the strength of a quite gratuitous interpretation of an obscure remark, he had, without warning, broken a sworn friendship. Worse still, he had enticed away his followers. Chingis-khan, who for the time being wished to avoid creating ill will, charged Arqay-qasar and Chaqurqan to go and tell Jamuqa of his accession. Curiously, Jamuqa, whether out of vestigial friendship for his childhood companion, or because he also at this point wished to avoid an open break, laid all the blame on the two great electors of the new khan, the princes Altan and Quchar. In fact, Altan and Quchar had tipped the scales by abandoning Jamuqa's party, to which they had at first adhered. Further, according to the Mongol epic it was they who, by their intriguing, had provoked the break between the two former *anda:* "Instead of seeking to divide us," Jamuqa declared, "why did you not elect khan Temüjin while he and I were living together? In electing him now what have your motives been?" And subtly—perhaps perfidiously—Jamuqa, now that the election was a *fait accompli,* urged the princes Altan and

Quchar to hold true to the oath they had sworn, to serve his *anda* with unfaltering loyalty.

These were words of prophetic irony, since no prophet was needed to foresee harmony would not reign long between the new Chingis-khan and the other princes of the blood who had made him king.

15

Prisoners Thrown into Boiling Caldrons

This correctness of Jamuqa's attitude to Chingis-khan's election proves that the two men, despite the break that had taken place, were yet still unwilling actually to do each other harm. The irreparable breach was to come between them through the actions of others, specifically of, on the one hand, Taychar, Jamuqa's younger brother, and, on the other, Jöchi-darmala, of the Jalair tribe, one of the vassals of Chingis-khan. Taychar was camped near the Ölegei spring, under Mount Jelama, in the region of the upper Kerülen. Jöchi-darmala was roaming in the district of Sa'ari Ke'er, "the donkeyback steppe." Taychar seized Jöchi-darmala's herd of horses. Jöchi-darmala set out alone to find his horses (his people being too scared to go with him). One steppe bandit, now, against another. Bent low, almost lying along his horse's mane, a man rides out at dead of night. He edges in toward the enemy camp, and watches till he sees the stealer of his horses. A whine, and Taychar falls, an arrow through his spine. Jöchi-darmala takes his horses back to his grazing grounds.

It was war. Resolved to avenge his brother, Jamuqa mustered the people of his tribe—the Jajirats, or Jadarans—and their federates (giving him up to 30,000 men), and set out across the Ala'ut-turqa'ut mountains to surprise Chingis-khan.

Chingis-khan was then camped before Mount Gürelgü, in the upper valley, that is, of the River Sangghur, where his people—likewise some 30,000 men—were split up among thirty groups of wagons and *yurts*. Very fortunately for him, news of the enemy's coming was brought him in time by two Mongols of the Ikires tribe, Mülke-totaq and Borolday. Battle was joined at Dalan-baljut ("the seventy marshes"), which Mongol scholars place near the sources of the Onon. Chingis-khan got the worst of it. He had to retreat toward the col of Jerene, also in the Onon basin. Jamuqa did not dare follow him, but wreaked savage vengeance on Chingis-khan supporters, the chiefs of the tribe of the Ne'üds, or Chinos (the "Wolves"), who fell into his hands: before turning back to his encampment, he had them boiled in seventy caldrons, an old torture from the "Warring States" period of ancient China. Chagha'anuwa, one of the Ne'üd chiefs, had particularly incurred Jamuqa's hatred when he deserted him to range himself among the first with Chingis-khan, at the division of the tribes. Jamuqa cut off his head, hung it from his horse's tail, and rode off dragging his sinister trophy after him.

Later, Persian tradition, retaining only a confused memory of all these horrors, reversed the deeds and gestures of the participants. Its version has it that in the battle of the Seventy Marshes Chingis-khan was the victor, and that it was he who had had the vanquished boiled in the seventy fateful caldrons. But it is indeed at Jamuqa's door these needless atrocities are to be laid, for they were what alienated sympathies from him, and brought the defeated Chingis-khan gains more valuable than victory, fresh recruits. Thus Jamuqa now forfeited to Chingis-khan two important Mongol chiefs, and with them their tribes: Jürchedei, of the Uru'uts, and Quyildar, of the Mangghuts. Prized converts, for in the hour of danger we shall see the admirable devotion of these two men to the hero's cause and person. At about the same time, the latter was rejoined also by his father's former friend, Mönglik. This return spoke volumes. It must have occasioned the conqueror particular, if ironic, satisfaction. Mönglik, indeed, it will be remembered, had been Yesügei's trusted aide. It was he the latter had charged, as he lay dying, to fetch home the future Chingis-khan. Regardless of this trust, the man had shrugged off any obligations as a guardian, had indeed evidently abandoned mother and child to their destruction. But yesterday, when the break came between Chingis-khan and Jamuqa, he had followed Jamuqa. Today here he was, he and his seven sons, returning. Such action on the part of so prudent a trimmer of sails proved that decidedly the wind was setting in Chingis-khan's favor. The hero, who knew how to let legitimate grievances lie when political interest required it, fêted all these new adherents, and his old followers, at a great forest banquet by the Onon.

If professions of allegiance flowed in now to Chingis-khan, it was because he was emerging already as the strong man it is safer to have as a protector than an enemy. It was also—strange as it may seem—because his rule had a quality of order, of moderation, of morality, almost of humanity, that his rivals' lacked. When hungry clans, who wavered between him and other chiefs, asked him to be allowed to participate in some great hunting roundup (for the life of these nomads always alternated between feasts and famine), he welcomed them courteously, and assigned to them more than their share of the game brought down. A politic generosity, certainly, aimed at creating popularity for himself among the tribes, increasing the number of his vassals. And it succeeded. From tribe to tribe the comparisons were passed of the scrupulous keeping of faith of the young khan, his generosity, his firm yet liberal exercise of royal power, with the brutal tyranny, the veerings of temper, the cruelties, of other contenders. "This lord Temüjin would take the garment from off his back to give it to you. He would get down from his horse and offer it to you. This is really a man fit to possess a country, able to feed his warriors, keep his house in good order." So the talk went in the steppe, at evening, in the felt tents, and men took him to their hearts, with a sincerity they were to prove when the testing time came.

16

The Brawl after the Banquet

But if the young royal authority of Chingis-khan earned the respect of the tribes by its equity and wisdom, the new master nevertheless thought in terms of strict obedience. The other Mongol princes who had elected him were clearly under the impression that they had appointed simply a commander in war, to preside over a grouping that was in its nonmilitary aspects more or less nominal. Their error was quickly made plain to them.

The first disagreement occurred at the banquet held in the forest of the Onon to celebrate the rallying of Mönglik and the other dissidents. As the chief guests were having set before them jugs of *qumiz,* two dowagers of the Jürkin clan, the ladies Qorijin and Qu'urchin, complained sharply at being served after the lady Ebegei, a mere "second wife" of Sechebeki, chief of that clan. And in their indignation they struck at the cook, Shiki'ür. The latter, shedding tears of humiliation, cried that never in the lifetime of Yesügei, Chingis-khan's father, would he have been treated thus. This was to reproach Chingis-khan himself with weakness. Mutual confidence was at the best of times never overmuch in evidence at these primitive eating and drinking bouts. Chingis-khan had charged his brother Belgütei to keep an eye on his own followers' horses. An important chief, Büri-bökö, had been given the same assignment with regard to the Jürkin horses. Now Belgütei surprised someone from the Jürkin party stealing a bridle from the Chingiskhanid equipment. Büri-bökö came to the assistance of his comrade. He and Belgütei grappled swiftly. Büribökö's saber gashed Belgütei's right shoulder. Belgütei for his part let the blood flow without making too much of the matter: naturally easygoing, he wanted to hush up the incident.

But Chingis-khan, sitting in the shade of a tree, a little apart from the other merrymakers, had seen it all. He bore down on them, furious. His prestige was at issue, and the affair took on a serious aspect, for the Jürkin princes, whose people comported themselves so insolently, represented the senior branch of the Mongol royal house. Their arrogance smacked of challenging the new khan's fresh-minted royal stature, of aspersions on the right of the junior branch. "What!" he cried to his brother Belgütei. "Shall we endure this?" The good Belgütei tried to calm him. "The wound was not serious. Now they have come to you, do not go and quarrel with them again because of me!" But Chingis-khan would have none of it. His prestige was involved! With branches from the trees, the batons they used to churn the butter, they fell on the Jürkins, "they beat them up." The two Jürkin dowagers who had been the first cause of the dispute were apprehended. Once he had taught the offenders their lesson, however, Chingis-khan asked nothing better than reconciliation, and straightway set free the two ill-tempered old women.

The authority of Chingis-khan benefited not long after this from misfortunes befalling his suzerain, the Kereit king Toghril.

Toghril, despite his house's Nestorian Christianity and his own translation into the famous, even legendary "Prester John," was an extremely bad kinsman. He was responsible, we know, for the death of several of his brothers. Only two had escaped his treachery, Jaqa-gambu and Erke-qara. Fearing for his life too, Erke-qara took refuge in western Mongolia, over by the Great Altay, with the Naymans. The Nayman king, Inanch-bilge, took up his cause; he drove out Toghril and set Erke-qara on the Kereit throne. Toghril went into exile in Turkestan, with the powerful king or *gur-khan* of the Qara-kitays, whose capital, Balasaghun, rose in the plain of Chu, west of Issyq-köl. But less than a year after, the *gur-khan* expelled him, and Toghril found himself forced to wander wretchedly in the Gobi, on the borders of the Uyghur and Tangut territories. Such was his plight that he was reduced to living on the milk of five goats and quantities of blood he took from a camel. In this pitiable condition, riding a blind horse—a brown horse with a black mane, we learn from our herders' epic, where chargers ever rate equal concern with men—he had come to Lake Güse'ür, one of the small lakes of the Gobi, between the Kansu or Ordos and the upper Kerülen, when he received a message by word of mouth from Chingis-khan. Stirred by pity, the Mongol khan sent two emissaries, Tarqay-ba'atur and Sükegei, with an invitation to come to him. Toghril came with all speed. Chingis-khan was camping at that time at Bürgi-ergi, on the banks of the upper Kerülen or the Sangghur, near the source of the two rivers. He came as far as Lake Güse'ür to meet the exile. Toghril confessed himself in the last stages of exhaustion, dying of hunger and fatigue. Chingis-khan installed him in the circle of wagons and tents that was his nomad capital, levied contributions in kind for his guest from the Mongols, furnished him with provisions and let him regain his strength; then, moving to winter quarters at Quba-qaya—still near the sources of the Kerülen—he took Toghril with him.

The following autumn (1197), Chingis-khan made an expedition against the Merkits and defeated them at Mürüche-se'ül near Mount Qa-diqliq. Their chief, Toqto'a, fled once again in the direction of Barghu-chin, on the eastern shore of Lake Baykal. Chingis-khan seized his *yurts,* his provisions, his horses, and made a present of them all to Toghril. In 1198, the latter was once more restored to leadership of the Kereit people.

These events produced an appreciable shift in relations between Chingis-khan and Toghril. Chingis-khan continued indeed to style him-self the latter's vassal, and to call him "father-khan;" but as his rescuer and restorer, he treated him now as an equal.

▲
▲▲

17

Chingis-khan in the Service of the King of Gold

And now, Chingis-khan benefited from an unexpected reversing of Chinese policy in Upper Asia.

It will be remembered that the first Mongol royal house had been overthrown by a coalition of the Tatars, nomads of similarly Mongol extraction who roamed the edges of Manchuria, and the "King of Gold," the *Kin* sovereign of Peking.[1] But the Tatars, whom the court of Peking had made use of to lay low Chingis-khan's predecessors, were not long in becoming thorns themselves in their protectors' flesh. And then Peking, in one of the somersaults it had a habit of executing in its relations with the nomad world, turned to make common cause against them with Chingis-khan and the Kereits.

A *Kin* army, commanded by Prince Wan-yen Siang, had attacked the Tatars from the southeast. Under their chief Megüjin-se'ültü, the latter were falling back with their herds towards the Ulja, a river flowing into Lake Bürün-torchi, between the Kerülen and the Onon—so drawing near the territory of Chingis-khan. The latter jumped at the opportunity to settle old scores with these enemy relatives. He harangued his followers, reminded them of how these Tatars had handed over his relatives Amba-qay and Ökin-barqaq, delivering them into the shame and lingering agony of death on the wooden ass. True, the actual martyring of the two Mongols had been the work strictly of the *Kin,* to whom the Tatars had sold them. But since here was an opportunity for vengeance on the Tatars with the aid of the rulers of Peking, let a start be made with them. And

[1] [The Jurchet dynasty of the *Kin* ruled over China from 1115 to 1260.]

indeed, without going back to these old memories, Chingis-khan had his own father Yesügei the Brave to avenge, treacherously poisoned by the Tatars at their board. "The Tatar people are our enemies. They caused our fathers' deaths. Here we have our chance to trap them in a vise!"

Their attack on the Tatars was to be a frontal one, down the Ulja valley, while the *Kin* army came up in pursuit from the southeast. Chingis-khan duly invited his allies the Kereits to join in. The Kereit king Toghril accepted willingly: he also had old scores to settle, for his grandfather Marghuz Buyruq, taken prisoner by the Tatars, had died an ignominious death. In three days he had mustered his army and joined Chingis-khan.

The two also invited the Jürkin chiefs Seche-beki and Taychu to participate, but the latter had not forgotten the unfortunate incidents of the Onon banquet. For six days they were waited for in vain. Then Toghril and Chingis-khan set out without them down the valley of the Ulja. The Tatar chief had barricaded himself behind an abatis of trees after the fashion of the forest tribes. Chingis-khan and Toghril forced his lair as hunters do their quarry's, killed him, and seized as booty his bed set with gold and pearls.

The *Kin* general Wan-yen Siang, delighted with his allies' victory, conferred on Toghril the title of *wang,* the Chinese term for "king." This word, pronounced *ong* in Mongol, was combined with the title khan, which Toghril already bore, to give the name *Ong-khan,* by which the Kereit sovereign will hereafter be referred to. Chingis-khan the court of Peking honored with a much more modest title, proving that for the Chinese the Kereits were still the most important tribe in Mongolia. Both leaders were for the rest warmly congratulated by the *Kin* representative: "By attacking the Tatars from the rear, by killing their chief, you have greatly served the King of Gold, and he will manifest his gratitude." Such words clearly class Chingis-khan as well as the new Ong-khan as modest federates in the service of the King of Gold, chiefs of savage tribes the court of Peking kept happy with titles and trinkets.

Chingis-khan and the Ong-khan paid themselves out of the booty from the Tatars, and it was loaded with spoils that they reached their respective *yurts* again. In his share, Chingis-khan had a little boy found abandoned in the Tatar camp, a child with a gold ring in his nose and a coat of damask lined with sable. He was given to mother Hö'elün, who adopted him: "He must be the son of some high personage. He will become so with us!" She named him Shigi-qutuqu and declared he should be her sixth child. Chingis-khan was also to grow deeply attached to this young brother by adoption; how deeply, he was to show a few years later. One day when his people were moving camp in their nomad fashion in severe cold and deep snow, a herd of deer made off from near their path. "Shigi-qutuqu, who was now about fifteen years old, told the *noyan* Küchügür, who had charge of him, that he would like to go after the animals, who were slowed down by the snow. He was given permission, and went off. In the evening, when they halted, Chingis-khan asked after Qutuqu. He was told he had gone off deer hunting. 'The child will die of cold!' he exclaimed in a rage. And he was so angry with Küchügür he struck him with a wagon shaft. But young Qutuqu came home, announcing that of thirty deer he had brought down twenty-seven. This youthful feat pleased Chingis-khan greatly. He sent to fetch the game, which were there indeed, stretched in the snow."

Chingis-khan Rids Himself
of the Mongol Princes

After his victory over the Tatars, Chingis-khan had returned to his encampment at Lake Qariltu, on the banks of the upper Kerülen. There
news awaited him that filled him with surprise and indignation. While
he was away, the Jürkins, taking advantage of his absence, had thrown
themselves on the people he had left behind, had robbed them, stripped
of their clothes some fifty men, and killed ten of them. Chingis-khan was
seized by fury. At the famous banquet on the Onon, the Jürkins had
struck his cook, Shiki'ür, and wounded in the shoulder his brother Belgütei. Pressed to join in the "national" expedition against the Tatars, they
had become evasive. Their failing in this respect had been the more crim-
inal in that Ökin-barqaq, the Jürkin chiefs Seche-beki and Taychu's own
grandfather, had perished at Tatar hands. And now it transpired that
these same Jürkins, not content to shirk their military duty, had descended in pillage on the *yurts* of the khan, entrusted to old men and
children during the holy war! It was the last straw! Chingis-khan
marched against the Jürkins, came up with them at Dolo'an Boldaq
("the Seven Hills"), near Ködö'é-aral, on the lower Kerülen, and took
them prisoner. Seche-beki and Taychu managed to make off with a few
followers toward the Pass of Telegetü, but Chingis-khan overtook and re-
captured them. He had them brought before him. He reminded them of
their military oath. They acknowledged they had betrayed it, that they
should be treated accordingly, and they "held out their necks." Their
heads rolled on the ground.

The execution of the Jürkin princes must have made a sharp impression on the tribes. Among the descendants of the glorious khan Qabul, they represented the senior line, Chingis-khan only one among junior ones. As eldest son of Qabul, their ancestor Ökin-barqaq had had time, at the sharing of the *ulus*,[1] to choose the most valiant warriors, the most infallible archers, and it was from this elite the Jürkins were descended. Now Chingis-khan had struck off the heads of their princes and subordinated their people. The proudest in origin of the clans had had to bow. The chief, once grudgingly elected by his peers to preside over a loose confederation of tribes in occasional joint hunting or raiding expeditions, had emerged as a relentless master, exacting from his subjects absolute obedience.

The Jürkin chiefs put down, Chingis-khan turned his anger on another Mongol prince, likewise descended from the hero Qabul, but belonging to the third branch: Büri-bökö. Büri-bökö (Büri "the Athlete") had once, it will be remembered, shown signal want of respect for Chingis-khan by wounding his brother Belgütei during the banquet on the Onon which had ended in a general brawl between the Jürkins and the followers of the khan. Chingis-khan had seemed for the moment to forget the offense, but he was biding his time. He used Belgütei to pay off the debt. One day, as if for amusement, he commanded Belgütei and Büri-bökö to wrestle before him. Büri-bökö, as his name indicates, was of Herculean strength, and in the normal course of things would have had an easy victory. But intimidated by the presence of the khan, he held himself back from exerting his full strength, was careful with Belgütei, and pretended to be overthrown by him. Belgütei, seizing him by the shoulders, jumped on his back. This was just what Chingis-khan had been waiting for. He gave Belgütei a prearranged sign—he bit his lower lip. Belgütei at once exploited his advantage; immobilizing his adversary—one knee on the wretch's back, hands gripping his nape—he broke his back. "Then he dragged the body outside, threw it on the ground and went away."

The other side of the coin was Chingis-khan's inspiring fanatical devotion. Among the former clients of the Jürkins was a Jalair warrior named Gü'ün-u'a. He came to present to Chingis-khan his two sons, Muqali and Buqa: "Let them serve as footmen before your threshold. If they abandon the service of your door, break their heels and pluck out their livers!" Gü'ün's two brothers, Chila'un-qaychi and Jebke, also ded-

[1] *Ulus* is a technical term for a land (and people) received as patrimony.

icated themselves to Chingis-khan. It was a family of heroes that thus entered his service. Muqali, notably, was one day to conquer for him Northern China. Jebke had found abandoned in the Jürkin camp a small boy, Boroqul. He presented him to mother Hö'elün, who adopted him. The great dowager had thus acquired through the hazards of war four adoptive sons: Küchü the Merkit, Kököchü the Besüt, Shigi-qutuqu the Tatar, and Boroqul the Jürkin. The excellent woman brought them up with diligence, "watching over them in the daytime with her eyes, at night with her ears." They too we shall find among the most devoted of the Conqueror's followers.

Surprise Assaults in the Mountains

The kingship of Chingis-khan, consolidated by the execution of his re-
fractory cousins, daily took more substantial shape. Re-established by
his aid, his erstwhile suzerain, the Ong-khan of the Kereits—whom he
continued to address ceremoniously as "father"—remained his loyal
ally, or at least appeared such. About 1199, the two launched an expedition together against the other great people of Upper Mongolia, the Naymans.

The Naymans, it will be remembered, were probably of Turkish descent and inhabited Western Mongolia. "They inhabited the Great Altay,
from the country in which later the town of Qaraqorum arose to the
upper Irtysh. They spread as far as Kereit country, and Kirghiz country
and Uyghur country." That is to say the ensemble of territories comprised today in the administrative area of Kobdo, Tarbagatay, and
Dzungaria. Since the death of their king Inanch-bilge they had split up
between the two sons of that prince, Tayang Tay-Buqa and Buyruq.[1]
The two brothers had quarreled over possession of a former concubine
of their father's. Tayang, we are told, ruled the clans of the plain and
Buyruq those of the mountain. Chingis-khan and the Ong-khan, for the
moment letting Tayang be, attacked Buyruq.

Buyruq was on the banks of the Soghoq, which is the upper part of the
River Kobdo, on the northeast slope of the "Great Mountain" (Ulugh-
tagh),[2] that is, of the Mongol Altay. Chingis-khan and the Kereit king,
crossing the Khangay range, moved, it would seem, into the region of the

---

[1] [The Tayang is also called Torluq in the *Secret History,* ¶ 198.]
[2] [This Turkish name, in the text of the *Mongol Secret History,* tends to confirm us
in our assumption that the Naymans were Turkish in origin, not Mongol.]

lakes, along a route perhaps not far off that taken by the Bouillane de Lacoste expedition.[3] This is wild country where grassland alternates with wastes of grey stone. Only the valley bottoms and the sides of the Kobdo River have the shade of clusters of birches and giant poplars. Buyruq, not feeling strong, abandoned the area and took refuge in the Altay. At the foot of the Altay, one of his lieutenants, Yedi-tubluq, apparently commanding his rear guard, was overtaken by the Mongol advance party: his saddle girths gave way and he was captured before he could reach the mountain. Taking nearby cols at 1,000 feet, passable from July to October only, Chingis-khan and his allies set out to cross the Altay, its basalt and porphyry ridge "like a jagged wall, with sharp, crumbling points," overhung by forty-five glaciers. Thence they came down on the south side into the valley of the Urungu, bordered with willow thickets, "into the country of Qumshigir." They came on the enemy near Lake Kizil-bash, the Ulungur as it is called today: a salt lake, circled by bare yellow hills. In this desert-like country Buyruq was crushed by Chingis-khan. The Nayman chief fled to the Siberian frontier, to the Kemkemjiüts of the upper Ienissei, in what is now the Tuvin region.

Chingis-khan and the Ong-khan, their victory won, took the road home. Their route, between the north slope of the Altay and the southern slope of the Khangay, led through the valley of the Baydaraq, the Baydarik of our maps, whose swift waters run down through the wild gorges of the Khangay, to end in the south in a salt lake, surrounded by reeds and sand with *saksauls* and tamarisks. Now one of the Nayman chiefs, the valiant Kökse'ü-sabraq, had stationed himself in one of the Baydaraq passes, intending to dispute the allies' passage. The two armies took up battle positions, but, as night was falling, Chingis-khan and the Ong-khan postponed combat till next day.

Then something extraordinary came to pass. In the middle of the night the Ong-khan, after lighting his fires to mislead all concerned, without a word to his ally, made off with all his force up the Qarase'ül valley, leaving Chingis-khan alone to face whatever the Naymans had in store for him.

What had happened, and what lay behind such a betrayal? The instigator was apparently the Jajirat chief Jamuqa, Chingis-khan's erstwhile

[3] [Bouillane de Lacoste, *op. cit.*, p. 4.]

"brother by adoption," become now his greatest enemy. Jamuqa indeed had followed the Ong-khan on this expedition. Riding at his side on the return journey, he had succeeded in arousing mistrust in the easily swayed soul of the Kereit sovereign. He insinuated that Chingis-khan had always kept up secret relations with the Naymans: "Even now he is not following you [perhaps there was a gap between the marching allies]. I, O khan, am like the white-plumaged bird, that, in winter as in summer, dwells in the north. My *anda* Temüjin is like the bird of passage, the lark or the wild goose, that, when the cold comes, takes wing for the sunny lands of the south. He must have gone back to the Naymans to tender his submission to them." Tradition has it that, like the ancient chorus, a Kereit noble, Gürin-ba'atur, protested in the name of loyalty: "How can you utter such calumnies of your *anda?*"

Meantime, Chingis-khan, who suspected nothing, spent the night preparing for combat. At dawn, he saw that the Ong-khan had deserted him. He realized the extreme seriousness of his position: "These people have left us here like burnt meats!" Swiftly, he made off in his turn, reaching, by an appreciable loop northward, on the other side of the Khangay, the valley of the Eder, and so securing his return unhindered to the Sa'ari Ke'er steppe—"the donkeyback steppe"—whence he had a few months before set out to war.

It was the Ong-khan who made a bad bargain by his treachery. He was withdrawing toward his usual encampments on the upper Tula when he was thrown back by the Nayman chief Kökse'ü-sabraq. The latter surprised the Kereits at the pass of Telegetü (Telegetü-amasar)—one of the passes of the Khangay chain—and captured a great number of them, with their animals and their provisions. The *senggüm* Nilqa, son of the Ong-khan, saw his wife and children fall into the hands of the enemy. The Ong-khan's fortunes went so badly that two important hostages he had in his train, the sons of the Merkit chief Toqto'a, escaped, and, making off down the Selenga, went to rejoin their father by Lake Baykal.

Chingis-khan's Magnanimity

In these straits, the Ong-khan was reduced to imploring aid from the same Chingis-khan he had a few days before so utterly betrayed. The Conqueror might at will have had his revenge, or, at the least, made Toghril pay dear for his help. He behaved, on the contrary, with remarkable magnanimity. Receiving the Ong-khan's entreaty, he sent to his aid his "four heroes": Bo'orchu, Muqali, Boroqul, and Chila'un. They were only just in time. In the meantime, the Nayman chief Kökse'ü-sabraq, having taken his loot off to a safe place, had returned to the attack against the Kereit *senggüm,* and was now making furious onslaughts on him in the district of Hula'anqut. Already two of the principal Kereit commanders, Teginquri and Itürgen-yudaqu, had been killed. The *senggüm*'s horse had had its thigh run through, and he was about to be taken. It was at this juncture that Chingis-khan's four lieutenants swept in, at full gallop. To the first of these, the faithful Bo'orchu, Chingis-khan had entrusted a steed beyond compare, "Grey-ear" (Chiki-boro), whose mane had just to be stroked gently with the whip for him to fly like the wind. In the battle Bo'orchu gave Grey-ear to the unhorsed *senggüm,* but the latter did not know the trick of stroking the mane, and the noble animal refused to budge. At last Bo'orchu remembered the instructions he had from his master, and gave Grey-ear "Chingis-khan's caress," and the charger rushed against the foe. The Nayman force took fright, and the Kereit king recovered all his men and all his goods.

The Ong-khan was magnificent in his thanks to his savior: "Once before, Yesügei the Brave gave me back my kingdom, and now behold his son has saved me once again." He called on the *Tengri* and the goddess Earth to witness his gratitude. He wanted also to reward Bo'orchu. It was a day when the fearless *noyan* was on guard over Chingis-khan, but the Conqueror bade him go to receive the reward for his services to the Kereit sovereign. The Ong-khan presented Bo'orchu with a robe of honor, and, furthermore, ten cups of gold. Bo'orchu, returning with these treasures, came to kneel before Chingis-khan and reproach himself, as with a crime, for having neglected, even for an instant, the service of his king to go to be laden with gifts by a foreign prince. Such was the absolute devotion the Conqueror inspired.

The Anti-Caesar Jamuqa and the
Battle in the Storm

It might seem that Chingis-khan, victorious over the Naymans and but-tressed by the alliance of the Kereit sovereign he had just saved, was on the eve of imposing his rule on the divers peoples of what is now Upper Mongolia. In reality, the hour of his final triumph was not yet quite at hand. Even among the Mongol tribes proper there was so far from being unanimity in his favor that a group of them soon set up an anti-Caesar rival to him in the person of his enemy, the Jajirat chief Jamuqa.

A curious personality was this Jamuqa, once the "brother by adoption" of Chingis-khan, now his worst adversary. All the chronicles point to the unstable, plotting, treacherous character of the man, his searing projects, his sudden disastrous fallings-short. It was he, we have seen, who had all but brought about a break between Chingis-khan and the Kereit Ong-khan. Now that, in spite of him, the Ong-khan and Chingis-khan were reconciled, he organized against them a veritable coalition of the tribes, a coalition that included the majority of the Mongol peoples with the exception of the immediate adherents of Chingis-khan. To it rallied all the Conqueror's old enemies: the Tatars of the lower Kerülen, the Merk-its of the lower Selenga, the Taychi'uts of the lower Onon; then the forest-dwelling Oyrats of the western shores of Lake Baykal and a great num-ber of lesser tribes revolving in the orbit of these others, notably the Qatagins, the Salji'uts, the Dörbens, the Ikires, the Qorolas, even the Onggirats of Buyur, the tribe of Chingis-khan's own parents-in-law. From western Mongolia the Naymans, or at least a section of the Nay-mans, came to join the league. Jamuqa was joined at the head of the movement by other former enemies of Chingis-khan: Toqto'a-beki, chief of the Merkits, Tarqutay-Qiriltuq, chief of the Taychi'uts, Qutuqa-beki, chief of the Oyrats, and lastly the Nayman Buyruq of the but recent trial of strength.

As the list shows, this was a confederation with support from every quarter of Mongolia, comprising as it did at once the Tatars of eastern Mongolia, from the flank of the Khingan, the Oyrats of the northern *tayga,* and the Naymans of the great Altay. The year was 1201. The tribes gathered near the source of the Olqui, whence they moved into the valley of the Argun. Where the little river Kan flowed into the Argun,[1] they proclaimed Jamuqa king with the title *gur-khan.* The election was to the accompaniment of religious ceremonies according to shamanist ritual. The chiefs of the confederates sacrificed a stallion and a mare. They bound themselves by a great oath: "May he among us who defects be cast down like this earth, cut in pieces like these trees!" and they crumbled earth into the river and slashed off branches with saber cuts. Then they made ready to surprise Chingis-khan.

But the secret was badly kept. One of the Qorolas tribe, named Qoriday, hastened to warn Chingis-khan, who was at Gürelgü, by the sources of the Kerülen, at the foot of the massif of Burqan-qaldun. Qoriday went at the gallop, on a swift horse. At nightfall, he came on a Taychi'ut camp with people of his own tribe. From them he got a change of horse, set out again, then almost fell foul of a troop of confederates carrying a white tent to the new *gur-khan.* By good fortune he escaped them, and came safe and sound to Chingis-khan.

Chingis-khan sent at once for help to the Kereit Ong-khan. The latter came to join his ally, and together they went down the Kerülen valley. Chingis-khan sent ahead as scouts his two cousins, the princes Altan and Quchar, and his uncle Daritay, while the Ong-khan similarly commissioned his son the *senggüm,* his brother Jaqa-gambu, and his lieutenant Bilge-beki. So traveling they came to the region of Mounts Chiqurqu and Chekcher and the district Köyten, south of the debouching of the Kerülen into Lake Kölen, between that lake and Lake Buyur. The Kölen, marshy-shored, is linked at high water with the Argun by a canal for the most part dry. The enemy came up the Argun valley. Heading them were the

---

[1] Long. 119°E, lat. 50°N. The Kan (or Gan) is a small eastern tributary of the Argun.

principals of the coalition: the Taychi'ut prince A'uchu-ba'atur, the Nayman chief Buyruq, Qutu, son of the Merkit chief Toqto'a, the Oyrat chief Qutuqa, all grouped round the anti-Caesar Jamuqa. As they came fanning out on to the plain of Lake Kölen, night was falling. Amid the cries of the advance guards, battle was put off till morning.

At daybreak, Buyruq and Qutuqa-beki, who were shamans, by their spellmaking, "pronouncing incantations and throwing stones into the water," produced a storm of rain and snow, intended to blind Chingis-khan. But, the *Tengri* aiding, the storm turned against the coalition. The air grew thick, and the supporters of Jamuqa, assailed at once by Chingis-khan and the anger of heaven, numb with cold, lost their footing. Men and beasts went hurtling in the murk to the foot of precipices. Those not killed outright were frozen stiff in the fiercely whirling snow.

Beaten, the coalition scattered. The Naymans took the road once more for the Great Altay, the Oyrats for their Baykalian forests, the Merkits for the lower Selenga, the Taychi'uts for the lower Onon. Jamuqa regained his camps by the Argun. Steppe bandit that he was, he did not hesitate to take advantage of the misfortune of his allies—the very men who had proclaimed him *gur-khan*—to pillage them, senseless conduct that finally lost him the last of his followers, and put conclusive end to his ephemeral kingship.[2]

2 1201-02.

22

Chingis-khan Wounded:
The Devotion of Jelme

Chingis-khan and the Ong-khan, after their joint victory, had split up. The Ong-khan had descended the Argun valley in pursuit of Jamuqa, while Chingis-khan went to throw back the Taychi'uts in the valley of the Onon. The Taychi'ut chiefs A'uchu-ba'atur and Qodun-orchang waited for him on the other side of the river. They battled fiercely till evening, an indecisive bout, following which, as night fell, the two armies bivouacked face to face.

Chingis-khan had been wounded in the neck by an arrow. The vein was touched, and he could not staunch the bleeding. In pain as he was, he stayed with the fighting to the end. When night finally came, he collapsed, exhausted. He had with him the loyal Jelme, of the tribe of the Urangquats, forest hunters of the Siberian *tayga*.[1] Jelme did all that could be done then for the wounded man. In the manner of the Mongol "doctors," he sucked the clotted blood from the wound, till his own mouth was all stained with it. Then he crouched down beside him and watched over him, for he was the only one with whom Chingis-khan, this terrible night, would trust himself. "Till midnight, he sucked the wound thus for fear the wound might be poisoned. About midnight, Chingis-khan came to himself and said: 'The blood has clotted at last. I am

---

[1] The Urangquats, Rashid ed-Din records, live in immense forests. They do not have tents, have no livestock, live by hunting and profess great contempt for pastoral peoples. For shelter they use only cabins made of branches and covered with birchbark. In winter, they hunt over the snow, tying to their feet small planks they call *chana,* and holding in the hand a stick they plunge into the snow as a boatman plunges his pole into the water.

thirsty.' " Jelme took off his headgear, his boots, his coat and jacket, then, clad only in his shoes, made coolly toward the enemy lines. Then he groped among the Taychi'ut wagons, in search of mare's milk, favorite drink of the nomads: in vain. The Taychi'uts, in fact, on their hasty march, had set loose their mares, without bothering to milk them. But finally he found in a wagon a bucket of sour milk. He grabbed it, and was lucky enough to get back with it unseen: the *Tengri* was watching over him! Then he added water to the curds, and gave his master to drink.

After three draughts, Chingis-khan murmured: "My eyes begin to see clearly." He spoke and sat up. Day was indeed beginning to dawn. The wounded man noticed, in the place where he had been lying, a pool of blood. He asked what it was. Jelme explained to him what had happened, how he had sucked the blood from the wound, then how he had gone, naked, to steal from the enemy the bucket of sour milk. "And if the enemy had caught you," asked Chingis-khan, "what would you have said?" "I had thought it out," answered the imperturbable Jelme. "I should have passed myself off as a deserter; I would have made out that you had meant to kill me, that you had stripped me of all my clothes but my shoes, and that in that state I had escaped. They would have believed me, looked after me, given me something to wear. Then I should have found a way to jump on a horse and gallop back here. That was what I was thinking, while I was looking for a drink to assuage the thirst of my master, he who is more to me than the apple of my eye."

Chingis-khan was moved by such devotion. "Before," he murmured, "when the Merkits had me surrounded on Mount Burqan-qaldun, you saved my life for a first time. Now you have restored me to life, by sucking my wound, and you have been, at the risk of your life, to fetch drink from an enemy camp to assuage the torment of my thirst. What you have done, I shall never forget!" With the simple grandeur of the exchange a breath of nobility wafts through this ferocious tale.

When it was fully light, it was seen that the enemy cavalry had disbanded, abandoning the rank and file. Chingis-khan, despite his wound, mounted and rode to round up and rally to himself all these men. Now he saw on a crop of rock a woman, dressed in white, weeping, who called on him loudly. It was the lady Qada'an, daughter of the Sorqan-shira who once in his childhood, when he had been wearing the cangue among the Taychi'uts, had saved his life. She called on him now for help, for Chingis-khan's warriors had seized her husband, and were taking him away to cut his throat. At her cry, Chingis-khan came to her at a gallop. He jumped down and clasped her in his arms. But, alas, he came too late: her husband had been butchered. Having rallied all these folk to his banner, Chingis-khan pitched camp for the night with his army. Full of compassion, he had Qada'an sit by his side. Next morning, Qada'an's father came to him, Sorqan-shira himself. "In the old days," Chingis-khan said to him, "you and your sons freed me from my cangue, my log of infamy. Then, you saved me. But since, why wait so long to join me?"—"In my heart," the old man answered, "I was already your follower. But if I had joined you sooner, the Taychi'ut chiefs would have massacred my wife and children, seized my herds and my possessions. . . . It is only now that we can at last come to join you." And Chingis-khan agreed that he had been wise.

"The Arrow that Wounded Your Horse, It Was I Who Shot It!"

At the same time as Sorqan-shira, there came to Chingis-khan another new recruit, a young man, this time, named Jirqo-aday. He was of the Besüt clan, a sept of the Taychi'uts. At the battle of Köyten, he had wounded with an arrow in the collarbone the war horse of Chingis-khan, a splendid brown creature with a white muzzle. Or rather, as, after the battle of Köyten, he was hiding with other Taychi'ut warriors to escape the victors, he happened to be caught up in Chingis-khan's hunt and enclosed by the circle of beaters. The Conqueror, seeing him, wanted to hunt him down, but Bo'orchu asked to be allowed the honor of pitting himself against so illustrious a fighter. For this sort of "archers' joust," Chingis-khan lent Bo'orchu his famous roan horse with the white muzzle. Bo'orchu let fly first, and missed Jirqo-aday. The latter's arrow, better aimed, found his adversary's horse, and then Jirqo-aday made off at a gallop. But now, without resources, he came to offer his services to the khan. The eagle eye of the Conqueror probed into his very entrails: "Who was it, after the Köyten day, wounded my war horse?" Jirqo-aday answered: "That arrow that wounded your horse, it was I, in the mountain, who shot it. The khan may punish me by killing me forthwith. My blood would stain but a little patch of earth, no bigger than the palm of a hand. But if you have mercy on me, I shall go at your behest to attack all your enemies. For you, I will cross the deepest torrents, I will split the rocks." The answer pleased Chingis-khan. "Ordinarily, a defeated foe takes good care not to boast of the damage he may have done you. But this boy, on the contrary, confesses it frankly. Let him be one of our companions: he has the mettle! He has been called till now Jirqo-aday. In memory of the arrow which wounded my horse, he shall be called henceforth Jebe ["The Arrow"], and he shall be himself as my war horse! Jebe, ride at my side!"

Thus it was that Jebe the Taychi'ut became the hero's companion. The name Chingis-khan gave him the young captain was to make immortal. In all the Mongol epic few were to become as famous as Jebe, who conquered for his master Semirechie and Kashgharia, and vanquished Persians, Georgians, and Russians.

"If You Had Delivered up Your Master to Me, I Would Have Put You to Death "

The Taychi'uts were thoroughly broken. It was this Mongol tribe, closely related to Chingis-khan's own, and formerly, moreover, subject to his father, that by its dissidence had made the hero's youth one of such hardship and uphill struggle. Now, he brought it by force to his heel. The Taychi'ut princes—A'uchu-ba'atur, Qodun-orchang, Qudu'udar—he put to death, with their children and their children's children, "and all their race was scattered as ashes." Their people he took to pass the winter with him in the district of Quba-qaya, near the sources of the Kerülen.

Nevertheless perhaps the most important of the Taychi'ut chiefs, Tarqutay-Qiriltuq, Chingis-khan's old enemy, persecutor of his childhood, the man who had once made him wear the cangue, had managed to hide in the woods. Three of his household—Shirgüetü, of the Ba'arin tribe, and his sons, Alaq and Nayaqa—took advantage of his weakness to betray his trust and take him prisoner. They hoisted him into a wagon and set out to deliver him to Chingis-khan. At that moment, the sons and brothers of Tarqutay-qiriltuq appeared, intending to set him free. Before they got to him, Shirgüetü climbed into the wagon, and, bending over his prisoner, drew his saber: "Your kinsmen are coming to save you. Whether I kill you or spare you it will make no difference, I shall be executed for having betrayed your trust. I might as well slice off your head!" He had his saber raised. Tarqutay-qiriltuq shouted with all his lungs to his sons to stop: "If you come closer, he will kill me. Turn away, if you value my life! . . ." He preferred to be handed over to Chingis-khan, telling himself he could touch the hero's heart with certain memories: in times of yore—doubtless in Yesügei's lifetime—it had been he, Tarqutay-qiriltuq, who had "taught the young Temüjin like a young two- or three-year-old colt." "Temüjin has not forgotten: for sure, he will not kill me!"

Shirgüetü, free of his pursuers, had gone on his way with his prisoner to Chingis-khan. His son Nayaqa, with more insight, made him see he was misjudging the nature of the Conqueror. The latter, it was known, had a horror of traitors. What he would say at sight of them could be forecast in advance: "These men have turned their hands against their rightful lord. What trust is to be placed in them? We cannot admit them to our company. There is nothing to be done but put them to death!" The words thus attributed to Chingis-khan were so much in line with what was known of his character that old Shirgüetü set his captive free on the instant. After which he came with his two sons to join Chingis-khan: "We had taken prisoner Tarqutay-qiriltuq to give him up to you, but we could not bring ourself to betray one who was our rightful lord. We set him free, therefore, and came alone to profess our loyalty to you!" The hero congratulated them: "You did well. If you had delivered up your master, I would have put you to death." Learning that the decision was due to the advice of the young Nayaqa, he praised the latter in particular. Nayaqa was later to become his trusted delegate in private missions of the most delicate kind.

Flashes of nobility like this are legion in the story of the Mongol conqueror.

The Extermination of the Tatars

Chingis-khan, in bringing to heel the Taychi'ut clans, had avenged wrongs done to himself. To avenge those done to his family, he had now to exterminate the Tatars, murderers of his ancestors, murderers of his own father Yesügei.

The Tatars, enemy-kin, as we have explained, to the Chingiskhanids, of the same pure Mongol stock, were divided into several tribes who wandered from near the lower Kerülen, and Lakes Kölen and Buyur, over as far as the Great Khingan, the range demarcating Mongolia and Manchuria. Chingis-khan, with the aid of the Kereit Ong-khan and the Peking King of Gold, had once already defeated them. He had also encountered them in every coalition formed against him, and they had been defeated by him then with their allies. Now—in 1202—he was of a mind to finish things once and for all with these eternal enemies. To do so he no longer needed allies; his own strength now sufficed. And it was a fight now to the death.

The decisive battle took place in the spring of 1202 in the area of Dalan-nemürges ("the Seventy Felt Cloaks"), which has been sited near the inflow of the River Khalkha to Lake Buyur. Chingis-khan had forbidden his troops to take booty of any kind till victory was complete: there would be all the time they wanted afterward to share out the enemies' goods. If the first assault was thrown back, they must, at whatever cost, return to the attack. "Who does not do so, will be executed." The Tatars were utterly crushed. Proceeding at once to one of those enveloping movements that were to make Mongol tactics famous, Chingis-khan surrounded the vanquished enemy near the Rivers Olqui and Shilügeljit, which run down from Mount Soyulzi, in the Khingan chain, to peter out in the Gobi. The four Tatar tribes—Chaghan-Tatars, Alchi-Tatars, Duta'ut-Tatars, and Aluqay-Tatars—were annihilated, chiefs and subjects.

But a serious breech of discipline had occurred. Contrary to the orders of Chingis-khan, his uncle, the vociferous Daritay, his first cousin Quchar and Prince Altan had turned to looting for their own benefit without waiting till the conclusion of operations and the general sharing out of booty. Evidently, they considered themselves, by reason of their birth, exempt from the prohibition of *yassaq* Chingis-khan had issued.[1] But precisely by reason of that it was vital that they should be made an example of, for indiscipline in such high quarters was likely to be contagious. Moreover, insubordination on the part of Altan might have particularly dangerous implications: was he not the son of the last Mongol khan, Qutula? Was this deliberate flouting not perhaps the prelude to rebellion in the offing? Inexorably, Chingis-khan had rounded up and confiscated the cattle the three princes of the blood had appropriated. Thus he re-established discipline, but neither Altan nor Quchar, nor even Daritay, ever forgave him this affront. Bitterly nursing their grievance, they were to carry on ceaseless stealthy agitation against the khan, till the day when they defected and went to fight against him in the ranks of the Kereits.

It remained to deal with the many Tatar prisoners. In this too Chingis-khan was relentless. He called his own followers to secret council, in a *yurt,* to take a decision. They pronounced categorically: "The Tatars caused the death of our fathers and forefathers. They shall be sacrificed in vengeance for our forefathers and our fathers; we will exterminate every male standing higher than a wagon axle. The rest we will make slaves of!" But on emerging from the council Chingis-khan's half brother, Belgütei, was unwise enough to let one of the Tatar prisoners, Cheren the Great (Yeke-Cheren), know the decision. Warning thus given them, the Tatars threw up the best defenses they were able. This was in the foothills of the Khingans, where the valleys are carpeted with grasses growing breast-high, easy concealment for a fugitive. This dense grass is furthermore studded with elms and willows, and groves of birch

---

[1] It will be remembered that Quchar was the son of Nekün-tayshi, himself brother of Yesügei and Daritay. Altan, as already stated, was the son of khan Qutula, who was the brother of Bartan-ba'atur, the same who was himself Chingis-khan's own grandfather.

and poplar grow halfway down the slopes. With wagons and tree cuttings it is easy to improvise barricades. The Mongols had to beat down this last-ditch resistance, and they lost a lot of men doing it. Then began the extermination of the Tatar male population, a methodical extermination, Mongol fashion. But even this slaughter was not one-sided, for the Tatars, knowing what awaited them, had hidden knives in their sleeves: before they died, many of them dispatched their executioners "to serve as a grave pillow."

Chingis-khan, furious with Belgütei for this indiscretion of his that had been the cause of such heavy losses, forbade him henceforth to attend council. Significantly, he extended the same prohibition to his uncle Daritay, whose attitude was becoming more and more suspect.

The Hearts of the Two Tatar Sisters

In his share of the booty, Chingis-khan accorded himself the fair Yisü-gen, daughter of the Tatar chief Yeke-Cheren. The story declares he felt much love for her. But the young woman was not jealous, or, at least, had a highly developed sense of family, for, the very evening of their union, as soon as she had assured herself of her master's heart, she told him that she had an elder sister, Yisüi, whose beauty was no less worthy of a king. "She was just now on the point of being married. But in the upheaval now, who knows where she may be!" "If she is as beautiful as you say," said Chingis-khan, "I will have them look for her. But if she is found, will you be willing to share with her your place beside me?" The good Yisügen having given her assurance, a search was made, and Yisüi was eventually found in a forest, where she was hiding with her be-trothed. The latter took flight, and Yisüi was brought back to the khan, who married her as he had married her sister. Yisügen, as soon as she saw her elder sister, had risen to give up to her the place she occupied in the hierarchy of royal wives, to take of her own accord a lower one. (Travelers in the East have described for us these hierarchical tiers of queens around the Mongol khans.) This good understanding greatly pleased Chingis-khan, who made no secret of the satisfaction it gave him.

The Tatars exterminated or made slaves, Chingis-khan held a great open-air banquet. He seated himself between his two new wives, Yisüi and Yisügen, and was drinking with them when he suddenly noticed Yisüi tremble. He suspected something and ordered Bo'orchu and Mu-qali to have lined up all the males present, tribe by tribe, and satisfy themselves as to their identity. At the end of the examination, there was one unknown whom none of the Mongol tribes recognized as belonging to them. He was a young man, fit and handsome-looking. Questioned, he confessed he was Yisüi's betrothed. He had returned and slipped in among the crowd to see his beloved again, thinking himself safe among so many. Alas, Chingis-khan was not one to make light of such matters, the less so in that he was himself greatly enamored of his new wife. "Why," he said, "does this boy come wandering here? Certainly to spy on us! There is one way to deal with him—as we dealt with his countrymen: cut him down before my eyes!" There and then, they cut off his head.

Nevertheless, his war with the Tatars almost cost Chingis-khan dear. After disaster overtook this people, one of their warriors, Qargil-shira, had managed to escape the general massacre, but, driven by hunger, he came back to wander around the Mongol camp. He finally presented himself as a supplicant at the *yurt* of the lady Hö'elün, mother of Chingis-khan, begging for alms. The dowager was goodhearted: "Since you ask alms," she said, "come and sit here," and she sat him in a corner of the *yurt,* behind the door. A little later, Chingis-khan's youngest son, Toluy, who was only about five years old at the time,[1] came in, then turned about and ran for the door. At that moment, Qargil-shira rose, seized him by the arm, and carried him off. He had his knife out ready to cut his throat. Hö'elün screamed. She and one of her friends, the lady Altani, threw themselves after the kidnapper. Altani caught up with him, grabbed him with one hand by the braids of his hair and with the other twisted his wrist, the one holding the knife, so that he dropped it. Near the *yurt* at the time were two of Chingis-khan's officers, Jelme and Jetei, slaughtering a young bullock. At Altani's cries, they ran, ax in hand, their fists still red with the blood of the beast, hurled themselves on Qargil-shira, and stretched him out stone dead.

Elimination of the Tatars gave Chingis-khan control of eastern Mongolia, while the Kereits and Naymans ruled respectively over central and western Mongolia. A measure of the advantage he was to derive from the extermination of the Tatars is that it was in the former Tatar country that he was to take refuge the following year, when, after quarreling with

---

[1] He was to die at the age of 39 in 1232. The extermination of the Tatars, then, according to the *Secret History,* would have taken place about 1198, but the other sources give 1202.

the Kereits, he had to abandon to them his territory on the upper Kerü-len. If in 1203 the Tatars had been still a force to reckon with, the hero would have found himself caught between his hereditary enemies and the Ong-khan, and would certainly have been crushed.

The Tatars' elimination thus reversed the balance of powers in Mongolia in favor of Chingis-khan, to the detriment of the Kereit Ong-khan. It did not take Chingis-khan long to become more peremptory in his dealings with the Ong-khan, or the Ong-khan to conceive a mounting distrust of Chingis-khan. Matters moved to a head.

"Our Daughters Are Ladies;
Theirs, Serving Women"

The break between the Mongol conqueror and the "khan his father," as he called the Ong-khan of the Kereits, has all the pattern of a classical tragedy, a mounting tension, clear-drawn characters. Chingis-khan was loyal to the end, or at least punctilious in outward loyalist allegiance to the "khan his father," albeit with a weather eye open for backslidings or even treachery on the Ong-khan's part. Indeed, the Ong-khan had on several occasions repaid his services in coin of the blackest ingratitude. When the Ong-khan, dethroned by his own brothers, was wandering wretchedly in the wastes of the Gobi, not only had Chingis-khan taken him in and re-established him, but he had made over to him all the booty from the Merkits of the lower Selenga. The Ong-khan, when on another occasion he pillaged the Merkits,[1] had on the contrary kept all for himself. Worst of all, in their joint campaign against the Naymans he had deserted Chingis-khan under cover of darkness, on the eve of a battle. It is true that when Chingis-khan had the magnanimity, after that, to save him from these same Naymans, the Kereit sovereign's better feelings seemed once again to come uppermost. At bottom, this weak character was swayed utterly by whomever he had been listening to last. A short while since, his son the *senggüm* Nilqa, who hated Chingis-khan, and the dangerous Jamuqa, who counseled the *senggüm,* had talked him into the blackest of treacheries against the Mongol conqueror. Now this

___

[1] He forced the Merkit chief Toqto'a-beki to flee to the bank of Barghuchin, eastern shore of Lake Baykal, killed Togus-beki, captured his two daughters, Qutuqtay and Chala'un, and two other of his sons, Qodu and Chila'un, with a great number of his people.

same Ong-khan, touched by the magnanimity of Chingis-khan who had just come to his rescue a second time, hovered on the brink of the opposite extreme: he all but disinherited his own son in favor of Chingis-khan. "I am getting old," he said to himself. "If I go to heaven, who will rule over my people? My younger brother Jaqa-gambu is without capacity. I have only the one son, the *senggüm,* and he is a nonentity. I shall adopt Temüjin as my eldest son, then I shall be able to grow old in peace!"

Steps were taken. The Ong-khan held a meeting with Chingis-khan in the Black Forest, on the banks of the Tula, and there solemnly named him his adoptive son. For a long time, indeed, in memory of Yesügei who had been the Ong-khan's adoptive brother (*anda*), Chingis-khan had addressed the Ong-khan as father (*echige*), that is to say, practically, as suzerain. But this time it seems that as well as the tie of vassalhood implicit in the term so far as Chingis-khan was concerned, there was now a new overtone setting him in a new relationship. Oaths were exchanged. "In war, we shall lead the attack together. In the hunt, we shall lead the beat side by side. If a serpent tries to insinuate itself between us to inject between us distrust and division, we shall afford no purchase for its sting, but will believe only what we have said to each other, in all frankness."

To seal this pact, Chingis-khan would have liked to obtain for his eldest son Jöchi the youngest daughter of the *senggüm,* Cha'ur-beki. He offered in return a princess of his house, Qojin-beki, for Tusaqa, the *senggüm's* son. But the *senggüm* could obviously not be expected to view with favor the understandings just arrived at. If his father treated Chingis-khan as his adoptive son, this could only be at the expense of the legitimate heir. He felt himself being maneuvered out of his inheritance. The *senggüm* refused outright therefore to assent to plans for the double marriage: "A daughter of our house," he declared proudly, "going to live with them, would set her eyes on the place of honor even if she had to stand at the door of the *yurt,* while one of their daughters, coming to live with us, even though she be given the place of honor, would keep watching the door," an image making the Kereit princesses out respectable *qatuns,* the Mongol princesses parvenus, and the projected union a misalliance.

This refusal stung Chingis-khan deeply. From this day on, the filial sentiment he seems long to have felt for the Ong-khan gave way to an ill-concealed rancor.

Nomads between Sworn
Allegiance and Treason

The cooling of relations that now set in was turned to account by Jamuqa, erstwhile chosen brother of Chingis-khan, now his worst enemy,
the anti-Caesar *manqué* who, having failed miserably in his bid for the
throne, was but the more jealous of his successful rival. Jamuqa at once
saw the advantage he could derive from events. In the spring of 1203 he
came to confer with the *senggüm,* and also with the Mongol princes Altan
and Quchar, who were firmly resolved to betray Chingis-khan to his enemies.

The surreptitious council took place in the region of Berke-elet
("sands of weariness") near Mount Chekcher, sited usually south of
where the Kerülen flows into Lake Kölen, a region where steppe modu-
lates into desert, with a sparse vegetation of *derissus* and *karagans.* The
meeting place was chosen undoubtedly at the request of the princes Altan and Quchar, and to avoid alerting either Chingis-khan or even the
Ong-khan in their respective encampments around, probably, the upper
Kerülen and the upper Tula.

Here, tongues were unleashed to vent accumulated hatreds. Jamuqa,
to fan these, accused Chingis-khan of being closely in touch with the
Naymans, the Kereits' hereditary enemies: "He calls himself the son of
Ong-khan, and see how he behaves!" Jamuqa succeeded particularly in
rousing the *senggüm* with warnings that on the death of the Ong-khan
Chingis-khan might try to seize the Kereit throne: "If you do not act
against this peril in time, what will become of you afterward? As for me,
if you march against Temüjin, you have my word I will attack him on the

flank." The dissident Mongol princes Altan and Quchar were no less vehement: "We will kill for you the sons of mother Hö'elün! We will leave their bodies lying in the steppe!"

Emboldened by this encouragement, the *senggüm* sent emissaries to his father to bring him round to his way of thinking. He reproached the old man with being deaf and blind to the ambitious designs of Chingis-khan, and proposed a sharp attack be mounted against the latter. But the Ong-khan showed a lively repugnance at the idea of betraying his oaths: "How can you plan such things against my son Temüjin? He has always helped us. He has even in the past saved me. Why all these slanders against him? If we break our words to him, the *Tengri* cannot protect us. And Jamuqa is anyway inconstant and a trifler; he speaks cleverly, but his word is worthless."

The *senggüm* refused to be discouraged. He went himself to his father and brought his major argument to bear: "While you are still alive, behold how little consideration Temüjin has for us. Is he likely, later, to leave me to claim my inheritance, this Kereit kingdom your father Qurjaquz labored so greatly to establish?" This time again the Ong-khan refused to consent to a break. Above all else he confessed his unwillingness to involve himself in the formidable hazards of such a war: "My beard is already white and I want to finish my days in peace. But you do not obey me." The *senggüm* went out in a rage "shutting the door sharply after him." In face of this anger, the old monarch yielded. He called back his son, and, weary of conflict, finished by giving the agreement asked of him, though insisting the rash young man must take responsibility himself for the breaking of the oath and the consequences: "If you think you can succeed, do as you have resolved, but do it yourself, and above all see that I incur no unpleasantness! But I doubt if the *Tengri* will favor you."

The *senggüm* asked nothing better. Already his allies, foremost of them Jamuqa, had been to set fire to Chingis-khan's grazing grounds. This brushwood fire however was not yet a final precipitation of hostilities. The *senggüm* had in mind, in fact, to take his enemy prisoner unawares. He thought he had found the way when in this same spring of 1203 he pretended to consent to the marriages earlier proposed by Chingis-khan; so inveigling the latter into attending a festive gathering to mark the compact, which was simply a trap. Chingis-khan, unsuspicious, set out with ten of his people. On the way, he stopped to pass the night in the *yurt* of the old man Mönglik, who had been, it will be remembered, the trusted confidant of his father. The prudent Mönglik showed him how unwise he was being: "When you asked for your son their daughter Cha'ur-beki, these people began by disdaining the union. And now they talk of a banquet for the betrothal? After such insolence, they give you the young woman? It looks to me highly suspicious! My son, decline the invitation! You have only to make the excuse that it is springtime, your horses are thin, they need to stay on the grazing ground, and say that you will come when they have had time to fatten."

Chingis-khan found this sound advice. He turned back, contenting himself with sending on in his place, to make his excuses to the Ong-khan, two of his followers, Buqatay and Kiratay. When he saw these two arrive instead of the hero, the *senggüm* knew his feint had been seen through.

29

The Two Herdsmen Save Chingis-khan

The trap having failed, the *senggüm,* who had finally been given carte blanche by his father, resolved to have recourse to surprise attack. Chingis-khan, assailed without warning out of the blue, would be encircled, put off balance for defense, surprised and slaughtered.

The council of war, consisting of the principal Kereit chiefs, which had come to this decision, had resolved to keep it strictly secret. It was evening. Next morning, the army would move off. Returning to his *yurt,* one of the Kereit chiefs, Yeke-Cheren, told his wife and son: "Tomorrow morning, at dawn, we are leaving to surprise Temüjin!" "Be quiet," answered his wife. "Suppose somebody heard you! They might think you were being serious!" Just at that moment, a servant called Baday, whose task was to watch the horses at pasture, was coming up to the *yurt* with mare's milk. He heard his master's words, and hastened with his news to his friend, Kishlik, also a horseherd. Kishlik went to listen in turn. What he heard froze him in terror. Yeke-Cheren was talking to his son Narin-keyen. As he sharpened his arrows, the latter remarked that if anyone overheard them, he must have his tongue cut out. A little while after, this same Narin-keyen ordered Kishlik to fetch from the grazing ground two of his best horses, "the white horse Merkitei and the brown with the white muzzle," adding that he had to be in the saddle before dawn.

Kishlik returned to Baday. "I have checked what you said. It is true. Let us go to warn Chingis-khan!" As soon as darkness fell, they killed and roasted a lamb, jumped into the saddle, and plunged into the night.

Before dawn, they reached Chingis-khan's camp, demanded to be taken at once to his *yurt,* and reported their news: "Alert, O khan! Your camp is to be encircled and yourself taken prisoner!" There and then, in the darkness, Chingis-khan gave his orders to the trusted men of his entourage. He woke his people, had everyone on his feet, and, abandoning everything that could weigh him down, part of his utensils, his scanty nomad's household goods, he fled at once eastward, making for the former Tatar territory, that is, for the basin of the River Khalkha and the foothills of the Grand Khingan.

30

The Affray by the Red Willows

Reaching Mount Mao-ündür, Chingis-khan left there a rear guard under the command of the faithful Jelme, of the Urangquat tribe, in whom he had full confidence. He himself continued his retreat east. Next day, in the afternoon, they halted near the sands of Qalaqaljit-elet, and had something to eat. They were now in the Khalkha river region, a zone of transition, cut into on the west by salt marshes and patches of desert, where the sands of the Gobi reach into the grassland. Far to the east the grassland begins again, getting thicker and lusher as it approaches the Khingan, while a little farther on, clumps of willow and elm, then of poplars and birches, herald the great forest that covers the inclines of the Khingan and the line of its crest on the horizon. Only the "powdering of sand," carried by the wind across the grasslands and even up on to the slopes, recalls the persistent presence of the desert to the southeast.

The army had not finished its meal when two horseherders of the Mongol chief Alchiday, Chigiday and Yadir, came up at a gallop. They brought the alarm: while they were grazing their horses in the new grass, they had seen in the distance a cloud of dust approaching, in front of the Mao-ündür mountains, along the site of the Red Willows (Hula'un-burqat): "No doubt about it, it is the enemy."

Chingis-khan thought so also. He had the horses brought in and ordered his men into the saddle. In the first rank of his followers rode the two tribes of the Uru'uts and the Mangghuts, counted among the proudest of the Mongol tribes, and whose chiefs were descended from the same mythical ancestors as himself.[1] The enemy—the Kereit army was now in sight—were taking up battle order also. The Ong-khan asked Jamuqa:

[1] From Nachin-ba'atur.

"Who are all the best warriors who surround Temüjin?" "They are the Uru'uts and the Mangghuts preparing for the fray. When they encircle the enemy their line never breaks; in their speedy retreats, their ranks stay intact. From their tenderest years they are trained to handling of saber and lance. For their banners, they have the tails of piebald yaks. Let us be wary of them!" The Ong-khan decided to match against them an elite, the Jirgin tribe, commanded by Qaday: "and behind the Jirgins shall come the Tümen-Tübegens under Achiq-shirun, and behind the Tümen-Tübegens the Olon-dongqayts, then Prince Qori-shilemün at the head of a thousand royal guards, then myself, the Ong-khan, with the main part of the army!"

At this point, a curious episode. The Ong-khan offered to Jamuqa command of the army, and Jamuqa declined it. Evidence of modesty on the part of Jamuqa, conscious of having never in the past succeeded in defeating Chingis-khan? Or did the Ong-khan's offer cause his ally to have doubts on the score of the Kereit army? Jamuqa ought surely to have accepted with joy the offer made him. It was he who was the instigator of this war, he who had long intrigued to set the former allies at odds. But such was the instability of this strange character that his thoughts were turning already to a reshuffling of alliances. Intelligence officers in our outposts in Africa know these sudden sharp veerings nomads are prone to. Jamuqa was telling himself, perhaps, that the Ong-khan was for him but a casual ally, while by the old Mongol customary law Chingis-khan, notwithstanding the present dispute, remained his "brother by alliance," the *anda* with whom nothing could destroy his ancient pact. Moved by this curious fidelity to their childhood memories, he sent word then to Chingis-khan of the dispositions of the enemy army and the plan of attack: "O my *anda,* be not afraid, but be on your guard!"

On his side, Chingis-khan had disposed his forces for the battle, not without noting the enemy's numerical superiority (the defection of his uncle Daritay and the Mongol princes Altan and Quchar cannot have failed to weaken his hand considerably). He turned first to old Jürchedei, chief of the Uru'uts. "Uncle Jürchedei, what do you think? I am thinking of giving you the advance guard." Jürchedei, stroking his horse's mane with his whip, was about to answer when Quyildar-sechen, chief of the Mangghuts, broke in: "It is for me to lead the first attack!" And he declared he would plant his *tuq,* his yak-tail standard, on the heights behind the enemy. To drive home his resolve to conquer or die, he asked that his orphans be looked after on his death. Jürchedei retorted: "Under the eyes of Chingis-khan we shall lead the attack together." At their command Uru'uts and Mangghuts drew themselves up in battle array. They had scarcely formed ranks when the enemy, the Jirgins at their head, attacked.

It was one of the direst battles of the time. In face of the charging Jirgins, the Uru'uts and Mangghuts countercharged. They forced the Jirgins to give way, they drove after them in hot pursuit. But as they did so they were themselves charged by Achiq-shirun of the Tümen-Tübegens. Achiq-shirun, making for Quyildar, struck him a blow so terrible it knocked him from his horse. The Mangghuts, turning back, rushed to surround Quyildar to protect him. Jürchedei for his part then headed a fresh charge that drove back the Tümen-Tübegens. As he was carrying all before him, another part of the Kereit army, the Olon-Dongqayts, threw itself against him, but he brushed it off in its turn. Then the thousand men of the Kereit royal bodyguard were seen to get under way, led by Qori-shilemün. But these also Jürchedei threw back.

Was the Kereit army, numerically superior, having the advantage of attack, nevertheless to fail? The Kereit crown prince, the *senggüm,* boiled with impatience. It was he who had wanted this attack, he who had forced the decision from his hesitating father, the Ong-khan. And now every charge his warriors made was brought up short against the wall of these men of iron. Without a word to his father, he placed himself at the head of his last squadrons and threw himself into the battle, but an arrow pierced his cheek—an arrow shot, it is said, by Jürchedei himself—and he fell from his horse. The entire Kereit army massed to surround and protect him.

▲
▲▲
───────

31

The Tears of Chingis-khan

The sun was setting behind the hills. The Mongols turned about. They could say theirs was the victory, but the day had been desperately hard-fought, and their losses were scarcely less than the Kereits'.

Among the Mongol chiefs, the heroic Quyildar was seriously wounded. Advancing dark and the exhaustion of both armies halted the combat. For the rest, Chingis-khan was under no illusions. With characteristically dispassionate decision, he abandoned the battlefield to the enemy and took advantage of the dark to get away. Some distance off, he called a halt.

That was a terrible night. The Mongols spent it in ranks, sleeping by their horses, reins in hand, ready to be in the saddle at the first alert. A night of anguish, for Chingis-khan did not know exactly what his losses were, even among those nearest to him. At first light he counted his followers. Three names were not answered to: Boroqul and Bo'orchu, his dearest comrades, Ögödei, his favorite son. This was a cruel loss. He struck his breast, raised his eyes to heaven. "Together they lived. Together they died." Or, in another version: "With Ögödei my two faithful ones stayed out there. Dead or alive, they could not leave . . ." [1] As he finished his words, a man was seen coming in the early light. It was Bo'orchu. At sight of him Chingis-khan, striking his breast again, gave thanks to the eternal *Tengri*. Bo'orchu explained what had happened to him: "In the attack, my horse was wounded by an arrow and fell. I ran away on foot. At that moment the Kereits turned to defend their

[1] [This passage is based on the account given in paragraphs 172–73 of the *Secret History*. Grousset's translation is incorrect, but as it does not affect the story I left it uncorrected.]

wounded *senggüm*. I saw a pack horse with a load that had slipped round. I cut off its load, jumped on it, headed in your tracks, and here I am!"

A few moments later a second horseman was seen approaching. Behind him hung the legs of another man. Drawing nearer, the two thus sharing a mount turned out to be Ögödei and Boroqul. Boroqul rode behind clutching Ögödei who had an arrow wound in the neck. Boroqul's mouth was still red with blood, for he had, in accordance with Mongol medical custom, carefully sucked the young man's wound. At this sight, Chingis-khan's heart tightened, and they saw the man of iron shed tears.

They learned what had happened. The wound Ögödei had received had pierced a neck vein. With the pain, the young prince had fallen from his horse. Boroqul had at once got down to protect and attend to him. He had spent the night at his side, busy sucking the clotted blood from the wound. In the morning, Ögödei could still not hold himself in the saddle. Boroqul had therefore hoisted him on to his own horse, then had mounted behind him, twining his arms around him to hold him there, and thus they had returned. Chingis-khan had a big fire lit and cauterized his son's wound. A cup of *qumiz* completed the young man's recovery.

▲
▲▲

32

"We Shall Gather up the Mongols Like Dung-pats."

All in all the battle had been inconclusive. The Kereits had certainly had a tough time. According to Boroqul, from the dust cloud he had seen in the distance, they could be taken to be moving along Mount Mao-ündür, in the direction of the Red Willows (Hula'un-burqat). Chingis-khan prepared himself for any eventuality: "If they come, we will face them. If we are borne down, we will re-form and attack again." Anything but reassured, he backed up the Olqui and Shilügeljit valleys and camped in the district of Dalan-nemürges, by our reckoning on the western slope of Mounts Obolo-khabala and Soyulzi, that is, on the western slope of the Great Khingan. Thus he found himself at bay at the very eastern limit of Mongolia, almost driven from Mongol country, on the brink of flight into exile and of taking sanctuary in Manchuria, property of the King of Gold in Peking. As he drew nearer the Great Khingan, away from the glum steppes of the lower Kerülen and the Buyurnor, he did come first on rich pastures, then forests, increasingly thick, that spread along the foot of the chain. Here his horses could build up resistance worn down by the forced marches of the withdrawal.

On their side, the Kereits had seen their surprise attack fail, and they had to think of new plans. At this stage, there came to Chingis-khan Qada'an-daldurqan, of the tribe of the Targhuts. He had left wife and children to come to join the Mongol hero. He had curious things to tell them of morale in the Kereit camp: the Ong-khan was reproaching the *senggüm* with having drawn him into an unholy war against a former ally, and already regarded the *senggüm*'s cheek wound as punishment.

His lieutenant, Achiq-shirun, comforted him as best he could: "O khan, formerly, when you had no son and wanted one, we made incantations and spells that your wish might be granted. Now that you have a son, we are resolved to defend him." Achiq-shirun also pointed out to the Ong-khan that a considerable proportion of the Mongol tribes—the greater proportion, he maintained—were fighting under Altan, Quchar, and Ja-muqa, alongside the Kereits. "As to those of the Mongols who have stayed with Temüjin, their plight is such that they have now but one horse to each rider, no led horses or pack animals, and that instead of tents all they have for shelter is the trees of the forest"—the last detail of partic-ular interest since it proves that Chingis-khan, driven from the Mongol steppe, had in fact been reduced to refuge in the verges of the great woods of the Khingan. "If they dare no longer march against us," the fiery Achiq-shirun said finally, "we shall march on them, and we shall gather them up like dung-pats." [1]

Not greatly comforted by these communications, Chingis-khan left the district of Dalan-nemürges, moving down the valley of the Khalkha, which flows from Mounts Obolo-khabala and Aruto-laku toward Buyur. At this point he called the roll of his army. He had only two thousand six hundred men left. He took thirteen hundred down the left bank of the Khalkha, sending the other thirteen hundred, including the Uru'uts and Mangghuts, down the right. During this march, they made hunting forays to provision themselves. The chief of the Mangghuts, the fiery Quyildar, whose wound was not yet healed, insisted, despite Chingis-khan's adjur-ings to prudence, on taking part in the hunting. His wound reopened and he died. Chingis-khan buried his faithful servant on the slopes of Mount Orno'u.

In this region, near the inflow of the Khalkha to Lake Buyur, lived the Mongol tribe of the Onggirats or Qonggirats, under its chiefs Terge and Amel. This was the tribe, it will be remembered, of the lady Börte, wife of the Conqueror. Chingis-khan sent Jürchedei to recall the old ties of kinship: "If the Onggirats still remember our alliance, let them submit. If they show themselves hostile, we attack!" Whether the name of the beau-tiful Börte worked on them, or whether they considered themselves too weak to stand up to Chingis-khan, they made their submission unresist-ingly, and allowed him to recoup his strength among them.

[1] [These were used as fuel by the Mongols.]

The Complaint of Chingis-khan

From here, Chingis-khan went to set up his tents on the banks of the little River Töngge, probably between the Buyur and Lake Kölen (little Dalay-nor). His horses completed their recovery in these grasslands with their willow groves, watered by underground springs. "I camp east of the Töngge. The grass is lush and our horses have developed their muscles again." From here he sent to the Ong-khan, and to the *senggüm,* to Jamuqa, to Altan, and to Quchar, two of his henchmen, Arqay-qasar and Sükegei-je'ün, with a message, or rather, writing being unknown in this society, with a recital for them, in verse, listing his grievances.

"The Complaint of Chingis-khan," as it has been called, turns out, under its guise of honor, emotion, old affection restrained with difficulty, to be a most adroit political manifesto: "O khan, my father," runs the hero's message to the Kereit king, "why were you angered against me and why did you make me afraid? The seat where I was wont to sit has been cut down; the smoke of my hearth has been scattered. . . .[1] Was it a stranger who incited you against me? Remember what we agreed once at the Red Hills (Hula'a-no'ut bolda'ut), near Mount Jorqalqun: that, even if a serpent sought to poison our relations, we would afford his sting no purchase, we would believe nothing of his insinuations without a frank and loyal explanation between you and me. If the wagon lose one of its two shafts, the ox can no longer pull it. If it lose one of its wheels, it can go no further. Was I not one of the two shafts, one of the two wheels of your wagon?"

Then, Chingis-khan enumerated all the services that his father Yesügei

---

[1] [Grousset gives a free translation of ¶ 177 of the *Secret History.* The smoke that is scattered has risen through the smokehole of the *yurt.*]

and he himself had rendered the Kereit sovereign, recounted here in this history. He did not spare the Ong-khan reminder of his cruelty, when he put to death his own two brothers Tay-Temür and Buqa-Temür, causing his uncle Gur-khan to drive him from the throne, where it had taken Yesügei's intervention to re-establish him. Then later, the Ong-khan had been driven out once again by another of his brothers, Erke-qara, whose death he had previously tried to bring about like the others', and this time it was Chingis-khan himself who had re-established him. Chingis-khan reminded him also, in the same tone of saddened friendship, of how the Ong-khan had deserted him during the campaign against the Naymans, at dead of night, in the presence of the enemy, on the eve of a battle; which had not prevented the Mongol hero from magnanimously saving the same Ong-khan, victim of his own perfidy. Finally, Chingis-khan claimed credit for having brought to heel at the time of their joint campaigns, and, as he put it, on the Kereit sovereign's behalf, the other Mongol tribes. "O khan, my father, I flew like a young falcon over Mount Chiqurqu, I crossed the Buyurnor, I took for you the blue-footed, grey-feathered cranes, the Dörbens and the Tatars; I passed beyond Lake Kölen, I took for you the light blue cranes with dark blue feet, the Qatagins, the Salji'uts, the Onggirats, and I gave them to you." Chingis-khan implied that when he was the Kereit king's vassal, all exercise of his sway was for him but the extension of that of the Ong-khan, his suzerain.

In this same message, Chingis-khan reproached his former *anda* Jamuqa with having, by his persistent jealousy, his intrigues and slanderings, sown discord between himself and the Ong-khan. "As you had failed to defeat me directly, you worked to alienate him from me." And this pleasant recollection: "In the old days, the first to get up in the morning was allowed to drink mare's milk from the blue cup of the khan our father [the Ong-khan]. Because I was always the first up, and always drank first, you began to be jealous of me. Today you drink alone from our father's blue cup"—a subtle image, alluding clearly to the fact that Jamuqa sought to oust Chingis-khan as adoptive son of the Kereit sovereign.

Altan and Quchar, the Mongol princes who had deserted him for the Kereits, Chingis-khan reminded that he had only earlier let himself be proclaimed khan because they themselves (who surely had better claims to the throne) had refused the honor and elected him instead: "Quchar, they wanted once to proclaim you khan, as the son of Nekün-tayshi, and it was you who refused. Altan, they wanted you, too, to rule us, as your father, khan Qutula, ruled, and you also declined. I myself, who am of no lesser breeding, as the grandson of the Ba'atur Bartan, I begged you in vain to accept the kingship, and it was on your withdrawal that I was raised to it." Chingis-khan recalled then to the two princes who had deserted him, after being his chief electors, the duties of a subject to his elected khan. "If it had been one of you two who was elected khan, the fair-faced girls, the fine-legged horses I won in battle, I should loyally have brought to you. The wild animals of the steppe or the wild animals of the mountains I killed in hunting forays, of these I should have offered you the finest portions!" Finally, he sought to reawaken in his two cousins the sense of Mongol solidarity in defense of the ancestral territory, at the headwaters of the Tula, Onon, and Kerülen. "Let not others ensconce themselves at the springs of the Three Rivers."

To the son of the Ong-khan, the *senggüm,* heir presumptive to the Kereit throne, Chingis-khan's message was this: "I also am the son of your father. There is this difference, that I am a son who was born to him clothed, while you were born to him quite naked, but the king our father had for us both the same affection. Fearful that I should insinuate myself between you and him, you conceived hate for me." Continuing on the same note, Chingis-khan invited the *senggüm* to cease harassing with their quarrel the old age of the khan "their father." He insinuated further that the *senggüm* was contemplating making himself king while the Ong-khan still lived, in other words, dethroning his father.

The various messages amount to diplomatic maneuvering of consummate artistry. The Mongol hero talks the right language, hits on the right argument, for every member of the coalition. With the Ong-khan, he grounds himself on loyalty, speaks as the faithful vassal, the adoptive son who has not deserved the unjust disgrace he has been cast into, and is hurt above all in his "filial" love. At the same time, he seeks to sow mistrust between the old man and his legal heir, the *senggüm,* implied to be nurturing plans for patricide. The Mongol princes gone over to the Ong-khan he shames by making them feel traitors to their forebears and people, pressing them discreetly to rally again to the standard to drive the Kereits from the fatherland. Under cover of the most irreproachable loyalty, the most touching good faith, enough insinuations are made to make breakup of the enemy coalition an eventual certainty.

In fact, he all but achieved his end there and then. On hearing the message, still so full of filial affection, of his "son" Chingis-khan, the Kereit Ong-khan was seized with remorse: "In truth, the saying is true, that one ought never to be separated from one's son." "His heart was wrung." He cried: "If I harbor ever again the slightest ill thought about my son Temüjin, may all my blood be shed as this blood is shed!" And, suiting his action to his words, he seized the knife he used for sharpening arrows, made a cut in his little finger, and filled with his blood a cornet of birchbark to go with the envoys to Chingis-khan.

But the *senggüm,* evidently furious at Chingis-khan's insinuations, killed what might have been reconciliation. "He calls you khan and father, but he makes no bones about calling you also your own brothers' executioner!" And beside himself, the *senggüm* demanded war without mercy: "Let Bilge-beki and Tödöyen raise the *tuq.* Let the horses be put to the best grazing that they may be ready for battle. No more hesitating!" The *senggüm* would seem even to have gone on to utter, as in classical tragedy, the rash words that committed him to fate: "Let the outcome of war decide. He who is the victor shall be supreme khan and shall take to himself the *ulus* of the vanquished!"

▲
▲▲

―――――

34

The Bitter Water of the Baljuna

Of the two messengers sent by Chingis-khan to the enemy coalition, one, Sükegei-je'ün, whose wife and children were with the enemy, did not care to return to his master. The other, Arqay-qasar, set forth again and carried back to the Mongol hero the answer, or rather the various answers, to his offers of peace.

On receiving these, Chingis-khan withdrew to the north. He set up camp on the shores of a small lake known as Baljuna (the "muddy" lake), to be found between the Onon and the Ingoda, toward the basin of the River Aga, or possibly farther east, between the northern bank of the Argun and Lake Tarei. To the northwest lay wooded steppe, the soil clay and sand, with an abundance of clematis and hemerocallis, broken by birch and willow; eastward, toward the undrained lakes of Tarei, ran steppe with *absinth* and *solonchak*. The lake of Baljuna was at this time of year almost dry. Chingis-khan—if we may believe later Persian tradition—was at one point reduced to drinking water pressed out from the mud. "Moved by the loyalty of those who had not left him in his distress, he promised them, hands clasped and eyes raised to heaven, that henceforth he would share with them the sweet and the bitter, asking that, if he went back on his word, he might become as the muddy water of the Baljuna. As he spoke, he drank of this water, and passed the cup to his officers, who swore in their turn never to leave him. These companions of Chingis-khan were known afterwards as the Baljunians, and were recompensed munificently for their loyal adherence." [1]

Chingis-khan, there should be no glossing over the fact, was now at bay on the extreme northeastern limit of the Mongol domain, on the

―――――

[1] [On the whole episode see Francis Woodman Cleaves, No. 39.]

verge of the *tayga* inhabited by the Tunguz peoples. Nevertheless, things for him were now slowly on the mend, while his enemies' affairs were taking a turn for the worse. Indeed, the coalition around the Ong-khan was beginning to break up. The nomads were capable of uniting in some temporary vendetta, where there promised to be spoils, under a war chief designated for the purpose. But in the absence of a completely exceptional individual, a leader of men of the stuff of a Chingis-khan, they fretted to take off into freedom again once vendetta had had its fling, and the more so when an adversary's resilience postponed the day of pillage indefinitely and made chances of booty dubious. Each had now but one wish: to leave the unlucky chief who had not succeeded in leading his confederates to victory. The process has been seen at work already as the seasonal leagues that had been mounted earlier against Chingis-khan and against the Ong-khan by the friends of Jamuqa disbanded. Now, it was Jamuqa and the other Mongol dissidents who had had enough of the authority of the Ong-khan. Among the dissatisfied was Daritay, uncle of Chingis-khan, who was beginning to regret having deserted his nephew; and the legitimate "pretenders," Altan and Quchar, as well as the eternal intriguer, Jamuqa himself. With them it was a case of all authority being irksome: "Let us seize the Ong-khan in a coup by night," they plotted, "and let us be kings ourselves, with no more bowing either to the Kereits' authority or to Temüjin's." But the Ong-khan, warned of the plot, anticipated them, and they were only just in time to escape. Jamuqa, Altan, and Quchar took refuge with the Naymans, in western Mongolia. Daritay, on the contrary, resolved to throw himself on the mercy of Chingis-khan. The latter pardoned him without any kind of reservations, for so far as we know no misunderstanding ever arose subsequently between uncle and nephew. About the same time, Cho'os-chagan, chief of the Mongol tribe of the Qorolas, rallied spontaneously to Chingis-khan.

Shortly after this there came to the Baljuna a Moslem trader named Hassan, who after a period in Öngüt country (on the *limes* of the Chinese province of Shan-si), had pushed on to the River Argun. He had with him a white camel, which he doubtless rode, and a herd of a thousand sheep. He had come down the upper Argun valley after sable fur and squirrel hide, both skins to be had in abundance on the threshold of the Transbaykalian *tayga*. He had made a detour to water his beasts at the lake of Baljuna when he met Chingis-khan, and the two men seem to have struck up a friendship. Indeed, three Moslems, the same Hassan, Ja'far-khodja and Danishmendhajib, were from now on to rank among the trusty "Baljunians."

More welcome still for Chingis-khan was the arrival on the Baljuna of his own brother, Jöchi-Qasar. Had he been earlier taken prisoner by the Kereits, or had he, like so many others, gone over to them? We do not know. What is certain is that, anxious to rejoin Chingis-khan, he escaped their surveillance, leaving among them, in a highly precarious situation, his wife and his three sons, Yegü, Yesüngge, and Tuqu. With a handful of companions he set out to look for Chingis-khan in the region toward the Qaraun-chidun mountains, lying, we take it, near the Boroshchovoks, whose chain, partly cedar- and larch-covered, divides the Onon basin from that of the Ingoda. Not finding him, he wandered wretchedly in these wild mountains, "reduced to eating the leather of his harness and his bow strings." After cruel hardship, he finally managed to find Chingis-khan on the Baljuna. The hero rejoiced greatly at his return. And it was now that the two brothers hatched the plot—a somewhat treacherous one, it must be confessed—that was to be the Kereit Ong-khan's downfall.

Night March and Surprise Attack

On the advice of Chingis-khan, Qasar sent to the Ong-khan two envoys, Qali'undar and Chaqurqan, charged with falsehood for the Kereit sovereign. "O khan, my father," Qasar's message ran, "I have sought everywhere my brother Temüjin, but I have been able to find no trace of him. I have called him and my call has remained without an echo. At night, I have for my only shelter the stars, for my only pillow the bare earth. My wife and my children are in the hands of the khan my father. If you give me assurance of safety and encouragement, I will return to you again." These lying words were to lull the Ong-khan's vigilance, for Chingis-khan informed the two messengers, who really were to act as spies, that the Mongol army would follow in their wake. He fixed a point where they should meet him again, at Arqal-geügi, on the lower Kerülen, and told them to come there, their message delivered, armed with all the information they could lay hold of.

So it was done. Chingis-khan, moving with his entire army, came down from the Baljuna into the valley of the lower Kerülen, where he stationed himself at Arqal-geügi. Qali'undar and Chaqurqan, going some days' march ahead of him, came to the Ong-khan, and delivered their message from Qasar. The Ong-khan, convinced that Chingis-khan had disappeared and suspecting nothing, had had set up his royal *yurt* "all of gold" and was holding a banquet. He welcomed the two envoys, believed the protestations of Qasar, and assured him of a good welcome. "Let him come without fear! I will send my assurance to him as guarantee, by my messenger, Itürgen." As token of reconciliation and pardon, he apparently charged Itürgen to take to Qasar (as once before to Chingis-khan) a little of his blood in an oxhorn. Itürgen, armed with these instructions, set out to go to Qasar. Qali'undar and Chaqurqan traveled with him.

It was essential that Itürgen, as they approached Arqal-geügi, should not perceive that Chingis-khan's army was drawn up there, or rather, that he should not perceive it until it was too late, when he no longer had time to go back to rouse the Kereit camp. What did in fact happen? According to one version, Qali'undar, watching the horizon, was first to see the *tuq,* the banner of Chingis-khan. Fearing Itürgen might see it also and make a sudden break, Qali'undar dismounted, pretending that his horse had something sharp embedded in its hoof, and asking the Kereit to hold the hoof while he extracted the foreign body, which gave him his opportunity to overpower the poor man. The *Secret History* tells a more exciting story: as they drew near Arqal-geügi, Itürgen had seen quite clearly the army of Chingis-khan. He turned sharply about, and made off as fast as his horse would carry him. Qali'undar, who had a fast mount, managed to overtake and pass him, but did not like to risk hand-to-hand combat with him and simply barred his way. Meantime Chaqurqan, bringing up the rear, let fly an arrow which struck Itürgen's horse in the hindquarters. The animal fell, and they made Itürgen a prisoner. They took him to Chingis-khan, who left it to Qasar to decide what was to be done with him. Qasar, a man who liked to get things over with, killed him on the spot.

Then and there, Qali'undar and Chaqurqan made their report to the Conqueror: the Ong-khan, all unsuspecting, was banqueting without a qualm of uneasiness; the thing to do was to take him by surprise forthwith. Chingis-khan agreed, and straightway issued his orders. The Mongol army sprang to horse and rode all night, Jürchedei and Arqay heading the advance party. The Kereits were camped at the exit from the pass of Jer-qabchiqay, by the heights of Chekche'er (Chekche'er-ondur). They were taken completely off their guard. Nevertheless, they put up a fierce defense. For three days and three nights they fought back. But they were completely surrounded, and had finally to lay down their arms, save for a handful of men who, with the Ong-khan and the *senggüm,* had managed to escape under cover of darkness.

Clearly Chingis-khan's victory was due to precisely planned tactics: after an approach by night kept carefully secret, the sharp onslaught with effect of total surprise; then the encircling of the enemy caught in a narrow pass, in a sort of mousetrap. It was the first of the great victories of Chingis-khan, but also without a doubt of all of them the most decisive, for it was with this one that he established definitively his authority among the nomads.

The first of his followers Chingis-khan thought to reward after the victory were the two horseherds Baday and Kishlik, who at the outset had saved his life with their forewarning of the Kereit surprise attack. The Mongol hero thanked them magnificently. He gave them the royal *yurt* of the Ong-khan with all that was in it: cups and dishes of gold, and the royal servants, who belonged to the Kereit class or tribe of the Ongqojit. In addition they received, with the title of *tarkhan,* the privilege of "quiver bearers," and also the privilege of "drinking from the cup," involving, it may be, the right to have their own guard of "quiver bearers," to bear their own arms at royal banquets, and to have each his drinking vessel for himself. Finally—another no less coveted favor —Baday and Kishlik were given the right to keep for themselves, in the hunt and at war, all the game they were able to bring down, all the booty they were able to seize, a particularly enviable privilege, since, with such very rare exceptions, all booty and all game had to be put into the general "board," to be apportioned out then to all and sundry by the khan or his generals. What heightened the value of these rewards still further was the magnificent citation with which the Conqueror accompanied them: "Baday and Kishlik, it is they who have saved my life! It is thanks to them, that, under the protection of the eternal *Tengri,* I have succeeded in crushing the Kereits and establishing my rule. I wish my successors, so long as their race retains the throne and down to the furthest generation, never to forget the services these two men have rendered me!"

The Mongol hero knew the way to men's undying devotion.

The Kereits had defended themselves valiantly. Now they rallied honorably to Chingis-khan. The attitude of one of their officers, Qadaq-ba'atur, of the Jirgin tribe, is characteristic. Brought before the Conqueror, after his people's surrender, he declared: "For three days and three nights, I fought. How should I have abandoned him who was my lawful sovereign? I held out as long as I was able, to allow him to save his life and escape. Now, if it is your will, I shall die. But if you are merciful to me, I will vow you my strength and I will serve you faithfully." Chingis-khan honored nothing so much as faithfulness and loyalty, even in an enemy: "The soldier who thinks of saving his life instead of serving his lawful master is not a man," he declared. "He alone is a man who shows himself faithful." And, praising highly the attitude of Qadaq-ba'atur, he accorded him mercy. As to the duties he assigned him, they are proof once again of the Conqueror's generosity. It will be remembered that in the first battle against the Kereits, one of Chingis-khan's best commanders, Quyildar, chief of the Manggut tribe, had received a wound from which he died shortly afterward. Chingis-khan did not forget his heroic lieutenant's widow and children. He appointed to their service Qadaq-ba'atur and a hundred other prisoners of the same Jirgin tribe. "And let the children of Qadaq serve those of Quyildar, and the children of their children until the furthest generation!" A hundred other Jirgins were assigned in like manner to the Mongol chief Tarqay-ba'atur, of the tribe of the Suldus. And the other Kereit tribes, Dongqayts, Tümen-Tübegens, etc., were similarly apportioned out among Mongol chiefs.

With the mass of the Kereit people, then, Chingis-khan took his precautions. He aimed to dissolve them as a political unit, to merge them into the Mongol nation, and he distributed the families as groups of servants or clients among the Mongol clans. At the same time, these measures appear to have been tempered in practice by considerable humanity, born of memories of an old comradeship in arms. In fact, numerous Kereits were later to hold positions of importance in the Mongol army and administration. Reflecting on the fate of the Tatars, and even, a little later, of the Naymans, the Kereits must be admitted to have been dealt with in their misfortune relatively lightly.

The Fate of the Kereit Princesses

There were doubtless contributory reasons for this attitude. One of the Kereit princes, Jaqa-gambu, the Ong-khan's own brother, had always been on terms of personal friendship with Chingis-khan. In earlier days he had once left his brother to join the Mongol hero a first time in an expedition against the Merkits.[1] And Jaqa-gambu had never been able to forget that the Ong-khan had put to death their other brothers. There had been a series of insurrection episodes. On one occasion he had with several Kereit nobles—El-qutur, Qulbari, Alin-tayshi—headed a veritable conspiracy against the Ong-khan: the plot discovered, he had had to take refuge among the Naymans.[2] On the Kereits' submission, therefore, Chingis-khan accorded him particularly favorable treatment. He left him authority over the section of the Kereit people ranking as his subjects. A double family union cemented this arrangement. Jaqa-gambu had two daughters, Ibaqa-beki and Sorghaqtani. Chingis-khan took Ibaqa-beki for himself and gave Sorghaqtani to his youngest son, Prince Toluy. It should be said at once that Jaqa-gambu did not long rest content with this regime of favor. He conspired later against Chingis-khan, and became an insurrectionary once more. The faithful Jürchedei was assigned to put an end to his activities, and lured him into a trap and captured him.

As for Jaqa-gambu's daughter, the Princess Ibaqa whom Chingis-khan had taken to wife, he did not keep her with him, but made a present of her to Jürchedei, with as little ado as if he were handing over to him some prize beast. He had indeed had it suggested to him by the spirits

[1] *Secret History,* ¶ 150.
[2] Op. cit., ¶ 152.

themselves that he thus dispose of her. One night as he lay beside poor
Ibaqa, his sleep was troubled by a terrible nightmare. He saw in this a
warning from heaven. On awakening, he told the young woman that he
had always been well pleased with her, but that in the dream he had just
had the *Tengri* had commanded him to give her up to another, and he
begged her not to hold it against him. And he called out to know who
was the officer of the watch at the door of his *yurt*. Jürchedei—for it was
he who was on guard duty—acknowledged the call. Chingis-khan ordered him to come in, and told him that he gave him in marriage the
Princess Ibaqa. As Jürchedei stood dumfounded, he assured him he
was speaking seriously, then, turning to the princess, made her his formal
acknowledgment that she had ever been above reproach in conduct,
cleanliness, and beauty, and presented to her the *ordu,* the palace of
tents she lived in, with the servants, effects, the studs and herds associated with it. He asked only to keep for himself half of the two hundred
young serving-women she had received as dowry. Her dowry had also
included two cooks, Ashiq-temür and Alshiq. They must have been very
good cooks, for Chingis-khan further asked Ibaqa if he might keep Ashiq-
temür.

Ibaqa's sister, on the other hand, Princess Sorghaqtani, was as wife of
Toluy, the Conqueror's son, to remain one of the Chingiskhanid family.
Her intelligence, her adroitness, her tact, and her political sense destined
her to play a major role in its affairs, and, fifty years later, to determine
the final orientation of the Mongol empire: she was to be the mother of
the great khans Möngke and Qubilay, and of the khan of Persia, Hülegü.
As a devout Nestorian, she was also an influential protector of the Christian Churches. The popularity Christianity was long to enjoy in the Mongol empire, in China and Persia as in Central Asia, sprang in large part
from the offices in this respect of the empresses of Kereit stock.

"You Have Trampled Underfoot the Head of this Dead Man!"

After his victory, Chingis-khan went to pass the winter (of 1203-04) near Mount Abji'a-ködeger, over toward the "steppe of the camel" (Temeen Ke'er), which has been sited in eastern Mongolia, between the mouth of the Kerülen and the River Khalkha.

In the meantime, the Kereit sovereign, the unfortunate Ong-khan, and his son the *senggüm,* had met with the sorriest of ends. In the three-day battle in which their army had been reduced to surrender, they had succeeded in escaping before their people's capitulation. The Ong-khan, riding right across Mongolia, east to west, came to the banks of the River Nekün (Nekunusun), which divided Kereit from Nayman country, and is perhaps the Nerün of our maps; a fast-flowing watercourse running north to south down from the Khangay, to peter out on the threshold of the Gobi in a salt lake surrounded by reeds, and sands with *saksauls* and tamarisks. The Ong-khan, almost dead of thirst, came down to drink right to the river bed. He found there a Nayman guard post, commanded by an officer named Qori-sübechi. This man arrested the fugitive. The Ong-khan told him his identity, but Qori-sübechi, not believing him and taking him for some brigand of the steppe, looked no further into the matter and put him to death.

Meantime, word of a stranger claiming to be the Kereit Ong-khan having been executed spread among the Naymans. The Nayman king, Tayang, wished to find out for certain what had happened. His curiosity was shared by the Nayman Princess Gürbesü, according to some texts Tayang's mother, to others, his wife, probably in fact one of his father's wives, now "honorary queen" in the household of the new sovereign; a woman notable, at all events, for her sagacity, and who seems to have enjoyed great prestige among the Nayman chiefs. When it was established that the fugitive the frontier guards had executed was indeed the Ong-khan, she showed signs of great distress: "He was a great king. Let his head be brought to us. If it is really that of the Ong-khan, we will offer sacrifices to it." Tayang, for his part, found Qori-sübechi gravely at fault in his death-dealing: "Why kill this great king, this old man? He should have been brought to me alive!" And he ordered the head to be set in silver and displayed enthroned on white felt. Gürbesü had drinks brought forth as for the royal banquets, had fitting airs played on the lute, and, seizing a cup, offered libations to the head. The head then smiled—or sneered. In the smile, at all events, Tayang saw an insult or an ill omen. He threw the head to the ground and crushed it with his heel. The best of Tayang's commanders, the valiant Kökse'ü-sabraq, at sight of this sacrilege, was seized with terror: "You have trampled underfoot the head of this king! Hear how the dogs howl warning of swift-arriving misfortune, imminent catastrophe!"

The *senggüm,* for his part, placing doubtless scant reliance on Nayman generosity, had preferred to plunge southwest into the sandy, stony wastes of the Gobi, the Móngol name for which was Chöl. There he led a precarious existence, moving from one water source to the next, and living by hunting. One day when he had dismounted to lie in wait for a herd of wild horses—"to be seen from afar, up and harassed by gadflies" —his groom Kököchü, weary of this life of hardship, seized his horse and rode off to join Chingis-khan. In vain Kököchü's wife tried to recall him to his obligations toward the *senggüm.* Kököchü came to Chingis-khan and sought favor for having thus come over. But the Mongol Conqueror, when he heard the story, was violently angry: "This man has abandoned in the desert his lawful master. How could one trust him?" And he had the disloyal groom's head cut off, at the same time giving orders for his wife to be rewarded. As for the *senggüm,* somehow he reached the boundaries of the Tangut kingdom, or Si-Hia, of the Chinese province, that is, of Kansu, toward the Etsin-gol, where he lived some time by brigandry. The Tanguts finally driving him away, he carried his brigand activities farther west, into Uyghur territory, toward the oasis of Kucha, and here the inhabitants killed him. So perished the last heir to the Kereit throne.

"These Evil-smelling Mongols"

With his annexing of Kereit country Chingis-khan was now master of central, as well as eastern, Mongolia. There remained western Mongolia, dominated by the Naymans from the chain of the Khangay to the Jungaria, its center the Mongol Altay and the upper Irtysh. The Naymans, passive spectators of the crushing of the Kereits, were now to take their turn.

The Nayman king, Tayang, ruled precariously, enjoying none of the prestige that had accrued to his father, Inanch-bilge. In his reproaches to him for his treatment of the head of the Kereit Ong-khan, his own officer, Kökse'ü-sabraq, drew bitter attention to the disparity. He recalled the words once uttered by Inanch-bilge: "My wife is young and I am old. My son is a weak youth. Has he it in him to impose his authority on my people and guard them from danger?" And Kökse'ü-sabraq did not attempt to hide the opinion the Nayman officers held of their present ruler, "whose talent was only for falconry, or big hunting forays."

Tayang, whatever his reputed inadequacy, had sensed the threat in the growing power of Chingis-khan: "In heaven there can be a sun and a moon. On earth there can be only one khan!" And he resolved, while there was yet time, to put down Chingis-khan. The prudent Queen Gürbesü strove to dissuade him from such a project. Not that she had any regard for the Mongols. She thought them savages: "These evil-smelling Mongols, with their black-looking clothes—it is fortunate for us they live some way away. May they keep their distance! We could fetch in their noblest girls, to milk our cows and ewes. Yet even for that they would have to be taught to wash their hands!" This was the scorn of the Nayman Turks, with the civilization that had rubbed off on them from their contact with the Uyghurs—they were already some of them Nestorians—for the savages of the upper Kerülen; but also the sound promptings of a farseeing woman all the more fearful of seeing her country bring down on itself invasion by these hordes.

Tayang nevertheless made his preparations for war. He boasted that he would himself invade the territory of the Mongols and "seize their quivers!" And, seeking allies, he sent an envoy named Torbitash to the Öngüts, a people, like the Naymans, of Turkish extraction, and also likewise Nestorians, established north of the Great Wall of China, in the region of Kuei-hua-ch'eng and Suei-yüan, to the north of the present Chinese province of Shan-si. He declared to the Öngüt chief his intention of attacking the Mongols, and asked the latter to take them in the rear from the south, or, to use the bard's figure, to be "his right hand." Now, Alaqush-tegin, notwithstanding the ties both of Turkish blood and of Christian faith that might have been expected to link him in fellow feeling with the Naymans, felt a greater inclination toward Chingis-khan. He at once sent off an envoy to him, a man called Yoqanan, or John—that is, by a Christian name—to warn the Mongol hero of Tayang's intentions: "Beware! Tayang is about to attack you. He boasts he will seize your quivers. He asked me to be his right hand. I have refused, but be on your guard!"

Chingis-khan, when this warning reached him, was in eastern Mongolia, in the Steppe of the Camel (Temeen Ke'er), near Tülkinche'üt, where he had organized a great hunting expedition. There in the hunting field they held council. Most of the generals pointed out—it was in spring—that at this time of year the horses were too thin for campaigning, and that a war expedition would have to be held over into the summer and autumn of, to be precise, 1204.[1] But the youngest brother of Chingis-khan, Temüge-otchigin, declared for immediate action. "The horses are thin? What is this excuse? For a first answer, mine are fat. How can we do nothing when we are brought such news?" He insisted they must not allow the Naymans the advantage of surprise: "It will be said of us:

---

[1] "The Mongols leave their encampments at the end of May and come down then into the plains, where the good, thick grass lets the herds make good, gradually, the almost total fast of the six months' off season. All along the riverbanks (of the Tula) we come on countless herds of horses, pitiably thin. These poor animals go head drooping, eyes dead, with hollowed flanks; all look wretched, and the young beasts have none of the gay, springy gait we are accustomed to in ours at home."
—Bouillane de Lacoste, *Au pays sacré des anciens Turcs*, p. 27.

'Behold, they who took Tayang,' and we shall be held in great honor!" [2] Belgütei, Chingis-khan's half brother, supported him: "The Naymans have boasted they will seize our quivers and arrows. Can any man worthy of the name let pass such an affront? They speak presumptuous words, but it is for us to prove them false, for us to strip them of their arms!" And he pictured the rich spoils awaiting the Mongol army; the great herds of horses in the Nayman country, the royal *yurt* of Tayang, that the enemy would have to leave behind when they fled to mountain and forest: "At our approach, their tribes will scurry to the tops of their mountains. To horse! It is the only answer!"

Chingis-khan approved this ardor. "With such men about me, how should I doubt of victory?" He interrupted the hunt, and set off from Abji'a-ködeger for the escarpments of Keltegei, near Orno'u, on the river Khalkha, where he called a halt to carry out a reorganization of his army, and in particular of his guard.

[2] These words are attributed by Rashid ed-Din not to Temüge but to Daritay, Chingis-khan's uncle.

En Route for the Khangay Mountains

Clearly Chingis-khan, though he had approved his brothers' counsels of attack, took his time. It was not until early summer, when his horses had had time to build themselves up, that he embarked on his campaign. The sixteenth day of the first month of summer—it was "the Year of the Rat" 1204—at full moon, he offered solemn sacrifice to the *tuq,* to the standard of his family, the white standard of nine tails, a pole decorated with horsehair—black hair from the tails of bay horses, Mongol tradition specifies. A vital ceremony, the shamanist peoples believed, for the standard was the dwelling place of the *Sülde,* the protector-spirit of the clan, who was solemnly invoked for the conduct of war.

Then the army moved on again, up the Kerülen valley. Riding ever westward, with Jebe and Qubilay ahead as advance guard, it must have crossed from the upper Kerülen region into that of the upper Tula, toward the upper Orkhon and the eastern foothills of the Khangay. It came thus to the "donkeyback steppe" (Sa'ari Ke'er). The hilly appearance of the country is more than once remarked on by the explorer Bouillane de Lacoste, who followed a similar route, and at just about the same time of year, around mid-June, when spring is still in evidence, at least so long as the traveler's road borders the upper Tula. "This immense prairie has not the desolate look one expects," writes Commander de Lacoste; "the grass is thick and studded with flowers. With the bright yellow of crucifers and buttercups, the mauve of thyme, scabious or iris, there mingles here and there the pure white of stellaria and the pale velvet of the edelweiss. The medley of colors is truly a joy to the eye." From south of the Tula to southeast of the Orkhon stretch in series the rounded hills which have given Sa'ari Ke'er its name. "One sees nothing in any direction but endless undulations, uniformly yellow," Lacoste goes on to write on June 21; "the soil is sandy; a short grass, half withered, grows in places." Farther on, to the west, is "yellow steppe, scarcely undulating, with here and there a dried-up salt lake [this is on June 25] making a great white patch that sparkles in the sun." Then, up at the level of the present Buddhist monastery of Doltzegen, come lines of bare hills, then again more undulating country, sand hills, high dunes with a scattering of bushes, and finally the first foothills of the Khangay barring the way to the upper Orkhon.

The "donkeyback steppe" behind them, the Mongol army saw the Nayman lookouts stationed high in the Khangay. While the Mongols were making their way to the Orkhon, the Nayman king, Tayang, had indeed advanced with all his forces from the region of the Altay to the Khangay massif, where he had set up his camp. The Naymans were at first full of confidence. They captured a Mongol horse that was in a bad state, and inferred from this that all the enemy horses were played out. They may not have been all that wide of the mark: to cross Mongolia, from the Khalkha to the Khangay, was something of an endurance test. Furthermore, Chingis-khan's army might well turn out to be outnumbered by the Naymans, who had been swelled by reinforcements in the shape of all the Conqueror's old enemies: Toqto'a-beki, chief of the Merkits, Alintayshi with a number of unsubdued Kereits, Qutuqa-beki, chief of the Oyrats, the indiarubber Jamuqa, and with them the remnants of the Dörbens, the Tatars, the Qatagins, the Salji'uts, all the vanquished of recent wars, all Chingis-khan's implacable, irreducible foes, with their ranks closed behind Tayang in this hour of decision.

In this situation, and while the main bulk of the Mongol army was halted at Sa'ari Ke'er, one of Chingis-khan's commanders, Doday-cherbi, urged him to caution. "We are few in number, and, as well, tired from our long march. Let us camp here, in the steppe of Sa'ari Ke'er, and graze our horses till they have regained their strength. Then, to hoodwink the enemy, let us light five fires to a man. So far as that goes, the Naymans are many, we know. But it is said their khan is a weakling who has never left his *yurt*. Our fires will mislead him as to our numbers. Then, as soon as our horses are fit again, we will overcome their outposts, throw them back on the main body of their army, and take advantage of the resulting confusion to pitch in to wholesale battle."

Chingis-khan approved this ruse, which turned out to be excellent. At sight of the countless fires that at nightfall sprang into life all over the vast steppe, the Nayman sentries up in their Khangay fastnesses whispered, appalled: "Who spoke of the Mongols being few? They have more campfires than there are stars in the sky." Tayang was camped in the Khangay near the River Qachir. Impressed by the reports of his advance posts, he passed them on to his son Küchlüg, advising him to temporize, even to make a strategic retreat. "It was claimed the Mongol horses would be played out, but they have more campfires than there are stars. Fighting with them will be terrible. They are such hardened warriors, they see a charge bear down on them without blinking an eyelid; you can pierce their cheeks and make their blood flow in streams, and they do not flinch. Is it wise to engage with them now? We should do better to withdraw in good order behind the Altay. Our horses are in good shape. Theirs will be brought to the last stage of exhaustion following us, and then we will fall on them."

It was sound advice enough, but it was not to the hearer's liking. Tayang's own son, his heir, the Prince Küchlüg ("the strong"), cried shame on what he called his father's cowardice: "Tayang is afraid like a woman! What is this about the numbers of the Mongols? The greater part of them has anyway lined up in our own ranks, with Jamuqa. But my father has never been to war. He has never ventured farther than a pregnant woman when she must urinate, or a steer grown fat as a wheel!" Tayang, bitterly, retorted: "Küchlüg is a youth full of conceit of himself. Let us hope that in the hour of combat, when death is at his elbow, this fine courage does not fade away!" But now Qori-sübechi, one of Tayang's principal commanders, threw in his insults: "Your father, Inanch-bilge, in the hour of combat, never showed the enemy his soldiers' backs or his horses' quarters. And you, you are already afraid? If we had known you were so cowardly, we would rather have given command of the army, though she is but a woman, to the Princess Gürbesü! What a misfortune that Kökse'ü-sabraq is too old! For you, weak Tayang, you are running away!" With which he shook his quiver, seized his horse, and was off.

Tayang had to give way: "Every life must end in death, every body is condemned to suffering. It is the fate of all men. Since destiny will have it so, let us fight!" He left his Qachir camp, went down the River Tamir as far as the Orkhon, which he crossed, and came to the eastern slope of

Mount Naqu, which apparently corresponds to the Mount Namogo of our maps, or rather one of the neighboring escarpments, north of Qara-qorum and Kosho-tsaydam.[1] The Naymans had thus reached the site of Chakirma'ut when Chingis-khan's lookouts saw them and gave the alarm.

[1] Probably opposite the junction of the Tamir and the Orkhon. Cf. the map in Bouillane de Lacoste, *Au pays sacré des anciens Turcs,* p. 54.

▲
▲▲

40

The Dogs of Chingis-khan
Eat Human Flesh

Chingis-khan drove off at once the Nayman scouts, drew up his army in battle array, and decided on his combat plans. The Mongol tactical specifications have in this case come down to us: we know that the order of march was to be "as thick grass," that the troops were then to take up the "lake" formation, and that they were to attack "drill-wise." [1] Chingis-khan himself took command of the advance guard, entrusting the center to his brother Qasar and the reserve cavalry to his other brother Temüge. The Naymans, however, their high-flown resolution to take the offensive proving short-lived, were already falling back from the Chakirma'ut position, and re-forming before the rocks of Naqu, Mongol advance parties harassing them as they went.

Tayang watched with anxiety these skirmishes, so disadvantageous for him, taking place before general action was engaged. Beside him stood Jamuqa, former "brother by adoption" of Chingis-khan, now his most consistent enemy. The Mongol epic has here a magnificent poem, in which the Nayman sovereign questions Jamuqa about the different bodies of the enemy army to be seen deploying on the plain. "Who are these," Tayang asks, "who pursue our advance guard as wolves pursue sheep right to their fold?" "These," Jamuqa answers, "are the four dogs of my *anda* Temüjin. They feed on human flesh and are tethered with an iron chain. They have foreheads of brass, their jaws are like scissors, their tongues like piercing awls, their hearts are iron, their whipping tails, swords. They feed on dew. Running, they ride on the back of the wind.

[1] [Mongol military terms, the exact meaning of which are unknown.]

In the day of battles, they devour enemy flesh. Behold, they are now unleashed, and they slobber at the mouth in glee. These four dogs are Jebe and Qubilay, Jelme and Sübötei." At his words Tayang shudders. He gives the order to fall back on both sides of the mountain, the Mongols on his tracks, "bounding in delight," as they seek to encircle his army.

At this sight, Tayang, in the epic, questions Jamuqa again: "And who are these people who rush to encircle us, like foals let out in the morning, full of mare's milk and gamboling around their dams?" "They," Jamuqa replies, "are the tribes of the Uru'uts and the Mangghuts. They hunt down like game warriors armed with saber and spear, they seize from them their bloody weapons, they throw them down and cut their throats, they carry off their remains!" Tayang orders further retreat up the mountain slopes. Then, halting, he questions Jamuqa yet again: "And who is this man one sees behind them, like a hungry eagle, fretting to swoop on his prey?" "That," Jamuqa answers, "is my *anda* Temüjin. All his body is cast in brass, forged in iron, without a chink an awl-point could pierce. Do you see him, taking off toward you, like a hungry vulture? You boasted once that if the Mongols dared come before you, there would remain of them not the skin of a lamb's hoof. Now, look!"

Tayang at this withdraws farther still up the mountain. He goes on questioning Jamuqa. "And who is this other chief coming against us down there?" "It is one of the sons of mother Hö'elün, reared on human flesh. His body is three fathoms long. He eats a three-year-old beast at a sitting. He wears triple armor. He can swallow a man whole, with his quiver, without choking, without losing his appetite. When rage takes him, and he lets fly his invincible arrows, he transfixes at one shot not ten but twenty men on the other side of the mountain. His arrows can find the foe at nine hundred fathoms. He is a being more than human, he was born from a dragon. That is Jöchi-Qasar!" Tayang, in terror, retreats still higher up the mountain. At this point he questions Jamuqa yet once more about a last Mongol chief he has just seen enter the fray: "That," is the answer, "is the youngest son of mother Hö'elün, Otchigin. They call him lazy, for he likes to go to bed early and rise late. But in the hour of battle he is never tardy!" This time Tayang in panic retreats to the very mountaintop.

What was going on in Jamuqa's head? Was this the primitive, shifty nomad soul, sensing that the Nayman cause was lost and already at work on schemes of *rapprochement* with Chingis-khan? Had some memory of their old friendship genuinely welled up in the man? Whatever the motive, Jamuqa deserted the Nayman army, and sent a messenger to the Conqueror lodging his claim to Mongol credit for it. "Tayang," his message ran, "terror-stricken at the account I have given him of your army, is in retreat to the mountain. His soldiers have no more heart for battle. As for me, I am abandoning them. Let my *anda* take measures accordingly!"

41

The Death of Tayang

It was evening. Chingis-khan had to put off further action till next day, but before night fell he was able to encircle Mount Naqu with his army. The Naymans tried to use the darkness to disengage and slip away over the mountain, but in vain. "They stumbled in the dark, fell from rocks; their bodies smashed at the foot of the precipices; the corpses piled up there, one upon another like felled trees."

Next morning, battle began again. The Mongol army hurtled to the attack on the Nayman positions. Tayang was seriously wounded. Qori-sübechi and his last faithful retainers struggled in vain to get him back into the field: the unfortunate Nayman king's wounds would not let him move. Vainly Qori-sübechi shouted to him that his wives and the Lady Gürbesü, above all, had adorned themselves in his honor and come forth to see him fight. Tayang was dying. Then Qori-sübechi said to the other warriors: "He has no more strength ever to rise again. Before he dies, let us return to the fray, that with his last glances he may see us dying valiant deaths." They went down and fought to the end. Chingis-khan, seeing their desperate courage, would fain have spared their lives, but they refused to surrender, and all died weapon in hand. The Conqueror, for whom the fighting man's loyalty to his chief was the supreme virtue, paid public tribute to their bravery. As for Küchlüg, Tayang's son, he had managed to get away, and had reached the valley of the Tamir, which, after a space of marshy grassland and bog, narrows rapidly, great granite promontories turning it into a series of larch-covered passes. The Nayman prince tried to make a hideout of this easily defended valley, but his Mongol pursuers were too close for him, and he had to take flight again.

Chingis-khan brought the Nayman country to submission as far as the Altay foothills. The Nayman queen Gürbesü, who was among the prisoners, was brought before the Conqueror. He reproached her with the contempt she had formerly shown for the Mongols: "Did you not call us evil-smelling?" But he took her into his household. Tayang's guardian of the seal, or chancellor, an Uyghur named (in Chinese transcription) T'a-t'a-t'ong-a, taken prisoner with his retainers, passed into Chingis-khan's service. Sole escapers from Mongol domination were those who had fled with Küchlüg and the clans, similarly in flight, of his uncle Buyruq.

The dissident Mongol tribes who had followed Jamuqa, namely the Jadarans or Jarjirats, Qatagins, Salji'uts, Dörbens, the last Taychi'uts and the Onggirats, made their submission to Chingis-khan. Jamuqa, thus abandoned by them, found himself reduced, like Küchlüg and Buyruq, to the wretched existence of the outcast.

42

The Advocacy of the Fair Qulan

The Merkit chief Toqto'a, who had to the end supported the Naymans, had escaped the disaster that overtook them. In the autumn of that same year, 1204, Chingis-khan set forth in pursuit of this chief, and defeated him near the Qaradal-huja'ur spring. The great bulk of the Merkit people, driven back into the "donkeyback steppe" (Sa'ari Ke'er), came under the Conqueror's yoke. But this time once again Toqto'a contrived to escape, with his sons Qodu and Chila'un and a few followers. They went to join the Nayman exiles Küchlüg and Buyruq, still holding out on the borders of Mongolia. Qodu's wives, the Lady Tugay and the Lady Töregene, fell to Chingis-khan: he gave Töregene to his third son, Prince Ögödei.

One of the Merkit tribes, a subsidiary one, the Uwas-Merkits, decided they had fought enough. Their chief, Dayir-usun, refusing to involve himself further in the destinies of Toqto'a, called a halt at the banks of the River Tar; resolved to find a way into the good graces of Chingis-khan, he decided to offer the latter his daughter, the fair Qulan. On his way, he met Nayaqa, one of Chingis-khan's officers, of the Ba'arin tribe, who undertook to guide them to his master: "The country is infested with brigands. If you go on your way alone, you will be killed, and your daughter might meet with disagreeable adventures." Out of prudence, before setting out, Nayaqa kept the young woman and her father three days with him. Then he set out again and brought them safe and sound to Chingis-khan, but when they arrived the Conqueror, finding the delay suspicious and persuaded that Nayaqa had abused Qulan, considered having him executed. In vain Nayaqa protested: "I have never thought but to serve the khan loyally. The girls fair of face and the horses fine of leg that I took among the vanquished, I have always brought to him. If ever I have done otherwise, let him kill me!" As torture loomed for the unfortunate man, the fair Qulan intervened, swearing that he was innocent, and that, if it had not been for his three days' and three nights' concealing of her, she would assuredly have fallen into the hands of bandits. "And indeed," this sensible young woman added, "you have only to test my virginity: I am still, by the will of the *Tengri,* as my father and mother made me." The test was made—most conscientiously, the bard assures us—and the results were entirely satisfactory. Chingis-khan, his mind set at rest, honored Qulan with all his love (as will be seen, she was one of his favorite wives, so much so as to be chosen to accompany him on his great Transoxania expedition). As for Nayaqa, he restored him to his position of trust, and even made public acknowledgment of his quality: "He is a fellow one may be sure of. He may be entrusted with important matters."

"These Merkits, I Hate Them!"

But Chingis-khan was not finished with the Merkits. After the submission of most of their clans, he had enrolled them in his army and charged them with guarding the baggage. But just as soon as his back was turned, they rifled what had been entrusted to their care, then turned rebels once again. They went off to barricade themselves in the mountains and forests of their country, toward the lower Selenga, south of Lake Baykal. The Uwas-Merkits entrenched themselves in the gorges of Quru-qabchal, the Uduyit-Merkits barricaded themselves in the "stronghold" known as "the summit hideout," Tayqal-qorqa, in a forest-dwellers' fortress of felled trees. Chingis-khan sent off to rout them out Chimbay, son of Sorqan-shira, who did so with troops of the left wing. To have done once and for all with these men of the woods, Chingis-khan ordered them to be completely dispersed.

Meantime, the Merkit chief Toqto'a and his sons, separated from the main body of their people, were wandering as we have said with the Nayman Prince Küchlüg near the western borders of Mongolia. Chingis-khan, setting out apace in pursuit of them, had arrived at the foot of the Mongol Altay, where he took up winter quarters (the winter of 1204-05). The war shifted now toward the massif of Ulandaban and Tabyn-ula, which, with its 13,000 foot peaks, links the Mongol Altay and the Russian Altay. On the eastern slope rises the River Kobdo which waters the lake region; on the western, the Bukhtarma, tributary of the upper Irtysh. A wild region, poorish in the north, toward Kobdo, where it supports only larches, and these only in the 7,500-8,000 feet band, but toward the south of which the forest spreads down to 3,300 feet or thereabouts, with cedar, aspen, willow, and pine. It was in the shelter of this imposing barrier, on the banks of the Bukhtarma, in the present-day Russian province of Semipalatinsk, halfway between the town of that name and the small market center of Altaysk, that Toqto'a and Küchlüg had collected what remained of their forces. In the spring of 1205 Chingis-khan arrived to hunt them out. Toqto'a was killed by a stray arrow. His sons, having no time to gather up his body, cut off his head "out of respect" to carry it away with them and pay it the last honors. Merkit and Nayman bands fled southwest. A great number of them drowned trying to cross the Irtysh, swollen at this season by the first melting of the snows. The survivors broke up. Küchlüg, crownless heir to the Nayman kings, went due south, across the Zungar steppe. He crossed the T'ien-shans, made his way along the borders of the Uyghur country on the Kucha side, crossed the Qarluq country, the present-day Semirechie, southeast of Lake Balkhash, and so came at last to the Qara-khitay empire, east of Issyq-kol, in what is now Russian Turkestan, where an unexpected future awaited him.

As for the Merkit princes, Qodu, Qal, and Chila'un, they also made their way to the edge of the Uyghur country, in the hope, probably, of making themselves masters of the fertile Uyghur oases, Beshbaliq, Turfan, Quarashahr, and Kucha. But the Uyghur king, the *iduq-qut* Barchuq, drove them off. The last Merkit bands, under Qodu, came back to the steppes north of Lake Balkhash, the former Qanqli country, where they roamed wretchedly for another ten years or so between the basin of the Imil and the Tarbagatay as far as the Steppe of Hunger.

One day—in 1217, according to some of our sources—Chingis-khan was to remember these last survivors of an enemy race. He ordered his best strategist, Sübötei, to bring them to heel. "After their defeat," he told Sübötei, "they ran away like wild horses with the lasso already round their necks, like stags with an arrow already in them. Catch them again. If they take flight skyward like birds, turn into a falcon and take them in mid-air. If they burrow into the ground like marmots, become a pick and dig them up. If they turn fish and take to the sea, become a net. To get to them, you will have to go through high mountain passes, cross wide rivers. Remembering the distance, eke out your provisions. Be careful not to be too hard on your horses. On the way you will see a lot of game. Do not let your men amuse themselves at will riding their horses hard hunting it; make beating forays only as often as is needed to supplement your stores, otherwise, before you have reached the enemy, your horses will be played out. See that the cruppers are not attached to the saddle and that bridles are not used. The mouths of the horses must be left free. If you give these orders, how can the men go at a gallop?" Then, the curious avowal that shows how bitter a memory had stayed with the khan of those grievous times of his youth: "These Merkits, I hate them, and have done so for a long, long time! I remember the day I had taken refuge on Mount Burqan-qaldun, and to take me they surrounded the mountain approaches. I was still so young, I was so afraid. . . . Today I have sworn to get them. However long it takes to hunt them down, however far they must be followed, I will have them! My thoughts go with you and may the supreme *Tengri* protect you!" For crossing the Altay and the Tarbagatay, Chingis-khan gave Sübötei "iron-framed wagons" (*temür-tergen*), specially built to withstand jolting in the gorges. Thus equipped, Sübötei carried out his orders. From the River Jam, to the Tarbagatay, to the northern bank of the Chu, in the Steppe of Hunger, west of the Balkhash, he gave chase to the last of the Merkits, and exterminated them.

This persisting hatred of the Conqueror's for the enemy Mongol tribe is to be noted. It had more than one root. It was the old hostility of the son of nomads for the "men of the woods," of the herdsman of the steppe for the trappers of the *tayga*. It was a personal bitterness also—let it not be forgotten—against those who had once carried off his wife, and whom he had perhaps to thank, alas, for the birth of his eldest child, Jöchi. It so happened, indeed, that when the youngest of the Uduyut-Merkit princes, Qultuqan-mergen, was taken prisoner by the Mongols, he was brought before Jöchi. Qultuqan-mergen was a remarkable archer. His skill and his youth interested Jöchi, who, taking a liking to him, asked for mercy for him from Chingis-khan. But the Conqueror was inflexible. The last of the Merkit princes must perish as all his family.

Pure Mongol stock as they were, the Merkits had ranged themselves with the unassimilable elements incapable of entering into the formation of the new unified Mongol nation.

▲
▲▲

44

A Note of High Tragedy:
Chingis-khan and Jamuqa

Following the crushing of the Naymans, their ally Jamuqa, Chingis-khan's personal antagonist, the old Mongol anti-Caesar, having lost all his following, had been reduced to the life of an outcast. With his five last remaining companions, he had taken refuge in the "Tangnu mountains," that is to say in the Tangnu range, with its 6,600 to 9,600 feet-high cols and ever-snowy peaks. The outcast was here at the very limit of his native country: the Tangnu mountains mark the dividing line between the "dry, pale steppe," characteristic of the Kobdo lake region, and the dense Siberian forest, the *tayga* of the upper Ienissei. It is hunting country *par excellence:* its forests of cedar, larch, white pine, and alder house a numerous fauna, the Wapiti stag of Siberia meeting its Mongol maral counterpart, the musk fallow deer of the far north, the wild ram or argali of the steppe. Reduced to living by hunting and chance, the exile was eking out here a highly precarious living, when the drama broke that was to decide his future: one day when he had just killed and roasted a wild ram, and was eating it, his five companions, weary of this life of hardship, threw themselves on him, bound him, and brought him to Chingis-khan.

The prisoner had doubtless no illusions as to the fate awaiting him. Nevertheless, it was as a king that he addressed Chingis-khan. First he demanded punishments for his treacherous subjects, the traitors who had given him up: "Like a base black crow attacking a great wild duck, so these vile slaves have dared to raise their hand against their overlord. Oh khan, my *anda,* how should you take them into your service?" Chingis-

khan, as we know, held traitors the vilest of the vile, and if there was a
principle he cherished, it was soldierly loyalty. Almost certainly he also
still harbored at heart an obscure affection for his one-time youthful
playfellow. His first act then was to accede to this. "How is it possible,"
he cried, "to let men who have betrayed their rightful chief go on living?
Such people should be exterminated, with their children and their children's children!" And he had the five traitors' heads cut off under
Jamuqa's eyes.

He did more. With the magnanimity that was so characteristic of him,
he offered Jamuqa pardon for all his sins. Plottings, betrayals, and the
ever-active enmity that had made the Jajirat chief the moving spirit of
successive coalitions against him—the Mongol hero was prepared to forget all. He wished to remember only their youthful friendship, the campaigns they had fought together, that one in particular, doubtless, in
which, when they were still both young men, Jamuqa had helped him recover the beautiful Börte. With restrained emotion, he called up these
memories, and in his greatness of soul invited the defeated foe to a re-
newal of their former friendship. "Before, we were closely united, inseparable as two shafts of the same wagon. And then, one day, you deserted
me. But now you have come back. Let us be united as before. Let us live
again together side by side. We had forgotten the memories of our youth,
let us bring them to life again. Since that time, you had cut yourself off
from me, but you were still my *anda,* my adoptive brother. When we met
face to face in the field of battle, I know that grief gripped your heart.
And indeed, in the battle against the Kereits, in the sands of Qalaqaljit,
did you not send me warning of the enemy's intentions? You did there a
service I do not forget. Nor do I forget, either, that before the battle
against the Naymans, with your words vaunting my strength, you sowed
fear in the hearts of their leaders."

Jamuqa's response to Chingis-khan's offer was a refusal of truly noble
dignity. "In times of yore, when we were young, when we became *anda,*
by the stream of Qorqonaq, we shared our meals, we said to each other
words never to be forgotten, we slept at each other's side. Then came
men who with artful argument set us against each other, and we hurled at
each other words of insult. But when I remembered the oaths we had
once sworn, I flushed red in shame, and I had not the courage to come to
meet you again, to look in the face of the *anda* of magnanimous heart.

And now lo, behold, in his mercy my *anda* proposes I should become once more his companion. But when I had a right to be at his side, I could not hold there. Today, oh my *anda,* you have united under you all the peoples round about. Heaven has chosen you for the throne of empire. Now that the world is yours, what use would a companion such as I be to you? Comradeship is something there could never again be between us. I should be like a louse in your jacket-collar, a thorn in your trousers. Because of me you would never sleep quietly. I have been unfaithful to my *anda,* and from break of day to sunset there is no one not aware of what I have done. You, my *anda,* you are a hero. Your mother is full of wisdom. Your brothers are full of ability. The seventy-three fine men who form your entourage serve you as so many loyal steeds. How inferior I am to you, oh my *anda!* A child still, I was abandoned by both father and mother; brothers I have none, and my companions have not been true to me. Heaven has bestowed its favor on my *anda,* who has surpassed me in all things. Now, oh my *anda,* you must be rid of me promptly, that your heart may be at peace. But if you decide I am to die, I must die without my blood flowing. On that condition, if you bury me near here on some height, my spirit will watch from afar over your grandchildren's grandchildren, and protect them forever. I was of noble, illustrious line, and if I am defeated, it is by an *anda* of yet more illustrious birth. Remember my words. And now, work your will quickly with me!"

Chingis-khan, when they told him these words, answered in deep sadness. "My *anda* Jamuqa has always gone away from us. Yet, I know of no harm he has ever thought to do my person. He is a man greatly experienced, of whom one might still learn much. But he is weary of life." Then, after this tribute paid to old memories, after he had tried and failed to save the erstwhile companion of his youth, Chingis-khan accepted the situation, the refusal of his offer, and the politician—I was about to say, the scrupulous jurist—took over: "A man like Jamuqa, such a man cannot be put to death without valid cause. But since he wants to die, I have found the indictment. Once, after Taychar stole Jochi-darmala's horses, we fought against each other, Jamuqa and I, at Dalan-baljut; he drove me in flight to the gorge of Jerene, and greatly frightened me. Today again I wanted him to become my companion, and he has turned away. I wanted to spare his life and he has refused. Let it be done as he wishes!

Put him to death without shedding his blood. Do not leave his corpse lying, but bury it with honor."

So it was done. The former Mongol anti-Caesar, the man who for a moment once set the fortunes of Chingis-khan in the balance, was buried with honorable ceremony on a height whence his spirit, according to the beliefs of the Altaic shamans, would keep watch over the descendants of his conqueror.

Such is the tradition set down in contemporary sources. Legend, however, is not content with this melancholy denouement. There Jamuqa has a more dramatic end. The story runs that Chingis-khan, not wishing his former *anda* to die at his orders, handed him over to his nephew Alchiday-noyan, and that at Alchiday's hands he died a ghastly death. "It is said that he ordered his limbs to be chopped off one by one, and that Jamuqa declared this was just, because this was how he himself would have treated his enemies if fate had delivered them to him. He hastened execution of the cruel sentence, proffering his joints himself to the executioner's sword."

45

The "May Field" of 1206
Proclamation of the Mongol Empire
Promotions and Citations

One or two cases of insignificant and peripheral dissidence apart, Chingis-khan was now master of all Mongolia. At this point he decided to have his accession renewed or confirmed by all the tribes. In the spring of 1206 he summoned for the purpose at the headwaters of the Onon a great *quriltay* or general assembly. He hoisted the white standard with its nine horsetails, the banner of the new Mongol empire, and had conferred on himself, a second time, the title of khan. The shaman Kököchü, or, as he preferred to be called, the Teb-Tenggeri, "the Very-Celestial," set the seal of his sanction on the proclamation. The power of Chingis-khan indeed corresponded to the will of Heaven; the Eternal Blue Heaven, supreme divinity of the ancient Turks and the ancient Mongols, had designated the new sovereign its representative upon earth. The latter's title reflected this consecration: he was "khan by the strength of the Eternal Heaven."

This "coronation" was followed by a series of promotions of generals, with magnificent citations recalling their exploits. A noble emulation worked in these heroes. Fearing to have pleased the master less than Muqali or Bo'orchu, Shigi-qutuqu, the abandoned child, long ago adopted by mother Hö'elün, recalled his devotion: "Have I been less devoted than another? From childhood, I have grown up at your threshold, and I have had no thought but for you. You have let me sleep at your feet, you have treated me as your youngest brother. What shall you give me now as a mark of your favor?" And Chingis-khan replied to Shigi-qutuqu: "Yes, I consider you as my sixth brother! While, with the aid of the Eternal Heaven, I was establishing my authority over all the tribes who live in tents of felt, you have been as my ears and eyes. Today, I charge you to take all these tribes, to count them out and to apportion them. Let none go against your decisions!" Shigi-qutuqu was in effect established in the office of grand judge: "Lay bare and punish all cases of fraud or theft. Those who have deserved to pay a penalty, mete them out their punishment!" Shigi-qutuqu's decisions were to be entered in "blue books" (or "in blue writing on white paper"), and these were to form a compilation of laws. "It is my wish," Chingis-khan said, "that unto my furthest descendants nothing be altered of dispositions made by Shigi-qutuqu at my orders and entered in the Blue Books!"

Chingis-khan had royal thanks for "father" Mönglik for having once saved him from walking straight into a trap set by the Kereits, when the future Conqueror of the World had been on the point "of throwing himself into a red-hot brazier, into an abyss of swirling water." Bo'orchu he sang the praises of at length, enumerating all the proofs he had given of devotion from the pursuit of the horse-stealers at the beginning of this story onwards. He recalled how that day Bo'orchu, still in his teens and prompted by an immediate sympathy, had left all to follow him. "To the comrade who asked your aid, you gave it unhesitatingly. . . . Your father was Naqu the Rich. You were his only son. You knew nothing of me yet on the instant you abandoned everything to follow me. . . . Later, during the campaign against the Tatars, at Dalan-nemürges, in the night, in torrents of rain, you sheltered me as I slept under your cloak of felt, and you stayed without moving thus till dawn, for fear of waking me. O Bor'orchu, O Muqali, you have helped me to the throne, because you have always given me good counsel, encouraging me when I was right, holding me back when I was wrong." And he had them sit on raised seats, above all the others.

Later, Mongol legend was not to rest content with the simple grandeur of this. It added romantic details, which by the seventeenth century have found their way into the account of the historian Sagang-sechen, himself a descendant of Chingis-khan. When he comes to the general distribution of rewards, at his great assembly of 1206, Chingis-khan pretends to forget, alone of his supporters, Bo'orchu. When evening comes, the Empress Börte reproaches the Conqueror for this: "Is not Bo'orchu your lifelong servant, the friend of your youth, the tried companion of your darkest hours?" "I only seemed to forget him," answers Chingis-khan, "to confound those who envy him, for I am sure that, even in this moment when Bo'orchu may believe himself passed over, he still speaks good of me!" And Chingis-khan there and then sends a spy to hear what is being said in Bo'orchu's tent. What is being said? The warrior's wife is complaining of the khan's ingratitude. And Bo'orchu counters: "It is not for reward I serve the khan. If he left me to die of hunger, I should continue to serve him with all my strength. May the khan's house of gold last for ever, that is all the reward I need!" Chingis-khan, to whom the words are reported, next day reassembles the *quriltay,* and his gratitude breaks forth in a magnificent gesture: "Oh my Bo'orchu, you who in the days of danger were my faithful companion, you whose heart never knew fear, you, my comrade when death stared us in the face in the battle, you to whom death or life was indifferent, let none here dare be jealous of you. Hear, you my princes and my nobles, hear, oh my people, and be witness, he it is I raise above all!"

Turning then to Muqali, Chingis-khan reminds him how once, at Qorqonaq-jubur, under the great tree by which khan Qutula had liked to dance, he, inspired by heaven, had prophesied the grandeur of the future conqueror. Chingis-khan will reward him presently with the title (taken from the Chinese) of *qu-yang,* meaning prince, "with the command of the left wing as far as the Qaraun-chidun mountains."

Another Mongol chief, Qorchi, of the Ba'arins, had also, in Chingis-khan's early days, prophesied his greatness to come, but, as a provident soothsayer, he had secured a promise, if events turned out as he foretold, of a harem of thirty pretty girls. Chingis-khan let him choose the thirty fairest of the defeated tribes. By way of more serious preferment, he was appointed to rule, in the northwest marches, the "forest-dwelling nations," that is the people of the Siberian *tayga* as far as the upper Irtysh area.

Jürchedei's great deeds were not forgotten. He was the recipient of Chingis-khan's public congratulations for having, at the battle of Qala-qaljit-elet, when the victory lay yet in the balance, put abrupt end to the enemy's attack by, with his own hand, wounding the Kereit *senggüm:* "If your arrow, that day, had not struck the *senggüm* in the cheek, what would have happened to us? It was from that moment that, by the will of the Eternal Heaven, the gateway to the empire opened before me!" Chingis-khan had no less praise for the pillar of strength the unshakable Jürchedei had been for him in the retreat to the Khalkha, and again in the decisive battle with the Kereits. "During the retreat," he told him magnificently, "you protected me like a high mountain; in the hour of the battle you were for me a shield." In supreme sign of imperial gratitude, Jürchedei, as already recounted, was presented with one of Chingiskhan's own wives, the Kereit princess Ibaqa-beki: "I give her to you in recognition of the services you rendered me when you helped me bring to heel the dissident tribes, reunite the scattered tribes."

The Conqueror did not forget praises for his four "fierce dogs," Qubilay, Jelme, Jebe, and Sübötei. "For me you have broken the necks of the strong and broken the backs of the athletic. When the order: 'Forward' sounded, you clove rocks and stemmed the wild torrent. In the day of battle, with such men before me," cried Chingis-khan, "I could rest assured!" And the citations continued, each receiving his word of reward. Now Qunan, of the tribe of the Geniges, "vigilant as the male wolf by night, as the black crow by day." He, and Kököchös, Degei, and "grandfather" Usun were saluted too for having faithfully informed their master of what they saw and heard. Now the loyal Jelme, brought by his father when still a child to be page to the future Chingis-khan, to keep guard over the entry to the royal *yurt.* "When I was born, my father had given me a bed of sable. Jelme and I were born about the same time. Together, we grew up. . . ." Now Önggür, for whom Chingis-khan had this tribute: "You, Önggür, with your Besi'uts and Baya'uts, you have protected me as a living hedge. You did not stray in the thick mist, you did not fail in the fray. In the rain you got soaked to the skin with me, in the bitter cold you shivered with me." His reward was freedom to reassemble under his own banner his scattered tribe, the Baya'uts.

Chingis-khan had a particularly affectionate word for the four "foundlings" adopted by "mother Hö'elün": Shigi-qutuqu, Boroqul, Güchü, and Kököchü. "You lay, abandoned; in the enemy camp; my mother picked you up, she set you on your feet, took you under her protection and raised you as her own children. Taking you by the neck and hoisting you by the shoulders, she has made men of you. For us, her own children, you have become companions as inseparable as our shadows."

And the Conqueror declared to these young "adopted brothers" that they had already repaid in loyalty and devotion the care that had been taken of them. "You, Boroqul, have been for me so attentive a companion that never, whether riding in the dark, in teeming rain, or encamped face to face with the enemy, have you failed to have food for me. . . ." Chingis-khan recalled also how two of his sons, Toluy and Ögödei, had been saved, the first by Boroqul's wife, from the hands of a Tatar assassin, the second by Boroqul himself in the first battle against the Kereits. "I owe him the lives of two of my sons. He has indeed redeemed the debt he owed my mother!"

In this time of triumph the hero did not forget those who, in the dark days, had died in his cause, like Quyildar and Chaghan-qo'a. "My friend Quyildar served me unto death. Chaghan-qo'a was killed by Jamuqa as he fought in my service. It is my will that their children and the children of their children, to the furthest generation, receive the aid the just due of the orphaned!" The son of Chaghan-qo'a, further, Narin-Toghril, received the right to reassemble his tribe, that of the Negüses. Lastly, Chingis-khan gave proof of particular affection for Sorqan-shira, who, it will be remembered, in the days of his youth had freed him from his cangue and saved him from the vengeance of the Taychi'uts. "That service, I have never forgotten. I think of it at night, in my dreams. In the daytime, the memory of it is always there in my breast. It is true, afterward you tarried a little before you left the Taychi'uts to join me. . . . But today I will grant you whatever you ask of me." Sorqan-shira asked for grazing grounds, exempt from dues, in the former Merkit country, around the River Selenga. On his two sons, Chila'un and Chimbay, was conferred the privilege of keeping for themselves in the hunt and in war all the game they could bring down, and all the booty they could seize.

So the Conqueror of the World, in these triumphant days of the spring of 1206, in the region of the upper Onon where he had been born, in this country of grassland and forest hymned by the Mongol bards, reviewed with emotion the hard vicissitudes of his youth, and associated magnificently with him in his triumph those who had been his comrades in arms.

46

The Old Guard

Then came the reorganization of the Imperial Guard. "Before," said Chingis-khan, "I had only a bodyguard of seventy for the daytime and eighty for the night watches. Now that by the will of Eternal Heaven I rule over all the Empire, the guard force must be enlarged to ten thousand warriors, recruited among the sons of the decurions, centurions, and myriachs." This elite body, held to a rigorous discipline, received special privileges: a mere rank and file member of the bodyguard took precedence over a chiliarch. Every member of the force was specially picked by the khan himself. They justified the confidence he placed in them. Haranguing them one day, Chingis-khan was to cry, in the magnificent rhetoric transcribed by the Mongol bard: "Oh, my trusty guards, grown white in my service! It is you who, in dark nights as in starlit ones, in snowstorm, in driving rain or intolerable cold, have kept watch round my *yurt* with its willow wattle and let me sleep in peace! When the enemy prowled about us, you were there watchful around my *yurt,* never closing your eyes, at the ready at the least rustle of a quiver! Thanks to you, I have reached supreme power!" And he conferred on their various regiments grand titles, that, as later in the Napoleonic army, fired their pride, and inspired them to noble emulation. The seventy bodyguards keeping the day watches under Ögöle-cherbi received the name "The Great Dayguards." The elite warriors commanded by Arqay-qasar were designated the "Old Braves." The archers of Yisün-te'e and Bugiday became the "Great Quiver Bearers."

This debt of gratitude to the Old Guard Chingis-khan intended should be binding also on his successors: "If they are true to my instructions, they will take as good care of you as I myself, they will hold you the good spirits of the Empire!"

Chingis-khan said also: "My quiver bearers are like a dark forest of innumerable trees. I wish to sweeten their mouths with fine sugar, to dress them in garments of brocade, to mount them on splendid steeds, to let them drink of delicious waters, to assure for their herds rich grazing, to leave no brambles in their meadows!"

But, beyond the army, it was to the whole Mongol people, united at last through his efforts, that the Conqueror's solicitude went out. "This valiant people that has given itself over to me to share my joys and my sorrows," his descendant Sagang-sechen has him say, "this people that has sworn its allegiance to me in all perils, this people of the blue Mongols, I will raise above all the people of the earth!"

As to the ideal of all these Mongols, it was still that of the nomad hunter, equal parts, alternating, of bonhomie and ferocity, such as explorers depict it, such as Chingis-khan would have formulated it himself: "In day-to-day life like a two-year-old fawn, at feasts and celebrations carefree as a young colt, but on the day of battle swooping to the attack like a falcon or a hawk. In daylight alert as an old wolf, in the night vigilant as a black crow."

In the Siberian *Tayga*

From the Khingan to the Altay, all the nomads of Upper Mongolia, "all those who dwell in *yurts* of felt," now formed but one army, under one flag. The great sedentary empires, in China, in Iran, were to have the fact sharply brought home to them. But before launching southward in conquest of the lands of civilization, the master of the steppes, the emperor of the nomads, wanted to secure the obedience of the forest hunters of the far north, in the Siberian *tayga*. Though in part of pure Mongol stock, these forest dwellers led, by the very nature of their habitat, a life in many respects peculiarly their own. "They do not live, like the other Mongols, in felt tents," writes a Persian historian, "they keep no herds, but live by hunting in their immense forests, and profess a great contempt for the pastoral peoples. All they have for shelter are cabins made of branches and covered with birchbark. In winter, they hunt over the snow by tying boards to their feet, and holding in their hand a stake they drive into the snow, as a boatman plunges his pole into the water."

Most considerable among these forest Mongol tribes were the Oyrats, who lived west of Lake Baykal, and to whom were attached the Buyrats, still a flourishing people today. The country, watered by the upper sections of the Rivers Lena and Angara, and the latter's southern tributaries (Belaya, Oka), is, except for the grassy steppe of Balagan, but one immense forest, of birch, poplar, and aspen, cedar, larch, and pine, thickly undergrown with mosses, rhododendrons, lichens. The fauna numbers elk and maral stag and wild reindeer, the red wolf, and the furred animals, bear, sable, ermine, marten, squirrel—profitable trading material for these hunting tribes. The Oyrats had joined in the old coali-

tions against Chingis-khan. Nevertheless, when the latter sent his eldest
son Jöchi to subject all these forest dwellers "as far as the country of
Sibir," the Oyrat chief Qutuqa-beki came spontaneously to offer his submission. He agreed even to act as guide to the imperial army. Jöchi came
thus to the district of Shiqshit, where "the ten thousand Oyrats" made
their act of vassalhood.

Jöchi then moved west, toward the country of the then Kirghiz, now
the Tubas, Turkish tribes who lived in the region of the upper Ienissei,
between Mounts Sayan and Tannu-ula. A wild region and one that, "except for the undulating steppe south of the Ulu-Kem and the lower
Kemchik, is covered with mountains, shrouded in snow from the month
of August." Huntsman's country also, with the forests of cedar, larch,
white pine, and birch sheltering the Wapiti stag, the musk deer, sable,
ermine, otter, and beaver. The ancient Kirghiz, like their descendants,
the present-day Tubas or Soyots, had since very early times domesticated
the wild reindeer, which supplied them with clothing, as birchbark supplied covering for their huts. These Turkish forest dwellers no more
offered to resist the army of Jöchi than had their Oyrat and Buyrat
neighbors. Their princes, Yedi-inal, Aldi'er, and Örebek-tegin, came
proffering tribute to Jöchi of white falcons, white horses, and black
sables. Turning homeward, his mission completed, Jöchi took all these
chiefs with him. The Conqueror welcomed especially warmly the Oyrat
chief Qutuqa-beki, who had been first to make his submission; in token
of his gratitude he gave in marriage princesses of his house to Qutuqa's
two sons, Inalchi and Törelchi: to the first, the Princess Checheigen, to
the second, the Princess Qoluyqan, daughter of Prince Toluy.[1] This
"policy of marriages" set the final seal on the submission of the forest
dwellers to the nomad emperor.

There was, it is true, still one tribe among these forest dwellers unsub-
jected: the Tümets—"the twenty Tümets"—who lived perhaps in the
wooded ranges of the Irkul among the headwaters of the Oka, perhaps
north of the Oyrats, near where Oka and Sima meet, between the Oka
and the Ija to the northeast of the Balagan steppe. All that is certain is
that they dwelt in mountainous country, and in the depth of the Siberian
tayga. "Save along the paths habitually trodden," writes Grenard, "the
tayga is scarcely less difficult to traverse than equatorial forest. Often
one has to take to the axe, especially where fallen trunks lie masked by

[1] It will be remembered that Toluy was the fourth son of Chingis-khan.

high grass and dense thickets of yellow acacia and wild currant. No heights to be seen from afar beneath the coating of forest; valley and stream to the eye indistinguishable; no point of orientation. Tales are told of hunting parties lost for ever in this fearful solitary expanse."

Chingis-khan sent out his faithful Boroqul to subject the Tümets. These men of the woods were ruled by the widow of their last chief, the Lady Botoqi-tarqun ("the fat lady"), not, it seemed, formidable opposition. Boroqul, unapprehensive, rode at the head of his advance party. One evening, as he was making his way thus in the dusk along a path, deep in thick forest, he was ambushed and killed. When Chingis-khan learned of the death of his adoptive brother, he was seized with rage. He wanted to set forth himself to avenge him. Bo'orchu and Muqali dissuaded him, and he confided the punitive expedition to Dörbey-doqshin, of the tribe of the Dörbets. Dörbey took his force in most orderly array to the edge of the enemy *tayga;* there he resorted to ruse; he made as if to enter the paths and passes he might normally be expected to take, then switched his route sharply and took to what was no more than a track trodden by animals. With axes, his men hacked a way along it, and in this way he came without an alarm being given to the top of a mountain —perhaps in the Karagasses—whence through a gap in the trees he could see below him—perhaps by the Uda, toward the present-day Nizhne-Udinsk—the Tümet people. The Tümets, indeed, all unsuspecting, had gathered for a banquet. Dörbey swooped down and had no difficulty in getting the better of them.

The coup was all the more fortunate in that the Tümets had not only killed Boroqul, they had also captured the Mongol general Qorchinoyan, and, as well, the Oyrat prince Qutuqa-beki, come over as we have seen into the service of Chingis-khan. Qorchi had indeed been taken in rather remarkable circumstances. It will be remembered that Chingiskhan had authorized him to choose himself a harem of the thirty fairest women of the tribes. Armed with the authorization, he had come merrily to exercise his right among the Tümet maidens, but they had had other ideas, and the ravisher had been thrown into chains. The Mongol army, naturally, set him free. Chingis-khan made up to him for his captivity by giving him his thirty pretty Tümet girls. Qutuqa he treated even better: he gave him the Tümet queen herself, "the fat lady" Botoqi-tarqun. But he also sacrificed a hundred Tümet warriors to the memory of him who had suffered misfortune, Boroqul.

48

Priesthood Versus Empire:
The Ambitions of the Grand Shaman

Chingis-khan, having joined under his rule the pastoral nomads of the steppe and the forest hunters of the *tayga,* was lord of all Mongolia. It was an outcome he owed undoubtedly to his personal qualities and those of his followers: as the saying went later, "the Empire was founded from the saddle." Nevertheless—and the proof is in the predictions the Mongol bard finds room for in his story—a contributory factor had been the good offices of certain of the soothsayers, or shamans, who, in the days before the advent of Buddhism, had so great an influence over the minds of the Altaic peoples.

Among these shamans, the most influential was Kököchü, son of Mönglik. We have seen the part played in the youth of Chingis-khan by Mönglik, who was of the tribe of the Qongqotats. It was Mönglik who had been charged by the dying Yesügei to fetch back the young Temüjin from among the Onggirats, and who had succeeded in the task. Later, it is true, he appears somewhat basely to have abandoned the child, and rallied but tardily to the Chingiskhanid cause. But equally is it true that he had a second time saved the life of the Conqueror, when he prevented his walking blindly into a Kereit trap. Now, in virtue of his eminent services, he had a place of prominence in his master's council. The prestige of his family was the greater in that the fourth of his seven sons, Kököchü, passed for the most formidable soothsayer of the day.

The supernatural "powers" of Kököchü were indeed considerable. The designation *Teb-Tenggeri,* "the Most Celestial," customarily coupled with his name, reflects the respect he was held in: was it not said that on his dapple-grey horse he went secretly to heaven to converse face to face with the divinity? He had played an important part in the great assembly of 1206 which had sanctioned Chingis-khan's elevation to the head of the Mongol empire. It was he, the Persian authors tell us, who had on that occasion confirmed in the name of the *Tengri,* the "sky-god," the imperial title assumed by Temüjin of "Chingis-khan." It is clear that the Conqueror, whether out of appreciation of his service or awe of his magic powers, went to some pains to be tactful in his dealings with him, and was ready up to a point, as we shall see, to fall in with him. But this state of affairs was not without its disadvantages. The influential position the soothsayer now found himself in puffed him up with presumption. He assumed the right to discuss anything and everything with Chingis-khan, to argue points with him, in a manner overstepping all bounds. Convinced it was he who had brought about the new khan's accession, that it was to his incantations that the master owed the throne, he was not far from thinking himself his equal. Strong by virtue of having six brothers at his back, he became daily more overweening.

One day, the seven brothers got together and had the audacity to beat up Qasar, Chingis-khan's own brother—Qasar, invincible athlete, invincible archer—an incident effectively demonstrating that the soothsayer's magic powers could intimidate even the imperial family.[1] Qasar, instead of taking his own revenge, came and cast himself on his knees before Chingis-khan to complain of his attackers: but the Conqueror displayed an irritation that ill concealed his embarrassment. "Were you not said to be invincible? And now you have let yourself be vanquished?" At such a welcome, tears sprang to Qasar's eyes. Without a word, he got up and went out. He was furious. For three days, he stayed away.

But matters did not rest there. The wily Kököchü came to Chingis-khan to sow suspicion in his mind about his younger brother. "A heavenly messenger came," he declared, "and, in the name of the Eternal Tengri, made this prophecy to me: Chingis-khan shall have the Empire. Then the same spirit came and spoke the same of Qasar. If you do not strike before Qasar, there is no knowing what may happen. . . ."

These treacherous insinuations made a strong impression on Chingis-khan. Persuaded that Qasar was out to supplant him and that Heaven

[1] Qasar was so strong, according to tradition, that he could break a man in two like a wooden arrow.

had sent him warning, he mounted his horse that very night, went to his brother and arrested him. Two faithful retainers of Qasar,[2] however, sped to warn mother Hö'elün of what was happening. The latter wasted not a minute. That same night, she harnessed a white camel to her wagon and took to the road. At dawn, she drew up before Chingis-khan's *yurt.* Qasar, hands bound, stripped of hat and belt, stood before the Conqueror, who was harshly interrogating him as to his supposed plotting. At the sight of his mother, her face a fury, bursting all unexpectedly into his *yurt,* Chingis-khan was thrown completely out of countenance and even frightened. The old woman went straight to Qasar, untied his bonds with her own hands, gave him back hat and belt. Then, unable to restrain her indignation, she sat down on the ground, cross-legged; she tore open her bodice, tumbled out her withered breasts, that hung to her knees. "Behold," she cried, "the breasts that suckled you. What crime has Qasar committed, that you would destroy your own flesh? When you were little, Temüjin would suckle one of my breasts, Qachi'un and Temüge would suckle the other, but only Qasar had the vitality to suckle both and relieve me of my milk. Temüjin's portion has been brain and ability, to Qasar fell strength and skill with the bow.[3] His arrows cast fear into the hearts of your enemies and brought them under your yoke. And now that all are subjected to you, you wish to see him no more!"

She spoke, and Chingis-khan was troubled. "My mother," he confessed, "makes me afraid; I feel ashamed in front of her. Let us go." And unable to meet the eyes of the great dowager, he went out, indeed, frightened and ashamed. He left Qasar at liberty and dared take no other action against his person. Yet the soothsayer's calumnies never faded from the Conqueror's mind. Without saying anything to his mother, he stripped Qasar of the greater part of all he held, leaving him only fourteen hundred subjects. When Hö'elün learned of it, it was another blow to the heart, and from that day, says the bard, her strength ebbed rapidly.

---

[2] Namely Güchü and one bearing the same name as the shaman, Kököchü.

[3] The skill of Qasar was proverbial. One day, Sogang-sechen recounts, Chingis-khan asked him to shoot a vulture. "Where do you want me to strike him?" asked the infallible archer. "In the head, between the yellow and black stripes," the Conqueror specified. Qasar let fly. The bird fell. They checked. The arrow had entered at that exact point. [This is a very free translation. Cf. a more precise version on pp. 66-7 of No. 33.]

49

Chingis-khan Breaks the Back of the Grand Soothsayer

Kököchü had, in fact, succeeded in bringing about the ruin of Chingis-khan's most important brother, and dividing the imperial family. Quite clearly, the Conqueror kept peace with him because he feared him. The "spiritual" power of the dangerous shaman was taking increasingly firm hold, and as a corollary his temporal prestige was mounting. Many were the subjects of Chingis-khan who joined the circle of Kököchü. Unmistakable indication of the trend, even clients of Temüge-otchigin, Chingis-khan's youngest brother, left his service to go over to the soothsayer. Temüge charged one of his officers, Soqor, to go and bring back his men. Kököchü beat Soqor, tied a saddle on his back, and sent him back thus accoutered to Temüge. Next day Temüge went in person to demand restitution of his people, but the shaman and his six brothers surrounded him, threateningly, and forced him to go on his knees and ask their pardon. Then they sent him home, without, of course, handing over a single one of his men.

The following morning, before Chingis-khan was up, Temüge was in his tent, and on his knees at the foot of the bed, telling in tears of his humiliation. Chingis-khan heard him in silence, still paralyzed, it would seem, by fear of the redoubtable soothsayer. It was his wife, Börte, who spurred him to action. Sitting up in bed, covering her breast with the bedcover, she cried to Chingis-khan: "How can this be that Kököchü and his brothers are free to commit such insolence? Not long ago they beat Qasar. Now they have forced Temüge to his knees before them! What a pass have we come to? You yet live, and hands dare to be raised against your brothers that are like pines or cypresses. What is to happen when your body, majestic as the trunk of a vast tree, slopes toward the tomb? What will become of your people that are like grass swayed by the wind, like a bird's song? Can you believe my poor children will then be able to rule? How can you look on impassive while your brother is treated thus?" And she broke down sobbing.

That clear-cut picture struck Chingis-khan. The future of his dynasty was at stake. On the instant, his superstitious fears vanished. He was again the man of action, the statesman they recognized. "When Kököchü comes here today," he said laconically to Temüge, "do as you like with him!"

Temüge had no need of more explicit instructions. He left and went to lay his plans with three men known to be mighty wrestlers. Not long after, Mönglik and his seven sons came to visit Chingis-khan in his *yurt.* Kököchü had scarcely sat down when Temüge had him by the collar. "Yesterday," he shouted at him, "you forced me to ask pardon of you. Now today let us see who is stronger!" And he dragged him toward the door. Kököchü struggled. They grappled. In the scuffle, Kököchü's cap rolled before the hearth. His father Mönglik, divining how things would go, caught it up, kissed it, and thrust it in his breast. Chingis-khan ordered the adversaries to leave, to go make their trial of strength elsewhere than in his presence. But the three athletes, primed by Temüge, were ready in front of the imperial *yurt.* Kököchü had scarcely stepped out when they fell on him, dragged him away a little, and broke his back. They threw the corpse in a corner, "near the wagon stand."

Temüge, his coup carried out, returned to Chingis-khan in his *yurt* and gave a version of his own of what had happened. "I wanted to pit myself against Kököchü, but instead of squaring up to me, he lay down and got out of it. An odd way to behave!"

Father Mönglik straightway understood what had happened. He dissolved into tears, with: "From the first day, oh khan, I have been your companion. . . ." But his six surviving sons displayed less resignation. They barred the door and surrounded the emperor threateningly. They had already dared to lay hands on him, pulling at his sleeves. Chingis-khan, seeing in what danger he stood, pulled violently away: "Stand off! Make way for me! Let me leave!" And, shaking them off, he did in fact get out of the *yurt,* calling for help. Quiver bearers and the day watch bounded forward and surrounded him, throwing a rampart around him with their bodies.

Having ascertained that the soothsayer was really and truly dead, Chingis-khan had the body carried to a tent, the door of which was then shut, and likewise the ventilation opening, while guards were posted all around it. The third day, at dusk, the ventilation hole opened "and the corpse came out through it of itself," the Mongol bard affirms.

Chingis-khan issued an official version of the miracle. "Kököchü beat and slandered my brothers; accordingly the *Tengri,* withdrawing its protection from him, has taken his life as now his body." But with Mönglik, the master was roundly frank. "You reared your sons ill. They wanted to make themselves my equals, and Kököchü has brought misfortune on himself. . . . I should have had you all suffer the same fate as Altan, and Quchar, and Jamuqa!" Mönglik and his six surviving sons quaked. Then Chingis-khan seemed to relent a little: born statesman, he was too much the politician to make a practice of useless executions, particularly of people hitherto so closely associated with his house. He had every intention of remembering the promises of immunity he had not long since made the Mönglik family. His word was sacred, as he was at pains himself to remind the accused: "He who gives his word in the morning and breaks it at evening is a man without honor. Accordingly, I grant you your pardon, and still my rage. But if you had but known how to hold that violent temperament in check, who knows to what heights the children of father Mönglik might have risen!"

The Conqueror was free now to show clemency: the summary execution of the shaman Kököchü had dealt Qongqotat prestige its death blow. They play no further part in this story.

Freed of the dangerous Kököchü, Chingis-khan looked for a grand shaman who would cause him no anxiety. He found one in Usun, an elderly representative of the clan of the Ba'arins. "According to our traditions," he said, "the *beki* [the ancient title of the grand shamans] takes precedence over all the dignitaries. Old Usun shall be *beki!* He shall be dressed in white, he shall ride a white horse, he shall sit in the place of honor, he shall be surrounded by the respect of all, and he shall choose for our enterprises the favorable years and position of the moon."

On the Approaches to China

Chingis-khan, having stamped out the last lingering notions of rebellion among the tribes, was master of the immense area that today constitutes Outer Mongolia. Pastoral nomads of the steppe and forest, hunters of the *tayga,* henceforth acknowledged the one master: himself; the one banner: the *tuq,* the pole with nine horsetails, in which dwelt the Guardian Spirit of the Army. The Conqueror now took all these tribes he had united as one people, and hurled them against the world of China.

China, indeed, was in truth a world comprising no less than three states within itself. Of these three, one only, that of Southern China, ruled by the national Sung dynasty, could claim to be purely Chinese. Northern China was divided into two "barbarian" dominions, of unequal size. The greater part had been for a century in the hands of a people of Tunguz stock, forefathers of the modern Manchus, and hailing, in fact, from Manchuria. This people, the Jurchets, was ruled by a dynasty whose kings had taken the Chinese name of *Kin,* which literally translated means "the Kings of Gold." From their capital at Peking the Kings of Gold reigned over the richest provinces of the Yellow River from the loess terraces of Shen-si and Shan-si to the alluvial Great Plain of the seaboard. The only regions not controlled by them in the interior were the March of the Northwest, since become known as Kansu, the Alashan steppe and the Ordos steppe in the great bend of the Yellow River, the last two areas forming part not, in fact, of China proper, but of what we should today term Inner Mongolia. Kansu, Alashan, and the Ordos country had fallen two centuries before to a people of Tibetan affinities, the Tanguts, who had founded there a kingdom more or less sinized, known by the Chinese name of Hsi-hsia.

It was against this kingdom of the Tanguts, or Hsi-hsia, that Chingis-khan directed the first of his attacks on China. Three times, in 1205, 1207, and 1209, he ravaged the country.

From the upper Tula, the heart of Mongol country, to Ning-hsia, the Tangut capital, there runs still today a track straight north-south, clear across the Gobi. The Gobi, indeed, particularly at this part, has never constituted an obstacle. "Gravel, sand and clay there make a surface hard and level as a race track," wrote Grenard. "Greyish dwarf iris, *kharmyk, budargan,* chance their arm in these arid plains. Here and there, very thin surface layers support a scant grass that is yellow from July on and scarcely distinguishable in the brownish expanse. In the full light of day all is pallid, drained of color, enveloped in a shroud of fine dust. Only in the early morning, the sky has gradations, moving through shades of blue steadily deepening into the mist of distance; and different hues can be distinguished in the ochre plain, marked here and there by the sharp shadows of a rock, of a group of tents, of a herd of horse or antelope, of a caravan skirting a hill, its leader in a high hat walking alone out in front with a rolling gait in his great boots. These vast stretches are easily traversed, practicable everywhere for horses, camels, wagons. There are few days the traveler does not come on grass and water for his beasts. In the center, there is an unwatered stretch of over seven hundred kilometers, but it is only necessary to dig, here two or three feet, there six or nine, to come on underground supplies."

Almost yearly, in autumn, "the time when the horses are fat," the Mongol horsemen, making their way without difficulty across these solitary expanses, came raiding the present-day Kansu. As they came on them fresh from the desert, the oases of the province must have appeared to the nomads of undreamed-of attractiveness and wealth; set in their surroundings of willow and poplar, orchards and meadows, fields of corn and millet. Further to the east, the Mongols made acquaintance with the Yellow River, the more impressive here in that in the immense curve it describes to enclose the Ordos steppe "it wanders in the empty expanse like a stranger lost in a hostile country." The Ordos plateau is, in fact, "but a piece of Mongolia," cut off from the rest of the steppes by the bend of the great river. Dunes of yellow sand and clay-salt plains; grasslands studded with fresh-water lakes or salt pools, bushy vegetation—so many features already familiar to the Mongols. The Tangut capital, the present-day Ning-hsia, lying on the river, between the Ordos and Alashan steppes, is an oasis under cultivation since remote antiquity, developed by the Chinese and irrigated by them by means of a skillfully designed network of artificial canals. It was an important commercial center: Marco Polo speaks of its camel-hair textiles and their export. Chingis-khan here for the first time came up against settled civilization. Ning-hsia was moreover a fortress-city, Chinese style, and the nomad army, all horsemen, was incapable of laying proper siege to it. It had not the war machines. Chingis-khan—in an inspiration of genius—had the idea of taking Ning-hsia by diverting the course of the Yellow River. But, here again, the Mongol army had not the engineers, and his plan failed.

The Tanguts nevertheless were at the end of their tether. The oases of Kansu, which were the heart of their kingdom, lived only by trade, as caravan stops on the great transcontinental route from China to Iran, the ancient Silk Road. The fighting, cutting their trade lines, was ruining them. The king resolved to accept Mongol suzerainty. In the same year, 1209, he gave one of his daughters to Chingis-khan in marriage (the Mongols found Tangut maidens particularly attractive), and paid over a tribute notable for the inclusion in it of considerable numbers of camels, the white camels of Kansu held by Marco Polo to be the finest in Central Asia.

Vengeance for Ancient Injuries: The War of Chingis-khan Against the King of Gold

Chingis-khan now had suzerainty, then, over the Tangut kingdom, over the modern Chinese province of Kansu, that is, and the Ordos and Ala-shan steppes. But this whole country amounts in fact to no more than a border area, lying almost outside Chinese territory proper. To win a real foothold in China, the Mongols had to attack the *Kin,* the "King of Gold" in Peking.

This was no small undertaking for the nomads, for the *Kin* kingdom, which comprised, with the exception of Kansu and the Ordos, the whole Yellow River basin, was one of the most powerful states of the period. Its masters, the old Jurchets, sinicized as they were, yet retained on Chinese soil the warrior qualities of their ancestors, the Tunguz forest hunters. These they could back, after a century of settlement in China, with all the resources of a thousand-year-old civilization. And here again, to an even greater extent than with the Tanguts, the nomads from Mongolia were to be faced with fortifications, a war of sieges for which they were totally unprepared. The Great Wall, moreover, with its flanking bastions, made, east to west, an almost unbroken defense line for the *Kin* kingdom.

But Chingis-khan, politician even more than soldier, had in this connection assured himself of help from precious allies. North of the Great Wall, the steppes of what is now Inner Mongolia were inhabited by a Turkish people, half sedentary, half nomad, the Öngüts, of special interest for us in that they professed Nestorian Christianity.[1] Here the Mongols were doubly at ease. The country, first of all, was strangely like their own: "Not a tree; grassy steppe stretching to infinity, with rivers running to brackish lakes. Grass country, as opposed to what the Chinese call corn country; the traveler moves through frightening solitude, till he comes on ten to twenty tents with camels and ponies grazing by them in the hundreds, and sheep and long-haired goats in thousands." And then Chingis-khan had long-standing ties of friendship with the Öngüt Turks who had made the area theirs. Their chief, Alaqush-tegin, had in 1204 done him most signal service by refusing to range himself against him with the coalition instigated by the Naymans, and by warning him of it. Chingis-khan had shown his gratitude by numbering Alaqush-tegin among the high dignitaries of his empire at the assembly at 1206. More: the Conqueror was to give his own daughter Alaqa-beki in marriage to one of Alaqush-tegin's successors, and this was to be but the first of a series of such unions between the imperial Chingiskhanid house and the royal Öngüt one, contracted throughout the thirteenth century.

This marriage policy secured Chingis-khan considerable advantages. The Öngüts, by their geographical position, by the ancient treaties that bound them to the King of Gold, were in the eyes of the latter guardians of the Chinese *limes,* sentinels beyond the wall. In allying them to him, Chingis-khan dismantled in advance the enemy defenses, and, without a blow struck, extended his empire to the very foot of the famous line of fortification.

By 1207, his plans here were sufficiently well advanced for him to take a high line with the court of Peking. An ambassador had just arrived to advise him of the death of the reigning sovereign and the accession of a new King of Gold, a communication of some importance, since legally the Mongol khan was still vassal to the *Kins.* Apparently somewhat abstractedly, the Conqueror asked the ambassador: "Who is the new sovereign?" "The Prince of Wei" was the answer. "I imagined," Chingis-khan then cried, "the King of Gold must be an eminent personage, designated by Heaven. How can an imbecile like the Prince of Wei perform such a role?" With which he spat toward the south (the direction of the *Kin* kingdom), mounted his horse and rode off, leaving the ambassadors dumbfounded.

[1] [On Christianity in Central Asia, cf. Nos. 66 and 67.]

Between the Mongols and the Kings of Gold of Peking lay a trench of blood, and, worse, inexpiable wrongs. No one, in the Mongol *yurts,* had forgotten the old affronts, the national khans ignominiously tortured by the Peking court, Khan Ambaqay, Prince Ökin-barqaq, nailed or impaled like common malefactors on the wooden ass. These were deaths that cried out for vengeance, and now that unity of the tribes was accomplished, the hour was at hand for the King of Gold to suffer his exemplary punishment.

In March 1211, accordingly, Chingis-khan mustered a great force in eastern Mongolia, on the banks of the Kerülen, to begin the attack on the *Kins.* His most distant vassals came to do him homage there, notably the Turkish princes of the west, Barchuq, king or *iduq-qut* of the Uyghurs, who ruled over the oases of Turfan, Qarashahr, and Kucha, and Arslan, king of Qarluq, from Semirechie, south of Lake Balkash. For this expedition against the King of Gold, the Conqueror prepared as for a national war, a holy war. In this spirit he made a pilgrimage to solicit the aid of the Eternal *Tengri* on one of the sacred mountains in Mongol country, probably Burqan-qaldun. Observing the ritual, he uncovered, threw his belt on his shoulders, beat the ground three times with his forehead. "O Eternal *Tengri,* I have taken up arms to avenge the blood of my uncles Ökin-barqaq and Ambaqay, put by the Kings of Gold to ignominious death. If you approve my action, lend me the succor of your arm, let men and spirits join here below to aid me."

And the Great War began. The Mongol army, boasting only horsemen, however, and being as yet unacquainted with the skills of engineering and incapable of mounting any systematic siege, marked time for a long while beneath the bastions of the Great Wall. The years 1211 and 1212 went by and they had taken only minor outposts. This was moreover rugged, tortuous country, descending in steps from the Gobi plateau to the Gulf of Pechili, but with the "descent" cut across by a series of ranges running southwest-northeast and ending in so many fractures, these ranges forming as it were the bars of a grille, the famous "grille of Peking." The Great Wall runs through these jagged, naked mountains, from the Gulf of Pechili to the Yellow River, flanked, at intervals, by a series of fortresses such as Hsüan-hua, northwest of Peking, and Tat'ung, in northern Shan-si. No matter for surprise, then, that, instead of resounding triumphs, the Conqueror chalked up here at first only plodding, hard-won minor gains. He did in fact have his victories, like that of February-March 1211 on Mount Ye-hu, between Peking and Kalgan. Nine years later the monk Ch'ang-ch'un found the ground there still strewn with white bones.

All the same, the Mongol conquest was still marking time in the frontier zone when the spring of 1212 brought Chingis-khan a stroke of political good fortune. Before it came into the power of the Tunguz Kings of Gold, Peking had been for two centuries in the hands of another barbarian people, the Khitay, whom the ancestors of the Kings of Gold had dispossessed. These Khitay belonged to a different race: while the *Kins* or Kings of Gold were of Manchu stock, the Khitay were rather relatives of the Mongols. Unlike the subjects of Chingis-khan, it is true, they had, in three centuries of life in Chinese territory, become almost completely sinicized. They cherished nevertheless memories of their former glory, and doubtless a desire for revenge on their conquerors, the Kings of Gold. And indeed, in the spring of 1212, one of their princes, Ye-lü Liu-ko, revolted against the King of Gold, gathered the people of his race, and came over to the Mongols. The Khitays' country of origin was in the region of Liao-yang, in the south of what is now Manchuria. Chingis-khan, quick to exploit the revolt, sent his lieutenant Jebe, "the Arrow," there with a task force. Jebe met with a reverse at first beneath the walls of Liao-yang; he pretended then to retreat, went to ground in the vicinity, returned to take the place in a surprise attack. Ye-lü Liu-ko could proclaim himself king of the Khitay under the suzerainty of Chingis-khan.

The Storming of the Great Wall and the Descent into the Great Plain

Genius is long patience. After two years' stubborn struggling, Chingis-khan at last, in the summer of 1213, brought off decisive successes.

He had to seize control of the historic Kalgan-Peking road that runs from level to level, pass to pass, between Inner Mongolia and the Great Plain of Eastern China. In July-August 1213, Chingis-khan succeeded in taking the first fortress-city on this road, Hsüan-hua, that, from the plateau whipped by the "yellow wind," where it is set surrounded by volcanic heights, controls the rugged, precipitous region between the outer works of the Great Wall and the Wall proper. Further to the southeast, along the same road, was the fortified town of Pau-an. Toluy, the Conqueror's youngest son, scaled the fortifications at the head of the attacking wave. The next town is Huai-lai. Here Chingis-khan scored a great victory over the *Kins,* and wrought such carnage among their troops that the ground for some ten miles around was for years still strewn with human bones. Southwest of Huai-lai was the entrance to the pass of Chü-yung-kuan or Nan-k'ou, a wild, gloomy gorge, over seventeen miles long, overhung by precipitous heights, and reinforced by a whole system of fortifications commanding the descent of the Great Wall toward Peking. The *Kins* were solidly entrenched here. The Mongol general Jebe, sent on with an advance guard, advanced as far as the entrance to the pass, then, using the old nomad·tactical trick, pretended to make a hasty retreat toward Hsüan-hua. As he expected, the *Kins* were unguarded enough to launch in pursuit of him. When he had lured them far enough from their positions, he turned about suddenly and charged them. Behind him, the whole Mongol army, commanded by Chingis-khan in person, charged too. From Huai-lai to Nan-k'ou they made a clean sweep of the passes. "The enemy corpses were piled up like felled trees." Chingis-khan came and set up his camp at Lung-hu-t'ai, "the plateau of dragons and tigers," at the entrance to the plain. Now there lay before him the Great Plain of eastern China, stretching in all its five hundred miles and more of cultivation from Peking to Nanking. And right beside him, scarcely eighteen miles off, rose the towers and palaces of the capital of the Kings of Gold, the present-day Peking.

Meantime, other Mongol detachments had gained control of the two other access routes to Chinese territory: taking in the northeast the fortress of Ku-pei-k'ou, commanding the principal pass in the descent from Jehol to Peking; in the northwest Ta-t'ung, military stronghold set between the two lines of the Great Wall, and dominating and defending from 4,300 feet the province of Shan-si.

At Ta-t'ung the Mongols found old friends who had suffered in their cause: the Öngüt princes. The Öngüt Prince Alaqush-tegin, who had formerly rendered such service to Chingis-khan in warning him of the Nayman threat, had been killed by the anti-Mongol faction. His widow and son had then taken refuge at Ta-t'ung. The Mongol victory released them, and Chingis-khan received them and overwhelmed them with favors. He would shortly give to one of the Öngüt princes, the young Negüdei, one of his granddaughters, daughter of his fourth son, Toluy. As we shall see, he was also to give to another Öngüt prince his own daughter, the wise and courageous Princess Alaqa.

Thus the Conqueror of the World, at the very moment when he towered most terribly for the enemies of his people, showed the sons of friends fallen in his cause the most touching, paternal affection.

The Mongol victories had had their repercussions at the court of Peking. One of the *Kin* generals, Hu-sha-hu, killed his master, the King of Gold Wei-shao, and set in his place another member of the royal family, who became King Hsüan-tsung (August-September 1213). Taking advantage of the disarray caused by this revolution, Chingis-khan that autumn launched a great offensive into the heart of the *Kin* kingdom. He had divided his forces into three armies, and never was a plan of campaign so clearly conceived or more systematically executed.

Chingis-khan, who was accompanied by his youngest son Toluy, himself took command of the army of the center, which was to invade the Great Plain. Others would have thought to take Peking by storm. With his sturdy common sense, he turned down the idea; the city was too strongly fortified and the Mongols not equipped for such a siege. He contented himself with masking it by a curtain of troops, and set off with his horsemen southward.

Imagine the astonishment of all these nomads, herders of the steppe or forest trappers, at the prospect that now opened before them. Away to infinity, from the walls of Peking to the Yellow River, stretched the Great Plain with its yellow-brown fields, where, for thousands of years, every inch of earth had been jealously cultivated by the same race of patient laborers, where farms and villages gave way to farms and villages, where fields of rice alternated with fields of millet, fields of *kauliang* with fields of maize. Through orchard and harvest the troop of horses drove, burning farm and mill, trampling the crop. Barely a halfscore of fortress-towns, strong behind their walls, held out against them. All the smaller towns they sacked, from Pau-ting, southwest of Peking, to Wei-hui, in north Honan. From Peking, the Conqueror had covered north to south more than three hundred miles, and he checked only because he was coming here to the Yellow River, wide as a sea inlet, and impassable for his horsemen.

But he did not limit his ride to Ho-pei. To the southeast, he made right across the fertile plain of Shantung, and took its principal city, Tsi-nan. At Tsi-nan the Mongol conqueror must have seen what a great Chinese city was in the thirteenth century, for the Shantung metropolis was already famous for its fine spurting fountains, its lake full of giant lotuses, the great trees of its parks, its "Mountain of the Thousand Buddhas" with statues going back to the seventh century, and for the luxury silk manufactures that were the basis of its extensive trade. Leaving on his east the sacred massif of T'ai-shan, Chingis-khan drove on to Lan-shan, latitude 35° North, at the extreme southern limit of Shantung province, on the threshold of the zone of inundated land and polders, through which, from 1194 to 1853, the Yellow River made its way to the sea. There, as in Ho-pei, the government of Peking had ordered the peasants to take refuge in the walled towns. But the Mongols, following a cruel practice they were later to adopt again in Iran, set their prisoners to work in siege operations and with them the local rural population. They pushed them to the fore as they attacked the fortified towns. The be-leaguered defenders, recognizing their unfortunate countrymen at the head of the assault columns, were reluctant to use their arms. Except for the really impregnable fortresses, all the cities succumbed one after an-other. Chingis-khan returned to the Wall with vast quantities of booty in gold, in silver, in luxury silks, in livestock and horses, not to mention the sad trains of chained youths and maidens.

While the Conqueror sacked the Great Plain, his three eldest sons, Jöchi, Jaghatay, and Ögödei, were heading a second force, "the right wing," the sources term it, since the Mongols were in line facing south. This army went down the western strip of Ho-pei, via Pau-ting and Shun-to, and drove on to near Huai-k'ing, in the part of Honan north of the Yellow River; then crossing the last southern foothills of the T'ai-hangs, it mounted the vast yellow-earth plateau that constitutes the old agricul-tural province of Shan-si.

The three Chingiskhanid princes thus entered the loess terraces of Shan-si from the southeast. They came to the basin of the Fen, the north-to-south course of which cuts the province in two. Moving up the longi-tudinal furrow of the river, they seized the principal towns strung out along its banks or in the vicinity: P'ing-yang, Fen-chen, and Hsin-chou. They also took, despite the system of fortifications and moats that had repelled so many assaults in the times of the old Chinese wars, the me-tropolis of the province, T'ai-yuan, a city wealthy indeed, as we know from Marco Polo and other thirteenth-century writers, as a center of both metallurgy and viticulture. The ease with which these places were captured shows the extent to which Mongol strategy had disconcerted the defenders. The latter had been expecting an attack from the north, and were taken completely by surprise when they saw the nomad horse-men bearing down from the south. Having sacked the towns, destroyed the farms, massacred the peasantry, fired the crops, the three Chingis-khanid princes made their way via Tai-chou and Ta-t'ung back to the Great Wall, to deposit their booty safely beyond the bounds of settled civilization, at the edge of the steppes, among their friends the Öngüts.

Chingis-khan had entrusted a third force of horsemen to his brother Qasar. Setting out, likewise, from near Peking, Qasar followed the coast northwest along the Yung-p'ing shelf. He subjected as he passed through it the country between the Pass of Shan-hai-kuan and Jehol, then went to do the same for the birthplace of the first Kings of Gold, the former Jürchets, that is to say upper Manchuria, in the region of the Rivers Nonni and Sungari as far as the Amur.

In April 1214, Chingis-khan brought his forces together again before Peking. His generals wanted to attack the city outright. More alive than they to the deficiencies of the Mongol poliorcetics, he disagreed. On the contrary, he sent a messenger to the King of Gold in Peking with a peace proposal: "All your provinces north of the Yellow River are in my hands. You have only Peking left. It is heaven who has reduced you to this state of impotence, but if I pressed you harder, who knows if it would approve? I am of a mind, then, to withdraw. Can you let me have the wherewithal to appease the wrath of my generals against you?"

The unfortunate King of Gold offered anything he wanted: gold, silver, silks—the three words recur like a refrain when settled folk are seeking to appease the nomads. He offered also five hundred youths, five hundred young girls, three thousand horses, and, for the bed of Chingis-khan, a princess of the blood, Princess Ch'i-kuo. The court of Peking thought for the moment it had averted disaster when the Conqueror, having deigned to accept these presents, recrossed the Great Wall by the pass of Chü-yung-kuan on his way back to Mongolia.

The Mongols Take Peking

In reality the King of Gold can have had no illusions. The peace so dearly bought was no more than a respite. Now that the Mongols had learned how to force the bastions of the Great Wall, they might at any moment return: Peking was too near the steppe. In June 1214 he accordingly gave up residence in the city, and retired behind the barrier of the Yellow River, to K'ai-feng, in Honan. His departure, however, was considered by his own subjects a desertion. On the way a part of his army mutinied, turned back northward, and went to place themselves at the disposal of the Mongols.

Chingis-khan did not let slip such an opportunity. In March 1215 he dispatched his officer Muqali with orders to lay siege to Peking. Just as the Conqueror had been against attacking the great city the year before when it had its full complement of defenders, so now he scarcely hesitated to embark on its blockade once he knew dissension was afoot among the enemy and part of the garrison had been withdrawn. A quality of his character comes out here. With his sturdy common sense, he never fails to draw the line between possible and impossible, to attempt only that which is strictly within his means. And this time again his judgment was sound. In a Peking abandoned by its king, the generals the latter had left there were now demoralized. One of them, Wan-yen Fu-hing, committed suicide in his despair. Another fled, taking his men with him. After his departure, the Mongols, led in fact by an enemy general who had come over to them, the deserter Ming Ngan, entered Peking (May 1215).

The Peking of the Kings of Gold was far from the size of the present city. It corresponded only to the present "Chinese town," or "outer town," the southern sector, that is, of the Peking of today. It was never-theless one of the greatest metropolises of its time, with its twenty-six-mile enclosure, flanked by twelve gates, and its four distinct "towns" that the Mongols had to take separately, one after the other. Besides the pal-ace of the Kings of Gold, which must have stood somewhere near the present Temple of Heaven, there was a Summer Palace, which has been sited over toward the present White Pagoda (Pai-t'a), near the "upper lake" of the modern "Imperial City." Around this summer residence, the area occupied today by the Inner City (the old "Tatar town") was then an immense park laid out for the delight of the King of Gold.

All this was razed. The carnage was what was to be expected. The Mongols set fire to the imperial palace, which burned for over a month. Chingis-khan, who to escape the heat of the Chinese summer had retired behind the Great Wall to near Lake Dolon-nor, did not even deign to inspect his conquest. Like all the Mongols, he had no conception of an urban economy, and, at least at this stage in his life, had doubtless no notion one might do otherwise with a conquered city than destroy it. He did, however, send three of his officers, Önggür, Arqay-qasar, and Shigi-qutuqu, to collect the "treasure of the Kings of Gold"—gold, sil-ver, precious stones, luxury silks. A *Kin* officer, named Qada, who had made his peace with the Mongols in time, had charge of these riches. He presented himself before the three emissaries, duly armed with offer-ings for them of personal booty, to win their favor, in the shape of bales of those gold-embroidered silks that, at the end of the century, were to be so much admired by Marco Polo. Önggür and Arqay allowed them-selves to be tempted, but Shigi-qutuqu proved incorruptible. "Before," he answered Qada, "all these treasures belonged to the King of Gold. Henceforth, they belong, like Peking itself, to Chingis-khan. How can you dispose of articles that are his? Do you dare to offer them to us? I will have none of them!" When they were back again before the Con-queror, the latter, who knew men, asked them point blank what Qada had offered them. Told what had passed, he severely reprimanded Öng-gür and Arqay, and rewarded Shigi-qutuqu with one of those magnificent encomiums he had the secret of: "You know your duty and you are true!"

Chingis-khan sought fully to exploit the fall of Peking by surprising the King of Gold's new capital, the town of K'ai-feng, in Honan. K'ai-feng was shielded by the course of the Yellow River, which the Mongol horsemen could not so much as contemplate crossing. They bypassed it and attacked Honan from the west, the Shen-si side. In the winter of 1216–17 the Mongol general Samuqa-ba'atur, moving down from Shen-si where he had sacked the ancient city of Hsi-ngan, "the Chinese Rome," came to attack the fortress of T'ung-kuan, which, set at the junction of the Wei with the Yellow River, south of the great elbow of the river, in a valley narrow as a gorge between the same river and the Hua-shan mountains, bars an invader's entry to Honan. Perceiving that the place was too strong for him, Samuqa moved a little farther south, toward the mountains. Eastward, the valley of the Yellow River, still as narrow as ever, was defended by the town of Lo-yang, our Ho-nan-fu. This Samuqa likewise left alone, continuing southward, through the Sung-shan mountains, whose steep heights and precipices presented great obstacles for his horsemen. He took, in this region, Ju-chou, south of Lo-yang, and came out eventually into the great agricultural plain of loess and alluvial soil that stretches south of K'ai-feng. The plan was well conceived and well executed. It failed, nevertheless, because the enemy had had time to mass around the town infinitely superior forces. Samuqa was only two and a half miles from K'ai-feng when he had to resign himself to retreat. By good fortune, the cold season falling early and with particular severity that year let him cross back to the other side of the Yellow River over the ice, and make his way north unimpeded.

About this time, as it happened, Chingis-khan lost interest somewhat in operations in China. Content to have driven the King of Gold south across the Yellow River, he made no further serious attempt to hunt him down there. Even north of the river, with the exception of the region around Peking that the Mongols kept a firm grip on, he tended to look on his Chinese possessions as little more than a kind of no-man's land, a zone of pillage for the troops he had left there. This attitude sprang in part from the Mongols' incomprehension of the urban habitat. The towns they captured, they then abandoned after thorough pillaging; the King of Gold moved in again when they had gone, and the next year they were back where they had started. In September 1218, Chingis-khan, becoming aware, doubtless, of the lack of consequence in these operations, appointed to direct activities in China one of his best generals, Muqali the Jalair, conferring on him a seal of gold and the princely title of *go-ong,* from the Chinese *kuo-wang,* "king of the country." Muqali grasped that for such a war of sieges, Chinese style, he must adopt Chinese methods, and in the first instance recruit an infantry of Chinese auxiliaries, even an "artillery" of native *ballistarii.* Tenaciously, for five years, he worked at the systematic occupation of towns, and when he died at his task, worn out, in April 1223, he had again practically driven back the King of Gold within the province of Honan.

54

Chingis-khan's Meeting with the Chinese Man of Letters

The forces of Chingis-khan in Northern China had at first done little but destroy. They were simply steppe herdsmen or forest trappers, and civilization was something they did not know existed. But Chingis-khan had now just encountered civilization, in the person of a Chinese nobleman taken at the fall of Peking. It was an encounter to have consequences so important for the destiny of the Mongol empire it deserves attention.

The nobleman was called Ye-lü Ch'u-ts'ai.[1] He was of the former royal house of the Khitay, kin to the Mongols, that had ruled in Peking in the tenth and eleventh centuries. His forebears, dispossessed in 1122 by the Kings of Gold, had rallied to their conquerors and had served them loyally. Ye-lü Ch'u-ts'ai himself had been counselor to the last King of Gold. It will be remembered that Chingis-khan had shrewdly presented himself to the Khitay as an avenger, and that a group of them had then, at his call, revolted against the King of Gold. Deliberately, when Ye-lü Ch'u-ts'ai was brought before him, he took the same line: "The house of Khitay and that of the Kings of Gold have always been enemies. I have avenged you!" "My grandfather, my father, and I myself," came Ye-lü Ch'u-ts'ai's reply, "have been subjects and servants of the King of Gold. I should be guilty of deception if I had harbored thoughts hostile to my recent sovereign." We know how high a value the Mongol conqueror set on dynastic loyalty, even in an enemy. The answer of Ye-lü Ch'u-ts'ai was particularly pleasing to him. The man pleased him too, with his

[1] [For more information on this important personage cf. vol. I, pp. 9-24 of No. 13. This was probably Grousset's source for what follows.]

height, his long beard, the impressive sound his voice had. Lastly, Ye-lü Ch'u-ts'ai was an accomplished astrologer. Chingis-khan attached him to his nomad court and was thereafter never without him. Before every expedition the Khitay minister had to consult the fates by examination of the cracks in a sheep's shoulder blades, the standard Mongol divination procedure.

But Ye-lü Ch'u-ts'ai was not merely a soothsayer as commonly understood in his place and time. He was a great Chinese scholar full of wisdom and humanity. He made noble use of the favor he found with Chingis-khan. While the other officers of the Conqueror thought only of pillage, he was content to appropriate from among the loot a few Chinese books, or medicinal drugs, with which it fell to him to save countless lives, in the epidemics bred from so many charnel houses. Through him, the influence of a centuries-old civilization began to make itself felt at the Chingiskhanid court. Discreetly, because he had the confidence of the master and used it only for good, he came to be able, as we shall see, to get barbarous orders retracted. He was to show the nomad conqueror that rather than ruining crops and massacring peasants, it would be in his own greater interest to obtain from them payment of a regular tax; that rather than destroying the urban agglomerations and looting the wealth that accumulated there, it would be more intelligent to preserve for the benefit of the empire the actual source of that wealth. The day was to come when he would dare to declare outright to Chingis-khan's son that the empire that had been "won from the saddle" could no longer be "ruled from the saddle." There was in him the stuff of a statesman, and it is to Chingis-khan's outstanding merit to have so quickly discerned and harkened to it: and this despite the cultural gap that yawned between the chief clothed in animal hides and the former counselor to the court of Peking.

Alexander the Great took with him on his campaigns the philosopher Callisthenes, nephew and disciple of Aristotle, but he ordered his death. Chingis-khan, who boasted certainly none of the Macedonian's culture, never swerved in his affection for his Chinese *literatus*.

On the Silk Road: The Uyghurs, Chingis-khan's Mentors in Civilization

The empire of Chingis-khan now embraced, as well as the Mongol steppe zone and the wooded mountains that bordered it on the north, part of northern China. His attention was to turn now to central Asia.

Central Asia, in the strict sense of the term, namely what is now Chinese Turkestan, is a region in process of "Saharification," its north a stony or salt-clay desert, an extension of the Gobi, its south given over to the immense sands of the Taklamakan. The Tarim, which runs west to east through the middle of these wastes, is a dying river that its tributaries now fail to join, or join only when already exhausted, and which is itself almost dried up by the time it comes to its indeterminate end in the marshes of Lobnor. But the twofold arc of the T'ien-shan mountains in the north, the Pamir in the west and the Altyn-tagh in the north, surround it with a zone of grassland, and even, in the case of the T'ien-shan and the Pamir, with forest-covered massifs. The rivers that run down from these ranges, before they come to peter out in the sands, in their upper reaches water a certain number of surprisingly fertile oases. These oases—Turfan, Qarashahr, Kucha, and Aqsu in the north, Cherchen, Keriya, Khotan, and Yarkand in the south—lie around the periphery in two arcs that meet in the west at the oasis of Kashghar. They are so many centers of intensive agriculture, gardened rather than cultivated, with maize and wheat fields, fruit trees and vines famous in history (a town in the neighboring region was to be called "Apple Orchard"). The hard-working inhabitants, though their language since the ninth and tenth centuries has been Turkic, are still peasants of Indo-European stock, brothers to today's Persians.

These agricultural, even market-gardening, oases were at the same time caravan stages of major importance for trade. Through them passed the ancient Silk Road that linked across the desert wastes the worlds of China and Iran, the Moslem world and Europe. The Alexandrian geographers of Ptolemaic times, Chinese Buddhist pilgrims of the early Middle Ages, Marco Polo at the end of the thirteenth century, all have left their descriptions of this famous road, the northern branch of which ran through Turfan, Qarashahr, Kucha, and Aqsu, the southern through Lobnor, Khotan, and Yarkand, the two meeting at Kashghar. From Kashghar the road ran over the passes of Alay and Transalay, north of Pamir, to come down again westward toward the agricultural plain of Ferghana, Samarkand, and Transoxania, the Moslem world. And a little farther to the northwest the wooded chain of the T'ien-shan, level with Üch-Turfan, between Aqsu and Kashghar, affords passage through its pine forests to another historic route, the one that leads down again to the Issyq-kol, "the hot lake," the waters of which, even though close by formidable glaciers, never freeze. Here again, another world begins, for west of the lake rises the River Chu, that after watering the fertile agricultural plain of Frunze, runs to ground in the "white sands" (*aq-qum*) over toward the Aral and the steppes of Sibero-Turkestan.

Dominion over this vast region, at the beginning of Chingis-khan's reign, was shared by two tribes of equal interest to the historian, the Uyghurs and the Qara-khitays.

The oases of the northeast—Beshbaliq (Dzimsa), Turfan, Qarashahr, and Kucha—belonged to the Uyghur Turks, the earliest civilized of the peoples of Turkic race. Having taken to settled living in the ninth century, the Uyghurs, some of whom were Buddhist, some Nestorian Christians, had evolved their own alphabet, based on Syriac, and later to serve, as we shall see, as prototype for the Mongol alphabet. They had made of their Turkic dialect a literary language: Uyghur literature has bequeathed, especially in the Buddhist domain, works of interest, some translated from Sanskrit.

Thus, the Uyghurs acted for the other Turco-Mongol peoples as their mentors in civilization. It was to them the tribes of the northern steppes came for the few scholars, the few scribes, they needed for their embryonic chancelleries. Over a great part of Upper Asia, Uyghur Turkic, the Uyghur alphabet, had become the language and script of the administration. Chingis-khan, when he wiped out the kingdom of the Naymans in 1204, found there, it will be remembered, an Uyghur scribe named T'a-t'a-t'ong-a, armed with a seal of gold. The Conqueror asked the meaning of this mysterious object. "Each time," answered T'a-t'a-t'ong-a, "that my master wished to levy silver or corn, or commission one of his subjects to do something, he marked his orders with this seal, to show their authenticity." In short, the Uyghur scribe was the Naymans' chancellor. Chingis-khan appointed him to perform the same functions in his service, and from that day official acts of the new Mongol empire began to be set down in Uyghur Turkic. Chingis-khan went further. Himself all his life illiterate, he insisted his four sons learn the Uyghur writing. He charged T'a-t'a-t'ong-a to teach them. Another scholar, Chinqay, by birth a Kereit but of Uyghur education, shared with Ta'-t'a-t'ong-a the task of organizing the Chingiskhanid chancellery, and it was in fact "prothonotary" or chancellor that he was called by western travelers. Already in the lifetime of the Conqueror, the nomad court had its quota of the "Uyghur offices" that were to assume such importance under his successors.

At this time the Uyghur kingdom, whose kings resided at Beshbaliq, that is, Dzimsa, in the northeast of the T'ien-shan, and bore the title *iduq-qut* ("Holy Majesty"), was ruled by a prince named Barchuq, evidently a person of astute perception. When the tribes of Mongolia united under the Chingiskhanid banner, Barchuq grasped at once the epoch-making character of the event. While others hemmed and hawed, he acted, and sent two messengers to bear to Chingis-khan his compliments. "It is with joy I have learned of the glory of my Lord Chingis-khan. The clouds have made way for the sun, the river is freed from the ice. Grant me your favor and I will dedicate my strength to you, I shall be as a fifth son to you!" On receiving a gracious reply from the Conqueror, the *iduq-qut* Barchuq, in the spring of 1211, betook himself to him in person. As token of his vassalhood he brought lavish tribute: gold, silver, precious stones, silks, damask, brocades, all the treasures of the ancient Silk Road the Uyghurs had piloted caravans over for four centuries. Chingis-khan was charmed with the eagerness of these overtures. He can scarcely have failed to be flattered also, for, all unlettered as he was, we know the prestige Uyghur culture enjoyed in his nomad background. He welcomed his visitor with especial warmth, and promised him the hand of the Mongol Princess Al-altun.

The two men must have parted well content with each other. Master of the Silk Road or at least of that road's northern section, the Uyghur prince had secured the goodwill of the immense nomad empire that had just come into being to the north, in the world of the steppe. And through the homage of the Uyghur, Chingis-khan had acquired control of that same Silk Road, axis of intercontinental relations. Let it not be thought the Mongol conqueror was too unsophisticated to attach importance to such questions. What we shall see of his attitude in the affair of the caravans of Khwarezm shows that, on the contrary, questions of trade were in his eyes of capital importance.

56

The Ride of Jebe the Arrow from
Mongolia to the Pamirs

The house that shared with the Uyghurs dominance of central Asia was that of the Qara-Khitays, the "black Khitays."

They were a branch of those Khitays, racially related to the Mongols, who had ruled from 936 to 1122 in Peking, where they had been profoundly sinicized.[1] The founder of the Qara-Khitays, when he was driven from Peking by the Kings of Gold, had come to try his fortunes west of the T'ien-shan (1128). Though of Chinese education, he had secured recognition of his authority by the Turkic peoples of the region, both those part "pagan," part Nestorian, part Islamized, of the "Country of the Seven Rivers," our Semirechie or Jeti-su, and those, almost all Moslem, of Kashghar, Yarkand, and Khotan. The Qara-Khitay empire thus founded had lasted from about 1128 to 1211. Its sovereigns bore the imperial title *gur-khan,* and their capital was the city of Balasaghun on the Chu, near the present-day Frunze.

But about the time Chingis-khan embarked on his conquest of North China, the Qara-Khitay empire had suffered a catastrophic upheaval. Its last sovereign, Ye-lü Che-lu-ku, had in 1208 given asylum to the famous Küchlüg, heir to the Nayman throne, driven out, as we have seen, by the Mongols. Not only did he receive the exile, he made him his son-in-law. He was ill repaid. Küchlüg, in 1211, revolted against him, took him prisoner, and seized power, then the throne. Now this wild Turk, descendant

[1] [The Khitays ruled over China under the dynastic title *Liao,* and gave to China its medieval name "Cathay." For further information on the history of this very interesting word cf. pp. 216-9 of No. 18.]

of the nomads of the Altay, had none of the qualities required to rule the already largely settled Turks of Issyq-kol, the peaceable agricultural population of Kashghar. To force the Kashgharian oases to accept his authority, he systematically, for two or three years, had his horsemen lay waste the harvest. Half shamanist, half Nestorian, as was commonly the case with the Naymans, and having thereto added marriage to a Buddhist Qara-Khitay princess, he took it into his head to persecute Islam, the majority religion in the country. He went so far as to crucify the chief of the imams of Khotan. Thus far had he alienated the sympathies of his subjects, when he went to war with the terrible Mongols.

The war was moreover at his instigation.

Among former vassals of the Qara-Khitay empire were two Turkic chiefs, Arslan ("the Lion"), king of the Qarluq, who inhabited the "Country of the Seven Rivers," and Buzar, king of Almaliq ("the Apple Orchard"), near what is now Khuldja, on the upper Ili. In 1211 these two princes, sensing the way the wind was blowing, had, like their neighbors the Uyghurs, transferred their homage to Chingis-khan. The appearance, to the north of Semirechie, of a Mongol division under "the great warrior Qubilay" had been the last spur required to effect Arslan's conversion: there and then, he had gone with Qubilay to Chingis-khan to make his act of allegiance. Buzar sent his son. Küchlüg would have been wise to turn a blind eye to these defections, to let Chingis-khan forget him. But he nursed an implacable hatred for the Mongols. He had forgotten neither his father killed at the battle of Mount Naqu nor the partial massacre of his people. It was the king of Almaliq, Buzar, he attacked first. Taking him by surprise as he was hunting, he had him put to death, but he could not take Almaliq. Buzar's widow effectively defended it, and their son Suqnaq-tegin went for aid to Chingis-khan.[2]

Chingis-khan, in 1211, had certainly not viewed with any favorable eye the passing of the former Qara-Khitay empire, the greater part of eastern Turkestan, into the hands of the last of the Nayman princes, son of an enemy race, himself a personal enemy of the Conqueror. The murder of the prince of Almaliq was a last straw, and precipitated Küchlüg's chastisement.

Chingis-khan entrusted vengeance to the speediest of his generals,

[2] This Suqnaq-tegin was later to marry a granddaughter of Chingis-khan, the daughter of his eldest son Jöchi.

whom he had himself surnamed Jebe, "the Arrow." This was in 1218. What route did Jebe take? What direction did he attack from? We do not even know where Küchlüg may have been as he awaited the final blow. It seems, however, that the Mongol horse made their way into Küchlüg's country from that of the Uyghurs through the T'ien-chan. Farther west, they could make use of Almaliq as a base, near the present-day Khuldja, on the upper Ili. In this prosperous "Apple Orchard," with Chingis-khan's loyal adherent King Suqnaq-tegin, they could recoup their strength at ease. From there, the Mongols had only to go down the valley of the Ili which widened out before them, an immense undulating plain, "mingling hummocks of sand with the verdure of reeds, grasses, and elm woods," and they were in the Land of the Seven Rivers, Jeti-su or Semirechie, the loess fields of which, wherever they are irrigated, yield an abundance of cereals, linen, flax, and early fruits and vegetables. The inhabitants, terrorized by Küchlüg, seem to have welcomed these terrible Mongols, elsewhere dreaded as a scourge from heaven, here greeted as liberators. Things went apparently the same way even west of Issyq-kol, where Balasaghun, capital of the former Qara-Khitay *gur-khans,* opened its gates without demur. The Mongols, charmed by the fruitfulness of the district, named it Go-baligh, "the pretty town."

And Küchlüg? Having so long provoked the Mongols, at their arrival he had taken flight. Dismayed by the invasion, he did not even attempt to defend Kashghar where the population, Moslem to a man, was intrinsically hostile to him, but plunged behind Kashghar into the mountains, in the direction of the 26,000-foot-high Mustagh massif, that dominates the approaches to the Pamirs. It was indeed in the Pamirs, on the "Roof of the World," that he thought to take refuge. But the Mongol horsemen, hot in pursuit of him, trailed him like a hunted animal. Among the precipices and sheer passes, in the silence of the alpine grass and the rarefied air of the high plateau, at the foot of the giant glaciers, the fantastic chase was played to its finish. The hunted prince had reached the high valley of Sary-kol, 10,000 feet up, when the Mongol vanguard overtook and beheaded him.

The main body of Mongol horsemen must have entered Kashghar just after Küchlüg had fled the town. Cleverly, Jebe, adopting exactly the reverse policy to Küchlüg's, forbade all pillage, an order that thanks to the strict Mongol discipline was obeyed absolutely. He did more. He put an

end to the measures of persecution against Islam, and formally authorized practice of the religion. The inhabitants, the vast majority of them
here in Kashghar, as in Yarkand and Khotan, Moselms, here likewise
welcomed the Mongols as liberators. Rallying to them, the Kashghari
peasants slaughtered the soldiers of Küchlüg who had taken refuge in
their houses.

In a matter of weeks, Jebe had conquered the whole former Qara-
Khitay empire, all eastern Turkestan. Chingis-khan feared lest his officer,
inflated by such success, should have thoughts of secession. In his first
message to him he warned him not to succumb to the pride that had been
the ruin successively of the Kereit Ong-khan, the Nayman Tayang, and,
now, Küchlüg. He did not know Jebe. The latter's loyalty to his master
was unshakable. It was not carving out a kingdom for himself he was
concerned with. It was something quite different, redeeming an injury he
had once done Chingis-khan. It will be remembered that in the days
before he had joined him, he had with an arrow struck down one of the
Conqueror's horses, a magnificent brown animal with a white muzzle, of
which the master had been especially fond. Chingis-khan had borne him
no grudge, for he had raised his former foe to be commander of his
army. But Jebe was still full of remorse, and, when he had subjected
eastern Turkestan, he hastened to requisition a thousand horses with
white muzzles, just like the one he had brought down, "to offer them to
the Emperor."

The Massacre of the Caravan

To the west of Semirechie and Kashgharia, now part of the Chingis-khanid domain, began a new world and a new civilization, the Moslem world, the Arabo-Persian civilization. The Mongol conqueror was now the neighbor of the empire of the shahs or sultans of Khwarezm.

This empire, which had been formed by a Turkish Moslem dynasty, originating from the former Khwarezm, today the country of Khiwa, south of the Aral sea, took in our Russian Turkestan, the greater part of our Afghanistan, and our Iran. It was an empire, in fact, of fairly recent date: the then ruling sovereign, the Sultan Mohammed (1200–20) had barely completed his last conquests when he came into conflict with the Mongols.

Chingis-khan had always wished to maintain good relations with the Khwarezmians. In 1216, receiving near Peking an ambassador from Sultan Mohammed, he had declared his conviction that the Mongol empire and the Khwarezmian, having quite distinct spheres of action—the one in eastern, the other in western, Asia—should live in peace and foster commercial exchange between them. But the subjects of the sultan, the rich merchants of Bukhara and Samarkand, considered the Mongols barbarians and made no secret of the fact. Three of these merchants came to Mongolia with a caravan laden with silks and cottons. One of them, brought to Chingis-khan, asked for the materials a price so clearly exorbitant that the Conqueror realized the trader thought to make a monkey of an ignorant barbarian. "Lo," he cried, "the man thinks we have never seen anything so beautiful!" He first undeceived his visitor by having brought forth for him to see the marvelous Chinese stuffs received as tribute from the King of Gold. After which he let the good man be despoiled of all his merchandise. The two other caravaneers, now more circumspect, declined to set a price on their materials themselves: they entrusted this to the khan's generosity. The latter indeed made them generous payment, and the first of the three as well. He had "new tents of white felt" put up for their use, and entertained them particularly well.

At the same time, Chingis-khan, in response to the Khwarezm sultan's embassy, sent to him three envoys whom he took care to choose from among Khwarezmian subjects in Mongolia: Mahmud of Khwarezm, 'Ali-Khoja of Bukhara, and Yusuf Kanka of Otrar. Among the presents they were charged to deliver to the sultan were an enormous gold nugget, gold ingots, objects of jade, ivory, and lengths of immensely valuable "wool" spun from the hair of white camels. The Sultan Mohammed received this embassy in the spring of 1218, probably at Bukhara.

A frankly pacific message accompanied the gifts: "I know your power and the vast extent of your empire," the Mongol emperor sent word to the master of Transoxania and Iran. "I have the greatest desire to live in peace with you. I shall look on you as my son. For your part, you are not unaware that I have conquered North China and subjected all the tribes of the north. You know that my country is an ant heap of warriors, a mine of silver, and that I have no need to covet other dominions. We have an equal interest in fostering trade between our subjects."

Sultan Mohammed found himself in a quandary. By calling him his son, Chingis-khan classed him outright as his vassal. On the other hand, the conquests of the Mongol frightened the Moslem prince. One night, he sent secretly for one of Chingis-khan's envoys, Mahmud, whom he knew to be Khwarezmian-born, and taking off a bracelet of precious stone and presenting it to him, adjured him to speak the truth: "Tamghach [North China], is it true that the khan has conquered it?" And again: "This reprobate who dares to call me son, who is he, what are the numbers of his troops?" His alarm grew visibly. For the moment, he judged it wise to send back Chingis-khan's three envoys with friendly answers.

Shortly after, Chingis-khan decided to take active steps to implement the program he had held out, and to send out to the Khwarezmian empire a great trading caravan, with, we are told, five hundred camels, laden with treasures of all kinds: gold, silver, Chinese silk, camel-hair materials, furs of beaver and sable. Those in charge of the caravan had been chosen, again, from among Moslem residents: 'Omar-Khoja of Otrar, Hammal of Maragha, Fakhr ed-Din Dizaki of Bukhara, etc. Chingis-khan sent with them a personal representative, a Mongol named Uquna. He had further required each of the princes of his family, the nobles (*noyats*), and the military chiefs to send with the caravan an agent, carrying cash with which to purchase Khwarezmian luxury products. His desire to intensify trade between eastern Asia and the Moslem world is patent.

The great caravan moved without incident across Upper Asia. It reached the Khwarezmian frontier at Otrar, on the mid-Sir-darya. There, the Khwarezmian governor Inalchiq Qadir-khan seized it: the treasures were looted and all who traveled with them—about a hundred people, at least—were put to death, including Uquna, Chingis-khan's personal representative.

Chingis-khan was angry. He had sincerely wished to establish peaceful relations, ties of steady trade, with the Moslem world, and this was the response! He was cut so deep he could not hold back his tears. We have seen how high a value he set on correctness in political dealings, on faithfulness to alliances and pacts as on faithfulness to a leader. And now his caravaneers, his ambassador, had been massacred in contempt of all law between peoples. It was he, the nomad clad in felt and animal hides, who found himself the defender of sworn faith, of respect for trading agreements, and the representatives of Turko-Persian civilization, of Islamic society, who behaved as barbarians. Once more, as on the eve of the campaign against the King of Gold, as before every grave decision of his career, he mounted one of the Mongol holy mountains, bared his head, threw his belt on his shoulders, and nine times beat his forehead before the Eternal Heaven, before the *Möngke Tengri,* supreme god of the nomads, to implore strength to avenge the wrong done him. And indeed his earlier goodwill, his desire for economic collaboration with the Khwarezmians, were to turn to relentless hate.

But—and it illustrates his self-control—whatever his anger, he wished to have right completely and unanswerably on his side. Possibly the governor of Otrar had acted unknown to his master? Chingis-khan sent one more embassy then to the sultan of Khwarezm, consisting of a Moslem, Ibn-Kafraj Boghra, and two Mongols, with an offer of peace if he would consent to hand over the culprit, Inalchiq. Not only did the sultan refuse to make the extradition, but he had Ibn-Kafraj put to death and—no lesser affront—sent the other two envoys back with their heads shaved.

The die was cast. The Mongol world and the Moslem world—the two halves of Asia—were now at war.

Whatever atrocities the Mongols subsequently committed in the course of this war, be it not forgotten it was righteous anger that sparked in Chingis-khan's heart at the massacre of his caravaneers and the unprovoked murder of his ambassador.

▲
▲▲

58

Before the Great War:
Chingis-khan's Testament

With the Khwarezm campaign there opens a new phase in the life of the Conqueror. Hitherto he had scarcely gone beyond his native Mongolia, for the Peking region where he had done battle is but an extension of the Mongol steppe. Now, as he crossed into the territory of Islam, he was stepping into a world unknown. The power of the sultans of Khwarezm, masters of Turkestan, of Afghanistan, and of Persia, appeared formidable, and, in fact, their armies were undoubtedly numerically superior to Chingis-khan's.

A kind of uneasiness, that the Mongol bard communicates to us, was ill concealed even in the Conqueror's immediate entourage. The fair Yisüi, one of his favorite wives, made herself the mouthpiece of the general disquiet. With the frankness only a favorite can permit herself, she pointed out to him the need to settle before they set out the question of the succession. "The khan is going out to cross by lofty passes great mountain ranges, he will cross vast rivers, he will lead far-flung expeditions, he will decide the destinies of many peoples. But every creature is mortal, every being short-lived. If your body, like to a great tree, one day leans toward the earth, what will become of your peoples, like to hemp stems or bird flight? Of your four noble sons, which do you appoint your heir? This question that I ask you, your sons, your brothers, your subjects are asking themselves also. We need to know your will. . . ."

These words made Chingis-khan thoughtful. Far from being angry, he was appreciative of Yisüi's courage: "You are only a woman, and you have just spoken wise words to me, words that neither my brothers, nor my sons, nor Bo'orchu nor Muqali have ever dared say to me. Yes, I was omitting to think about that, as if I myself had succeeded peacefully to my predecessors, or as if I were never going to die. . . ." And there and then he turned questioningly to his eldest son Jöchi: "You are the eldest. It is for you to speak!" But Jöchi kept silence, or rather, before he could open his mouth, his brother Jaghatay, who hated him, broke in to bring brutally into the open what everyone there was doubtless thinking: "You turn to Jöchi," he cried at his father; "is it he you want to name as your successor?" And, not mincing his words, he reminded him that Jöchi's birth was more than doubtful. Was Jöchi son of Chingis-khan or of the Merkit warrior who had carried off his mother? "He is simply a bastard picked up in Merkit country. Should we let him take the throne?" Jöchi, bounding up at the insult, seized him by the collar. "Our father," he shouted, "has never made any difference between us, and you, you dare to treat me thus! By what right? What qualities have you, what have you ever done, that would make you superior to me? You are superior only in your unlikability and stunted mind!" And he challenged him to a kind of trial before God. "If you beat me with the bow, I will cut off my thumb. If you beat me wrestling, I will not rise from where I have fallen! But let our father decide: it is for us only to obey."

Squaring up to each other, they were already half at grips. Bo'orchu and Muqali rushed in and separated them. Chingis-khan preserved a bitter silence. Kököchü, one of the old servants of the Conqueror, finally found the right words: "Why this violence, oh Jaghatay? Before you were born, the Mongol world was all trouble, everywhere there was war between tribes, no one dared take his rest, each made off with what was his neighbor's, the world was in turmoil, rape and murder were on every side." An only too realistic picture of the anarchy that had reigned among the Mongols before the establishment of Chingiskhanid order, an anarchy sufficient to permit the empress Börte's abduction by the Merkits. Speaking of Börte, the old warrior found moving words to touch Jaghatay and his brothers: he recalled "the heart, tender as butter, of their saintly mother, her soul pure as milk." "Are you not all issued from her entrails, have you forgotten the warmth of her breast? In speaking as you do, Jaghatay, you smirch the honor of your mother, you revile and slander her!" And he recalled the years of hardship: "In that time your father founded the Empire. He shed his blood in streams. For pillow he had his sleeve. He had his saliva to quench his thirst, his gums to appease his hunger, and in his daily struggles sweat streamed from his brow to the soles of his feet. Your mother shared his trials. She denied her own mouth food to feed you. Carrying you round her neck, she had but one thought: to make you men. Such she was, who reared you till you reached the soldiers' shoulders and the horses' croup. Our saintly empress, her heart is pure as the sun and like a lake!"

Chingis-khan, emerging finally from his silence, called Jaghatay to order: "How can you speak thus of your brother Jöchi? Is he not the eldest of my sons? In the future I forbid you to speak such words!" At the paternal reprimand, Jaghatay retracted: "Jöchi and I," he said to his father, "are your two eldest sons. Together we will prove our devotion to you. That one of us who fails his duty, may the other cut him down with an ax! If one of us is tardy, may the other split his heels!" And to solve the impasse, he proposed that he and Jöchi should alike stand down in favor of their brother Ögödei—third of Chingis-khan's sons—known for his good sense and generosity: "He is a youth of deliberation, we would gladly obey him. Let him stay close to your side to learn how to be khan."

Jöchi supported the suggestion, notwithstanding its transference of the right of seniority from himself to the younger Ögödei. The uncertainty that still hung about his birth made it difficult for him to take any other attitude. For the rest Chingis-khan, with his forthright good sense, was anxious to forestall any future disagreement between the brothers. "You should not live side by side. The motherland is vast, rivers and streams many. I will divide up the Empire in such a way that you have each your separate governments, and, for your tribes, clearly marked off grazing grounds."

Then Chingis-khan gave the floor to Ögödei, who had just heard himself named heir-presumptive. Ögödei was in fact the son he liked best, and the one, too, who most resembled him. He had the soundness, the sturdy good sense of his father, with less genius, doubtless, and, in compensation, more bonhomie, an easy temper, a childlike generosity with which a penchant for drinking (but this was a vice common to all the Mongols) was not perhaps entirely unconnected. He answered simply that since he could not refuse the honor offered him, he would do his best to justify it by his zeal. Toluy, youngest of the Conqueror's four sons, promised in his turn always loyally to support Ögödei: "If he forgets something, I shall be there to remind him; if he falls asleep, I shall wake him. I shall be like the whip of his horse. In long campaigns as in sudden scrimmage, I shall fight at his side!"

These problems of succession settled, and all eventualities thus provided for in case of misfortune, Chingis-khan set forth to conquer the Moslem empire.

In Moslem Country

The Mongol army mustered in the summer of 1219 on the southern slope of the Altay, near the sources of the Irtysh and the Urungu. A grandiose setting, well befitting the human tempest gathering there. To the north, the jagged, sharp-peaked barrier of the Altay, covered, from 3,300 to 8,000 feet, in splendid forest, mingling Siberian larch and T'ien-shan pine, to say nothing of cedar, aspen, poplar, and willow. Below this, the lush pasturage grazed over today by Torghut herds. Running down from the Altay, rushing, waterfall-broken streams "cast their dark blue waters amid the damp green of forests and fields." Of them is born the Irtysh, its deep, limpid waters making at once westward, toward Siberia. Farther south, the Urungu runs a parallel course, albeit one taking it soon, with its bordering willow clumps, into a zone of hills bare of vegetation, heralding the desert of Dzungaria. From here, taking the valley of the Emil, at the foot of the Tarbagatay, then the "gate of Dzungaria" between the Balyk and the Dzungar Ala-tau, the Mongol army moved down into the low-lying plain of Semirechie or Jeti-su, "the Country of the Seven Rivers."

This was territory of the Qarluq Turks, whose king, it will be remembered, was Chingis-khan's vassal. When the Mongol army came to Qayalik, an area between what are now the towns of Lepsinsk and Kopal, it was joined by Arslan. Also to Qayalik came two other of the Mongol emperor's vassals, the *iduq-qut* Barchuq, king of the Uyghurs, bringing with him from the region of Turfan a contingent of ten thousand men, and Suqnaq-tegin, prince of Almaliq, near present-day Khuldja. The Mongol army must have numbered at this point between a hundred and fifty and two hundred thousand men. Chingis-khan had left behind in Mongolia, as "keeper of the hearth," his youngest brother, Temüge. Foreseeing a long absence, he had brought with him, to charm away the vexations of the campaign, one of his second wives, the fair Qulan. The reconnaissance forces were entrusted to generals whose worth had been proven in the recent wars: Jebe, "the Arrow," led the foremost advance guard, followed, at intervals, by Sübötei and then Toquchar.

In the face of the Mongol threat, the Sultan Mohammed, not knowing where the attack would be made, had apportioned the main part of his army among the principal fortresses covering his frontiers in the north, along the line of the Sir-darya, and east, toward the Ferghana gap. The rest was distributed among the garrisons of Transoxania, such as Bukhara and Samarkand, or of Khwarezm proper, such as Urgenj near Khiwa. The effect of this dispersion was to let the Khwarezmian army, over-all numerically superior, be outnumbered at any given point.

The Sir-darya, the course of which formed the Khwarezmian empire's northern boundary, is a great river more than 1,750 miles long, carrying, below Khojend, when the water is low, from November to March, 13,630 cubic feet, and when it is high, in about June, 47,420 cubic feet. After it leaves what is now the town of Turkestan, it turns into a real desert river, with the desert already bordering it on the southern bank from there on lying on both sides. It was just about here that in the autumn of 1219 Chingis-khan made his attack. Coming from Semirechie, he must have ridden between the Alexander and the Qara-tau mountains, through the pass of Aulie-Ata; he appeared with all his army before the town of Otrar, on the northern bank of the river, some fifty miles to the south of the present Turkestan. He left there a division commanded by two of his own sons, Jaghatay and Ögödei, supported by the *iduq-qut* Barchuq, king of the Uyghurs. Otrar was only to be taken after long siege, for the governor was still the same Inalchiq who the year before had slaughtered the caravan sent by Chingis-khan; knowing he could expect no mercy, he put up the defense of despair. When the town fell, he held out another month in the citadel. "Borne down upon from all sides, he retreated to a terraced roof, followed by two soldiers he soon saw die at his side. Out of arrows, he went on hurling bricks that the women handed him from the tops of the walls. At last, overwhelmed by numbers, after fighting like a maniac, he was taken, bound, and led before Chingis-khan. In vengeance for the death of the men of the caravan who had died victims of his cupidity, the Conqueror ordered molten silver to be poured into his eyes and ears."

A second Mongol division, under Prince Jöchi, Chingis-khan's eldest son, descended the left bank of the Sir-darya and camped before Sighnaq, opposite the present-day Turkestan. Jöchi sent the Moslem Hasanhaji with an invitation to the townspeople to open their gates. Without waiting to hear the message, the inhabitants, calling on the name of Allah, put him to death. Jöchi at once gave the order to attack, and to press on regardless until the place was taken. "Fresh troops relieved those who were tired. After seven days' daily onslaught the Mongols entered Sighnaq and slaughtered all the inhabitants." Pushing on, Jöchi appeared before Jend, near what is now Perovsk. "The inhabitants trusted to the height of their walls, but soon their confidence gave way to consternation. The Mongols, setting up their ladders, scaled the walls and entered the town on all sides." As the inhabitants of Jend had not defended themselves, Jöchi spared their lives, but he forced them to let their town be pillaged for seven days. He left there as governor a Moslem caravaneer who had been taken into his father's service, 'Ali-Khoja of Bukhara.

While Chingis-khan's eldest son was thus bringing to heel the communities of the lower Sir-darya, a Mongol detachment of five thousand men, under Alaq-noyan, Süketü-cherbi, and Taqay, was pushing into the upper part of the river valley, and attacking Benaket, west of Tashkent. This town was defended by Turkish mercenaries, of the Qanqli tribe, who after three days asked to surrender. "The Mongol commander promised them their lives, but when they had given themselves up and the Benaket population had been driven from the town, the mercenaries were segregated from the citizens and killed by saber or arrow. The craftsmen were then apportioned among the Mongol companies, and young men carried off en masse to be used in the siege of other towns."

Continuing up the Sir-darya valley, this division appeared before Khojend, at the gates of Ferghana. The governor, one of the most famous of the Turkish paladins of the time, Timur-melik, "the Iron King," withdrew with a thousand picked men into a fortress in the middle of the river. Faced with this determination, the besiegers sent for a reinforcement of twenty thousand Mongols and fifty thousand prisoners. "The latter, divided up into squads and companies and commanded by Mongol officers, were set to bring stones from a mountain twelve miles away and cast them in the river. On his side, Timur-melik had had built twelve great boats with decks (the Sir-darya at Khojend is 450 feet across). Each day, several of these boats made toward the shores and riddled the besieging army with arrows." At last, at the end of his resources, Timur-melik managed to escape with his followers in his fleet down the Sir-darya, breaking a chain thrown across the river at Benaket. Farther down, however, by Jend, Prince Jöchi had barred the way again, this time with a pontoon bridge. Before he reached this block, the Iron King landed on the left bank, and made off at full gallop across the Red Sands (Qyzil-qum), where attempts to catch him failed.

The episode proves the Khwarezmian armies had no lack of valor. But they were badly commanded, and, as already pointed out, their dispersal among the different strong points condemned them in advance.

▲
▲▲

60

The Wind of Anger and the Taking of Bukhara

Meantime Chingis-khan was active. While his sons and officers were taking one after another the towns on the Sir-darya, he, with his youngest son Toluy and the main body of the army, had driven from Otrar toward the valley of the Zerafshan that is the heart of ancient Transoxania. Moving along the southeast of the Red Sands, the Mongol advance guard, under Dayir-ba'atur, reached the small town of Nur-Ata. They came at night. The Mongols crossed the gardens that surrounded the place, and in the morning were there before the town. The inhabitants were so far from suspecting their approach they took their patrols for a friendly caravan. Without a hope of defending themselves, they opened their gates to Sübötei. "They came out themselves, bringing only their agricultural tools and their livestock, after which the Mongols pillaged the houses. Beyond this, Chingis-khan was satisfied with a payment of 1,500 dinars, a sum equivalent to the usual tax payment under the Khwarezmian regime." In February 1220 Chingis-khan came to Bukhara.

This was one of the great cities of Islam. It had three parts: the citadel, nearly a mile around, the city proper, or *shahristan,* and the suburb or *rabad.* Contrary to the arrangement in most of the other towns, the citadel lay not inside the city, but outside. The city, built on a raised section, in the center of the present town, was enclosed by a wall which had seven gates, evocatively named—Gate of the Bazaar, Gate of the Spice Merchant, Gate of Iron, etc. Famous mosques drew the faithful: the cathedral mosque, rebuilt in 1121, the Friday mosque, likewise a century old, the mosque of the Syrians. The suburb itself was surrounded by a second wall, with eleven gates. The principal streets of the town were paved with stone, in Islamic country a highly distinctive feature. Numerous *ariqs* or derivation canals led off from the Zerafshan served the town and its outskirts. The chief of these was known, very aptly in this dry country, as Rud-i-zar, "the River Bearer of Gold." An expertly maintained system of locks and reservoirs effected distribution of the water. On the outskirts, the canals irrigated innumerable gardens with a profusion of pleasure pavilions that testified to the wealth of the oasis. This wealth derived largely from flourishing industry, notably from the famous "Bukhara carpets." Between the citadel and the Friday mosque was a great textile factory (*kargah*), the products of which were exported as far away as Syria, Egypt, and Asia Minor. The Bukhara bazaars were equally famous for their copper goods, notably their fine lamps.

When Chingis-khan arrived there, the garrison of Bukhara numbered between 20,000 and 30,000 Turkish mercenaries. The Conqueror invested the town completely, then attacked it without pause for three days. According to their usual practice, the Mongols pushed to the forefront of the attacking ranks captives they had taken among the population round about. The third day, the chiefs of the Turkish garrison, among them a certain Inanch-khan Ogul, losing confidence, agreed to make a general sortie during the night, to force the blockade and escape. Their plan almost succeeded, but the Mongols recovered themselves, made off after them, and caught up with them on the banks of the Sirdarya: most of the escapers were killed.

Abandoned by their defenders, the townspeople decided on surrender. A deputation of imams and prominent citizens came to bring Chingis-khan the town's capitulation. The Mongols entered Bukhara between the tenth and sixteenth of February 1220. Four hundred Turkish horsemen still held out in the citadel. "The Mongols proclaimed that all the inhabitants of Bukhara capable of bearing arms should present themselves on pain of death to fill in the moats of the citadel. . . . Then they set up catapults. When these machines had made breaches in the wall, the Mongols went into the fortress and left not a man alive."

After the taking of the citadel, the inhabitants were told to leave the town taking nothing with them but the clothes on their backs. The town evacuated, the Mongols set systematically to pillage it, killing all those who in spite of the order had stayed behind. The imam 'Ali Zandi, seeing the Korans trampled by the Mongol horses, voiced his grief to another Moslem personage, Rukn ed-Din Imamzada. "Be silent," the latter answered him. "It is the wind of God's omnipotence that bloweth, and we have no power to speak." [1]

Later popular imagination was to return to this conception. One romanticized account places it in the mouth of Chingis-khan himself. As he entered the town, the Conqueror is said to have ridden his horse into the cathedral mosque. "He asked if it was the Sultan's palace. He was told it was the house of Allah. He dismounted before the *mihrab,* mounted two or three steps of the *minbar,* and declared loudly: "The countryside is empty of fodder. Feed the horses." [2] People went to look for corn in the shops of the town. The cases containing the Korans were brought by the Mongols into the mosque courtyard to serve as feeding troughs, and the sacred books of the Moslems were trodden underfoot by the horses. The barbarians set down their jars of wine in the middle of the mosque, and brought in the singing girls of the town. They themselves sang till the walls resounded, and while they gave themselves over to celebration and debauch, the leading citizens, the doctors of the law, the leaders of religion, had to obey them as slaves and tend their horses. Then Chingis-khan made his way to the Place of Prayer (near the gate of Ibrahim), where on solemn occasions the inhabitants assembled to pray together. At his orders they had been assembled there. "He went up into the *minbar* and asked who were the richest persons in all this crowd. Two hundred and eighty were pointed out to him, of whom ninety were foreign merchants. He had them come forward and addressed them. Recapitulating the hostile acts that had forced him to take up arms against their sultan, he went on: 'O people, know that you have committed great sins, and that the great ones among you have committed these sins. If you ask me what proof I have for these words, I say it is because I am the punishment of God. If you had not committed great sins, God would not have sent a punishment like me upon you.' When he had finished speaking in this strain, he continued his discourse with words of admonition, saying, 'There is no need to declare your property that is on the face of

[1] [A. J. Boyle's translation of Juvaini. Cf. No. 7, p. 104.]
[2] [*Op. cit.,* p. 105.]

the earth; tell me of that which is in the belly of the earth.' Then he asked them who were their men of authority; and each man indicated his own people. To each of them he assigned a Mongol or Turk as *basqaq* in order that the soldiers might not molest them and, although not subjecting them to disgrace or humiliation, they began to exact money from these men; and when they delivered it up they did not torment them by excessive punishment or demanding what was beyond their power to pay." [3]

This, Juvaini's colorful, dramatized sequence, is not in the accounts of the other historians. What is certain is that grievous things took place. "It was a day of horror," wrote Ibn al-Athir, "there was nothing to be heard but the sobbing of men, women, and children torn apart forever, the Mongol troops sharing out the population. The barbarians did violence to the modesty of the women under the eyes of all their unfortunate menfolk, who in their powerlessness could only weep. Not a few chose death as preferable to the sight of these horrors. Among these were the *qadi* Sadr ed-Din-Khan, Rukn ed-Din Imamzada, and his son, who, forced to look on at the dishonoring of their women, provoked their own deaths by fighting." At the height of the pillage, a fire broke out that consumed most of the town (it was built of wood), with the exception of brick structures such as the cathedral mosque and one or two palaces.

[3] [Op. cit.]

61

Toward Samarkand

Chingis-khan left "the smoking ruins of Bukhara" to march on Samarkand. He moved up the Zerafshan valley, all country houses, gardens, orchards, fine meadows, watered by many canals. Two forts alone—Dabusiya and Sar-i-Pul—attempted resistance. He left detachments to take them, and continued on his way, accompanied by a vast train of citizens of captured towns or peasants of regions he had passed through, whom the Mongol horsemen drove before them to serve in the coming sieges: any who could no longer keep up with the horses were promptly killed.

Samarkand lies four and a half miles south of the Zerafshan. Numerous canals (*ariq*), running off from the river, ensure the loess of the oasis its fertility, which contrasts sharply with the aridity, the bareness, of the countryside around. As all Transoxanian towns, Samarkand was made up of three parts, ranged here south to north. In the south, the citadel (*quhandriz*), then the town proper (*shahristan*), then, lastly, the suburb (*rabad*). The thirteenth-century *shahristan* stood on the site of Afrasiyab, north of the present town. The town was surrounded by a wide wall pierced by four gates, including, on the east, the China gate, its name recalling the ancient relations of Transoxania with the Silk Road, and, on the south, the Greater Gate (*Bab kish*), near which lay the bazaar quarter—notably the metalworkers' section—the caravansaries and the warehouses. This was the most populous quarter, but the whole community numbered some five hundred thousand inhabitants. Despite the crowding of the workers' quarters and the bazaar, Samarkand was very much spread out, a great deal of space being given to gardens, with every house of any size set in its own. The many irrigation canals had made possible indeed considerable horticultural development. "The delights of Samarkand," as one came on it out of the desert, lay above all in its flowers, and in the charm of its canals, its ponds and fountains. Arab geographers have praise also for its monuments, notably the cathedral-mosque, the ruins of which have been found by Barthold to the west of the citadel, in the Afrasiyab quarter.

The looms of Samarkand were famous throughout the Orient. They produced the famous silver-lamé fabrics of Samarkand (*simghuns*), and also tents used by caravans all over central Asia. The metalworkers' quarter exported vases in copper and cups of marvelous elegance; the saddlers' quarter, harnesses vied for from Kashghar to Shiraz. Another specialty of Samarkand workshops was rag paper, the technique of making which had been learned from the Chinese in the eighth century, and which took the place, in the Moslem countries, of papyrus and parchment. Samarkand further exported silks and cottons and even garden produce: "Samarkand melons, in lead boxes packed in snow, were sold as far away as Baghdad."

Such was the great city Chingis-khan, in this month of May 1220, came to lay siege to. The sultan of Khwarezm had left there a garrison of some fifty thousand Turks commanded by his uncle Tughay-khan. The fortifications of the wall, and especially those of the citadel, had been repaired and increased. The Conqueror accordingly acted circumspectly. He was rejoined near the town by the three other sections of his army, who, the conquest of Transoxania behind them, brought him enormous contingents of prisoners to serve in his siege operations. Thus his sons Jaghatay and Ögödei, who had just taken Otrar, drove before them people of the middle Sir-darya. All the captives were divided into groups of ten, each group bearing a standard, as if these were Mongol warriors, a trick to deceive the defenders as to the strength (in any case in itself very considerable) of the besieging army.

Chingis-khan, who had set up his headquarters in the Blue Palace (*Kök-seray*), in the suburb, spent two preliminary days making a personal inspection of the place and examining its fortifications. The third day he gave his troops the order to move in, pushing before them the unfortunate prisoners disguised as soldiers. The townsmen—Tajiks, for the most part—came out to fight. The Mongols, adopting their usual tactics, withdrew, and lured into an ambush this improvised militia, foot soldiers that their cavalry had no difficulty cutting to pieces: nearly fifty thousand Samarkandis died.

This defeat sapped the defenders' courage. The Qanqli mercenaries, who made up the greater part of the garrison, thought that, as Turks, they would be treated by the Mongols as compatriots. The fifth day of the siege, they presented themselves at the Mongol camp, complete with baggage and families, Tughay-khan at their head. Deserted by the garrison, the townsfolk could only surrender in their turn. The *qadi* and the *sheikh-ul-islam* came to Chingis-khan with a message to that effect. They took back satisfactory guarantees enough, and opened the gates. The Mongols made their entry into Samarkand by the northwest gate, the "Prayer Gate," on March 17, 1220. They proceeded at once to demolish the ramparts. As always in such cases, the inhabitants were made to evacuate the town, so that the Mongols might pillage more freely. Chingis-khan had given safeguards not only to the *qadi* and the *sheikh-ul-islam,* but also to other doctors of the law and members of the Moslem priesthood, to a total of several thousand. These were scrupulously respected. The citadel still held out. The Mongols began by cutting off its water supply by blocking the canal serving it. Half the defenders—about a thousand men—succeeded in making their escape during the night. The rest gathered in the cathedral mosque for a last desperate resistance. All were killed, "to the last man," and the mosque burned down.

As for the Turkish mercenaries who had given themselves up in the first instance, they had miscalculated. We know how great a horror Chingis-khan had of treason. He had all put to death, thirty thousand of them, including their chief, Tughay. The townspeople, mainly Tajiks, were better treated. Doubtless Chingis-khan respected these citizens for their courage and their loyalty to their prince. He contented himself with commandeering the craftsmen, in all thirty thousand, whom he apportioned among the *ordus* of his sons, his wives, and his high officers. An equal number of men were requisitioned for military tasks. There remained some fifty thousand prisoners. These Chingis-khan allowed to buy back their freedom for 200,000 dinars.

62

At Urgenj: Attack Through a Town in Flames

The Mongols had a great deal more difficulty in taking the capital of Khwarezm proper, the town of Urgenj, the former Gurganj.

Urgenj lay near the delta of the Amu-darya on the Aral Sea, some ninety miles northwest of Khiwa. Here also a system of *ariqs,* or derivation canals, carefully maintained, assured the fertility of the oasis in a region disputed by marsh and sand. The town was famous in the thirteenth century for its silk manufactures, and also as a trading center and caravan stage—a role that had brought it considerable wealth. The Turkish garrison were resolved to fight to the end. Their attitude was shared by the civilian population, profoundly attached to the Khwarezmian dynasty.

Chingis-khan sent against Urgenj a powerful army, commanded by three of his sons, Jöchi, Jaghatay, and Ögödei, backed by veteran generals such as Bo'orchu, Tolun-cherbi, and Qada'an, in all, apparently, some fifty thousand men. Jöchi tried to persuade the inhabitants to surrender without a fight. "He sent word to them that his father had granted him Khwarezm proper as his domain, that he wanted to preserve its capital intact, that it would pain him to see it destroyed, and that he was giving proof already of his good intentions in treating with care the gardens and suburbs." But his invitation had no success.

Since the countryside, all marsh or sands, furnished no stones for projectiles, the Mongols cut down the mulberry trees of the town outskirts and hacked these into shape to fill the bill. Then, they made the prisoners fill in the moat, an operation completed in ten days. As soon as this had been done they began to mine the walls, but after that they had still then to conquer the town quarter by quarter, or rather street by street. In this new kind of war for them, they used pails of petroleum with which they set fire to the houses. But the town was cut in two by the Amu-darya. Three thousand Mongols hurled themselves on the bridge spanning the river. They were repulsed, and died to a man, which did not fail to raise the spirits of the defenders.

Behind the Mongol failure lay the poor relations between Jöchi and Jaghatay. The two brothers, as has been seen, detested each other. On the eve of the expedition's setting forth, they had only just been prevented from flying at each other's throats. The siege of Urgenj revived their quarrel. Jöchi, who knew that the town would form part of his portion, sought, as we have seen, to spare it damage. Jaghatay reproached him violently for this. The discipline of the troops suffered from their ill feeling. They finally took their grievances to their father. Chingis-khan, greatly displeased with them, answered by placing them both under the authority of their brother Ögödei, a measure in line with the recent decision about the succession. The Conqueror did the right thing. "Ögödei contrived by his gentle reasoning to restore harmony between the two brothers, and by his severity to restore the troops to the discipline that made them invincible."

The attack was resumed. Hell raged. Women, children, old men, knowing they could now expect no mercy, threw themselves into the defense and never drew breath. The Mongols went on bombarding the houses, now so many fortresses, with vessels of flaming petroleum. In the light of the fires, the attackers advanced in waves over piles of horrifyingly burned corpses. At last, after seven days, the defenders, at bay in the last three districts still surviving the flames, sent the *faqih* 'Ali ed-Din Khayyati to beseech Jöchi's mercy. "Show us your mercy having shown us your fury!" But Jöchi was now exasperated by the losses inflicted on his army: "How can they speak thus, when it is their fury that has killed so many of my soldiers! It is for us now in our turn to show them our anger!" He made the whole population go out into the plain. The young women and children were taken as slaves. The craftsmen were set aside to be deported to Mongolia, to serve the khan. The entire remainder of the masculine population was divided up among the Mongol companies and ruthlessly slaughtered by arrow and scimitar. As a finishing touch the

Mongols breached the dykes containing the waters of the Amu-darya, and submerged the town (April 1221).

If we are to believe the Mongol epic, Chingis-khan was highly dissatisfied at the lack of dispatch with which his sons (Jöchi in particular) had gone about their taking of the town. And to add insult to injury, they had shared out among the three of them prisoners and spoils, without reserving for their father his lion's share.

When, the town finally taken, they waited on him, he refused for three days to give them audience. His old companions, Bo'orchu and Shigi-qutuqu, had to intervene in their favor: "The taking of Urgenj has increased our power. The *Sart*[1] is defeated, your great army rejoices. Why, O khan, are you still angry? Your sons have acknowledged their fault and are full of repentance. Show clemency, and pardon them." Chingis-khan then allowed himself to be mollified a little, and received the three princes, but not without delivering himself of a severe reprimand. As they stood before him not daring to move, the sweat of fear on their foreheads, the three "quiver bearers," Qongqay, Qongtaqar, and Chor-maghan, interceded in their turn: "As young hawks about to be trained for hunting, the three princes came out to learn the trade of war. Why do you reprimand them in this way on their return? From the rising to the setting sun we have a world of enemies. Unleash us your savage Tibetan dogs, and with the aid of Heaven and the goddess Earth we shall vanquish these peoples, we shall bring you back gold and silver and silks and riches, and we will conquer for you populations and towns. Do you wish us to go to attack the Khalif of Baghdad?" These words finally appeased the Conqueror. In fact, only Jaghatay and Ögödei had rejoined their father, and their relations with him were ever after perfectly affectionate. Jöchi, after the fall of Urgenj, stayed on in that region and the steppes of the present-day Kazakstan that constituted his territory. He lived there apart, taking no further hand in the war, and his relations with Chingis-khan grew, as we shall see, steadily cooler.

[1] [Central Asian name for Moslems.]

Manhunt: On the Track of the Sultan

While his empire crumbled, Sultan Mohammed of Khwarezm, aghast at the catastrophe his ill faith and arrogance had so deliberately provoked, and veering between the wildest boasting and total prostration, had first not reacted at all, then fled south of the Amu-darya, toward Balkh. Thence, he reached eastern Khorassan, sought refuge there at Nishapur, and finally, more and more terrified, scurried to Qazwin, in the northeast of Iraq-'Ajemi, at the opposite end of his domains.

But Chingis-khan pursued him with relentless hate, born of the slaughter of his envoy, that day when the Mongol caravan was sacked at Otrar. "Wherever he betakes himself," he declared to the *qadi* Wahid ed-Din Bujhenji, "I will rout him out. I will devastate any country that gives him refuge!" He unleashed in pursuit of the fugitive his two best officers, Jebe and Sübötei, and also Toquchar, bidding them take twenty thousand of his horses. And the epic hunt was on.

Jebe and Sübötei crossed the Amu-darya north of Balkh. Up here, the width of the river varies greatly: at the chalk barrier of Kelif, it narrows from 5,000 feet to 1,500 feet. The two Mongol generals came to the other bank, in any case, without bridge or ferry, doubtless in the manner described by Plano Carpini: the soldiers rolled effects and equipment in leather bundles that floated like leather bottles, which they then attached to the tails of their horses and clung on to as the horses swam across.

Landing on the southern bank of the Amu-darya, Jebe and Sübötei were in what is now Afghan Turkestan, in the vicinity of Balkh. The dignitaries of the town sent a delegation to them with gifts. The two generals had orders from Chingis-khan not to hold up their pursuit taking towns, but make capturing the sultan their absolute priority. Faithful to their instructions, they declared themselves content with the protestations of friendship of the people of Balkh, and pressed on westward toward the Persian province of Khorassan, where they had been advised the sultan was to be found. Their colleague Toquchar, however, failed to resist the temptation of pillage. He was relying doubtless on his personal position, having married a daughter of Chingis-khan. But the Conqueror was not to be trifled with in matters of discipline. He spoke of nothing less than of having his son-in-law beheaded, and at all events relieved him of his command.

Meanwhile, Jebe, covering in a few days over 430 miles, had arrived before Nishapur. He sent for the local authorities and handed them a proclamation from Chingis-khan, in Uyghur script, very expressive of the Conqueror's state of mind. "Commanders, important men, people," ran this document, "know that God [the *Tengri*] has given me from east to west, the empire of the world. Whoever shall submit shall be spared, but woe to those who resist: they will be slaughtered, with their wives, children, and all their dependents." Despite the threatening terms of this, the Mongol general did not break his march to attack the town. The other great city of Khorassan, lying a little farther east, was Tus, near what is now Meshed, on the Kashaf-rud, "the River of Turtles." It also was served by a system of irrigation canals, assuring the fertility of its fruit trees. Arab geographers speak of its manufactures (its striped textiles were famous) and its turquoise mines. Sübötei here again asked only a purely formal submission to be on his way, but the magistrates making him an insolent reply, he went into the town—without any great difficulty, apparently—and proceeded with the regulation massacre.

Jebe and he set out again at once, ever fiercely determined to come on traces of the sultan. Acting on information received, they followed the track that, still, today, serves nothern Khorassan, north of the great salt desert, by Sebzevar, Shahrud, and Damghan, whence it runs on to Iraq-'Ajemi, and through Semnan to the present-day Teheran. The towns that offered resistance, such as Damghan and Semnan, were sacked by Sübötei, who, from Semnan, marched directly on Ray, while Jebe made a detour by Mazenderan, where he sacked Amol. The two generals joined up before Ray. Since they left Nishapur, they had come over 430 miles.

Ray, the former Rhages, five miles southeast of our Teheran, was the greatest town of Persian Iraq. It exported all over the East its silk materials and its magnificent polychrome ceramic ware, decorated with exquisite miniatures. The Mongols, swooping in a surprise attack, killed many people in the outskirts; in the town itself the *qadi* tried to parley with them, but could not prevent their sacking the bazaar and killing many there. But here again the Mongols did not tarry. They had just learned that the sultan, still fleeing before them, was now in the northwest, at Resht, on the shores of the Caspian, in the province of Ghilan.

Their information was correct. But at the news of the sack of Ray, the sultan, instead of assembling the few hundred thousand troops the Persian provinces offered to put at his disposal, once again lost his head. Such indeed was the terror the Mongols inspired that part of his men deserted him. He rushed from Resht to Qazwin, where one of his sons had mustered a force of thirty thousand. With this, it would still have been possible for him to harass the Mongols, who moved scouring the country in isolated detachments, but once again the "Mongol terror" operated, and far from attempting to surprise his enemies it was he who, near Qarun, was all but taken by surprise by them. His horse was hit by arrows and he himself barely escaped. Thinking then to take refuge in Baghdad, he galloped to Hamadan with the fearsome Mongol horsemen ever on his tail, and indeed, in the suburbs of that town, actually skirmished with their troops, but without their recognizing him. Now he had once again changed his mind, and was trying to head back to the Caspian. This sharp switch of direction threw Jebe and Sübötei for a while off his track. He was thus able to reach the shore of the Mazenderan. But the Mongols had already picked up the trail again. Their advance guard was almost on him. He had just time to throw himself into a boat and gain the open sea under a volley of arrows. He took refuge on the little island of Abeskun, near the mouth of the Gurgan, west of Astrabad. Here the erstwhile potentate of Islam, one-time sultan of Turkestan, Afghanistan, and Persia, died of despair and exhaustion in January 1221.

The man who had dared defy Chingis-khan, had massacred his caravaneers and refused satisfaction, was no more. The mission with which the Conqueror had charged Jebe and Sübötei was accomplished. If they had not been able to take the sultan alive, they had harried him like a hunted animal till he dropped, finished. They, on the contrary, despite their fantastic chase—since crossing the Amu-darya they had traveled at the gallop over a thousand miles—were as fresh as the day they set out.

And, their task accomplished, Chingis-khan immediately assigned them another: to press on, in an immense reconnaissance sortie, around the Caspian Sea, across northwest Persia, the Caucasus, and Southern Russia.

We shall tell the story later of this unbelievable ride. Meantime, we have to retrace our steps to accompany the Conqueror of the World across the Afghan mountains. The Chingis-khan of this campaign, seen, as just now at Bukhara and Samarkand, through Arabo-Persian sources, comes across, it must be confessed, somewhat differently from the hero of the coverage of the first part of his life in the Mongol epics. This is the difference in sources at work, of course, Arab and Persian annalists being unable to forget the depredations wrought on the lands of Islam by the man they looked on as the Attila of the Moslem world. But there is more to it than that. The Chingis-khan of the Mongol bard's portrayal is not indeed belied. The Mongol hero remains the same demigod, generous, magnanimous, and great, moderate in all things, balanced, rooted in common sense, human, in a word, even humane, that he has ever been. He has taken up arms only in the justest of causes, because the Khwarezmians have massacred his caravans and slain his ambassadors. But this righteous war the Mongols have been driven to, they fight Mongol style, as the nomads they are, and also as the half-savages of remote steppe or *tayga*. There is no contradiction here. Chingis-khan continues to show himself personally the equal of the greatest of the "makers of history;" it is not his fault if the Mongol Alexander commands troops of the approximate level of cultural development of redskins of the seventeenth-century American prairie.

Which courtesies having been observed in respect to strict historical objectivity, let us make no bones about our horror at the appalling butchery. Lock, stock, and barrel—need we say it?—we are with the Arabo-Persian civilization that the barbarians set out—and failed, heaven be praised—to annihilate.

64

The Wind of Anger Blows over Khorassan

After the taking of Samarkand, Chingis-khan passed the heat of the summer of 1220 south of that town, at Nasaf, the present-day Qarshi, which is indeed, at that season, the most pleasant place to be in Transoxania. The oasis, well sheltered by the Hissar mountains, has, compared to Samarkand, the advantage of foliage and shade, and its magnificent gardens surpass those of the Transoxanian capital. In these grasslands, the Conqueror let his horses recuperate, weary after so long continually on the move. In the autumn, he moved towards the Amu-darya and came to lay siege to the town on the northern bank of the river, opposite Balkh, Termez or Tirmihd. "The high officials having refused to open the gates, the town was carried by storm the eleventh day. All the inhabitants were forced to come out, and were divided up among the Mongol companies to be slaughtered. One old woman, just about to receive the fatal blow, cried out that, if they did not kill her, she would give a fine pearl. They asked her for it. She replied that she had swallowed it. At once they slit open her stomach, and pulled out, in fact, several pearls. Thinking others' might perhaps have swallowed pearls, Chingis-khan gave the order to slit open all the dead." [1]

Meantime, as we have seen, the wings of the Mongol army were on the move harrying the enemy everywhere; in Khwarezm, Jöchi, Jaghatay, and Ögödei were taking Urgenj; in Persia, Jebe and Sübötei were hunting to his death the defeated sultan. Chingis-khan, who from the banks of the Amu-darya directed operations over-all, spent the winter of 1220-21

[1] [A paraphrase of Juvaini's account. Cf. No. 7, p. 129.]

upriver from Qarshi, at Sali-Saray. It was not until the spring of 1221 that he crossed the river near Balkh and embarked on decisive conquest of Afghan Turkestan, the ancient Bactria, of which Balkh was the capital, then on conquest, or rather, destruction, of Khorassan.

Balkh, once Bactria, has always tempted conquerors. An oasis of irrigation in the midst of desert steppe, it had hitherto survived all invasions behind its wall of beaten earth, seven and a half miles around. As already recounted, Jebe and Sübötei, who had made an earlier appearance before the town, had been content with a purely formal submission. At the approach of Chingis-khan, the prominent citizens came to do homage to him. But then the Mongol sovereign, fearing the town might become a rallying point for his enemies, ordered all its inhabitants to come forth, ostensibly to be counted, and massacred them. The fortresses of the region that attempted resistance were taken one after the other, always by the same method, of making a bevy of prisoners fight in the front ranks, those who hung back being killed.

Meantime, Chingis-khan had sent his fourth son, Toluy, to conquer, or complete the conquest of, Khorassan. Jebe and Sübötei, who had ridden across the country the previous year, had here also merely extracted nominal submissions. This time, the conquest was really driven home.

Khorassan, the name of which, in Persian, signifies "the East" (of Persia), is a long strip of steppe scattered with oases, watered by streams running down from the ranges of Paropanisad, Pusht-i-Koh, and Binalud, that then promptly lose themselves in the great desert that, there as elsewhere, gnaws at all the interior of the plateau of Iran. Cultivation, that is, is possible there only by dint of unremitting work maintaining the irrigation canals, and defending against the encroaching steppe the gardens, orchards, vineyards, the corn, rice and barley fields, the screens of elm and poplar, that constitute "the smile of Khorassan." By the period of our story, long centuries of patient toiling had secured the country wealth, and out of the soil of this material prosperity had blossomed the flower of Persian culture. Near Tus was born the Homer of Persia, the immortal Firdusi, author of the epic of the *Shahnameh;* Tus was the birthplace also of the philosopher Ghazali, "the Moslem Pascal"; Nishapur nurtured the poet Omar Khayyam, whose pessimistic sensualism is clothed in all the grace of oriental lyricism.

With the advent of Prince Toluy and his nomad warriors in these privileged oases there ensued one of the most grievous dramas in human history: destruction of a culture, and with it destruction of the oases themselves, "the death of the earth."

The first town to suffer the blow was Nisa, near Ashkabad. This, too, was an oasis possessed of the supreme treasure: ample water, and, in consequence, much verdure and many gardens (it crouched at the northern edge of the Kopet-dagh range, whence flowed many streams). "The ten gates of the town were drowned in foliage," which to the traveler fresh from the sinister Black Sands (Qara-qum) of Turkmenistan, must have seemed "a contrast virtually miraculous." Toluy sent against Nisa a force of ten thousand Mongols, under Toquchar, Chingis-khan's son-in-law, now restored to favor. By this time the Mongols, the sieges of so many towns behind them, had made astonishing progress in the art of this kind of warfare, especially in ballistics. "Against the walls of Nisa, Toquchar brought into action a battery of twenty catapults worked by captives and conscripts. These unfortunates were also made to advance the battering rams, those who hung back being slain. After two weeks' unremitting attack, the engines having made a wide breach, the Mongols made themselves, during the night, masters of the wall. At dawn, they entered the town and drove out the inhabitants. When the latter were all in the plain, they ordered them to tie themselves together with their hands behind their backs. The unfortunates obeyed without thinking what they were doing. If they had scattered and fled to the mountains close by, most of them would have escaped. When they were tied, the Mongols surrounded them and shot them down with arrows, men, women, and children indiscriminately. The number of the dead was about seventy thousand."

Toquchar then moved on Nishapur. This was one of the finest towns in Persia, the capital of the province of Khorassan, then at the height of its prosperity. From the River Sanghawar, which flows down the range of Binalud, to the north of the town, the beneficent water was channeled by twelve canals, and worked, the Arab geographers affirm, twelve mills. "Not only all the gardens, but also most of the houses, had abundant provision of water." The fields of the oasis yielded rice and cereals, the outskirts were famous for their turquoise mines. Politically, lastly, Nishapur still remembered the time not long ago when it had been one of the capitals of Iran under the great Seljuq sultans.

Jebe, a few months earlier, had confined himself to "lecturing" the town. Toquchar attempted to storm it, but he was killed on the third day of the attack by an arrow from the ramparts (November 1220). The general who succeeded him, judging that he had not sufficient strength to take the town, withdrew, deferring vengeance. In the meantime, he divided his troops into two parts. With one he marched on Sebzevar, a town some sixty-two miles to the west of Nishapur, took it in three days, and slew the entire population, seventy thousand persons. The other division made toward Tus and took the fortresses of the area, putting all the inhabitants to the sword.

Toluy himself did not enter the fray till the beginning of the following year. He moved at first on Merv, the great oasis of the lower Murghab. The industrial and commercial activity of this town explained the important role it had played politically in the preceding century as capital of the Seljuq sultan Sanjar. The oasis was celebrated for fine cotton which it exported, unworked or woven; and for the attention given to sericulture, with the export both of raw silk and silk textiles. The weavers' quarter, and those of the coppersmiths and potters, were ports of call for caravans from all over the Middle East. One of the marvels of the town was the mausoleum of Sanjar, the great turquoise blue cupola of which could be seen a day's march away.

Toluy arrived before Merv with an army of seventy thousand men, in part made up of conscripts from the conquered territories. Two sallies by the defenders having failed, they offered their surrender (February 25, 1221). Toluy ordered the inhabitants to come out from Merv, with the most precious of their possessions. Seated in the plain, on a gilded seat, he first had brought before him the soldiers of the garrison, and saw them beheaded. Then it was the turn of the civilian population. Men, women, and children were separated. The air rang with their sobs and lamentations. These unfortunate people were apportioned among the troops and almost all slaughtered. Only four hundred craftsmen were spared, and a certain number of children of both sexes, intended as slaves. The two hundred richest of the citizens, merchants or owners of land, were tortured until they declared where they had hidden their treasure.

The Mongols destroyed the dam on the Murghab that assured the irrigation round about, and the flourishing oasis reverted to desert. Of the former city of the Arabian Nights, there remained only a few mounds where the palaces had stood, enormous piles of glazed bricks, and the ruins of the brick wall and towers of the "Fortress of the Sultan" (Sultan-qal'a). Sole memorial more or less intact to a glorious past, the mosque of Sandar was left raising its stripped dome to heaven.

From Merv, Toluy passed to Nishapur, twelve days' march away. The young Chingiskhanid burned to avenge the death of his brother-in-law Toquchar, slain by the inhabitants five months before. The latter, aware that they could expect no mercy, had done their utmost to reinforce their walls. "Their ramparts were furbished with three thousand ballistas or machines for hurling lances, and three hundred catapults. The Mongols made no less substantial preparations. They brought up three thousand ballistas, three hundred catapults, seven hundred machines for throwing burning naphtha, four thousand ladders, and two thousand five hundred charges of stone." Confronted with such "artillery," the defenders soon lost heart: a delegation came to Toluy imploring mercy. The latter refused all compromise and ordered the attack. Battle was waged all day and all night. At morning, the moats were filled in, the wall was breached in seventy places, and ten thousand Mongols had scaled it. On every side the troops of Toluy pushed into the town, and streets and houses were for the rest of the day so many battlefields. On Saturday, April 10, 1221, Nishapur was completely in the hands of the Mongols.

Toquchar's widow, daughter of Chingis-khan, then made her solemn entry into the town with an escort of ten thousand men "who slaughtered indiscriminately all they saw." The carnage went on for four days. Even dogs and cats were killed. Toluy had heard that when Merv was sacked, many of the inhabitants saved their lives by lying down among the dead. To make quite sure this time he ordered decapitation of all the corpses. Pyramids of heads were built of different "materials": pyramids of men's heads, of women's, of children's. . . . "The destruction of the town went on for two weeks." Toluy left alive only, as was his custom, the principal skilled craftsmen—four hundred of them—to deport for work in Mongolia.

The daughter of the Conqueror could leave Nishapur her soul at peace, Toquchar had been avenged.

From Nishapur, Toluy moved southeast—south of the chain of Paro-pamisus—to lay siege to the town of Herat, another oasis amid the

steppes and deserts, or rather center of the line of oases running along
125 miles of the valley of the Herirud: "The villages succeed one another each side of the mountains, surrounded by corn fields, vineyards,
orchards; here and there, the Aleppo pine and the elm lend variety to the
landscape; along the rivers, poplars grow in veritable woods." The Mongols sent into Herat with a summons to surrender. The governor executed their messenger, and for eight days the town held out against all
assaults. But the same governor having been killed, the Iranian burgesses
offered to surrender on condition their lives were spared. Toluy promised
this and kept his word. He contented himself with massacring the Turkish soldiers of the garrison, twelve thousand men. Then he set out to
rejoin Chingis-khan under the walls of Talaqan.

▲
▲▲

65

Storm over Afghanistan

After taking Balkh and Talaqan, Chingis-khan had gone off to spend the summer of 1221 in the mountains of Bactria. Then he moved southward and crossed the high mountain barrier that runs almost unbroken east to west from the Hindu-kush to the Paropanisads to divide the former Bactria from central Afghanistan. At the heart of this mountain network, just where on the north the Paropamisus joins the Hindu-kush, while on the south this chain is continued by that of Kɔh-i-baba, the town of Bamiyan held a position of major strategic importance. Places charged with history, starting from the high cliff honeycombed with the former Buddhist grottoes, whose giant statues, 116 to 176 feet high, looked out—as they had done for almost ten centuries—over the fresh valley of the Bamiyan, with its water courses, its tilled fields, its clumps of poplar and willow. Opposite the Buddhist cliff, on the plateau of Shar-i-golgola, rose "like a solitary sentinel" the thirteenth-century Moslem citadel.

No fortress was to cost the Conqueror more dear. One of his grandsons whom he greatly loved, Mütügen, son of Jaghatay, was killed by a defender's arrow. Impatient to avenge him, Chingis-khan ordered the attack. He took part himself, "bareheaded," a later chronicle was to declare. His troops, fired by his anger, took the fortress by scaling the walls. He ordered that every living thing, man or beast, should be killed, the child slain in its mother's womb; that no booty should be taken, everything should be inexorably destroyed, so that, after this day of death, no creature should ever again inhabit the place, which became known as the "Town Accursed." His orders were carried out to the letter, and the desolation of Shar-i-golgola today still bears witness to the Conqueror's grief and anger. "On the drear, deserted hillside," writes M.

Dollot, "nothing has changed since those tragic days. I climbed the difficult path to the top between the ruins, among which still rise a few stretches of keep wall, last remaining trace of the citadel, simple mud walling that seven centuries of the inclemencies of this climate have not reduced. In the grim chaos one catches the sparkle, among the pebbles once incorporated in the buildings and the homely bits of earthenware, of fragments of glazed faience bearing the decorative motifs of Persian ceramic ware."

The siege of Bamiyan has an epilogue, an episode vividly characteristic of the Mongol Conqueror. "When the young Mütügen was killed, his father Jaghatay was not there. He returned when they were demolishing Bamiyan. Chingis-khan ordered Mütügen's death to be hidden from him. A pretext was accordingly found to account to Jaghatay for the young prince's absence. A few days later Chingis-khan, at table with his three sons, Jaghatay, Ögödei, and Toluy, flew into a pretended rage with them, accusing them of no longer being obedient to his commands, and, as he spoke, gazed fixedly at Jaghatay. Affeared, Jaghatay went on his knees and protested that he would die rather than disobey his father. Chingis-khan accused him in the same fashion several times, and asked him finally: 'But do you speak the truth? Would you keep your word?' 'If I fail to do so,' cried Jaghatay, 'may I die!' 'Well,' Chingis-khan replied, 'your son Mütügen has been killed, and I forbid you to show any sign of grief.' Struck as by a thunderbolt, Jaghatay yet had the strength to hold back his tears, but after the meal he went out to give way a moment to his grief."

Meantime, the fugitive heir to the former Khwarezmian empire, Prince Jalal ed-Din, had found sanctuary about ninety miles to the southeast of Bamiyan at Ghazni, a veritable eagle's nest, a spur of rock, rising in solitary isolation from the high steppe of the Ghilzai country that is dominated to the north, at 7,600 feet, by a new tangle of mountains running to the Koh-i-baba horizon line. At Ghazni, Jalal ed-Din rallied an army of ten thousand horsemen, Turkish mercenaries and native Afghans. A Mongol detachment that was laying siege to a fortress in the nearby mountains was cut to pieces with the loss of a thousand men.

Chingis-khan, learning of the reappearance of Jalal ed-Din, had sent a reconnaissance force out in this direction of between thirty and forty-five thousand men, under the command of his adoptive brother, Shigi-qutuqu. The clash came near Parvan—not, probably, the present town in the Pandshu valley, north of Kabul, but an older site of similar name at the headwaters of the Lugar, south of the Afghan capital. Battle was waged all day without any decisive result, and, toward night, the two armies retired each to its own camp. During the night Shigi-qutuqu, to make the enemy believe he had received reinforcements, ordered each Mongol horseman to set a felt dummy on his led horse. This stratagem almost succeeded, for next day Jalal ed-Din's officers, seeing the Mongol cavalry mustered for the fray in a double line, thought other detachments had joined up with it, and spoke of retreat. But Jalal ed-Din stood firm. He had his horsemen dismount, and each man tie his horse's reins to his belt, then he awaited, impassively, the Mongol attack.

And battle recommenced. The Mongol cavalry charged, but was met by a cloud of arrows that drove it back to re-form. A second charge was on the point of breaking the enemy lines, when Jalal ed-Din sounded a trumpet. All his troops remounted, and, exploiting their numerical superiority, hurled themselves on the Mongols with great shouts, extending their line to encircle them. "Shigi-qutuqu had urged his side not to lose sight of his *tuq,* his standard, but, seeing themselves surrounded, they fled in disorder, and the plain being cut across with gullies and their horses falling into these, they were sabered by the better-mounted horsemen of Jalal ed-Din, so that the greater part of the Mongol army was destroyed." The victors distinguished themselves by atrocities crueler even than the armies of Chingis-khan could be accused of. One of the ways they amused themselves was hammering nails into the Mongol prisoners' ears.

Parvan had seen the invincible Mongols put to flight. Was the charm broken? Chingis-khan, on hearing of his officer's defeat, displayed the self-control that was one of the secrets of his genius. He declared calmly that Shigi-qutuqu, spoiled by victory hitherto, should profit by his lesson. But he acted promptly. He made at once for Ghazni, with such speed his troops had for two days no time to cook their rations. Reaching the battlefield, he had Shigi-qutuqu explain to him the disposition of the two armies. He found fault with the measures he had taken, reproached him with not having dictated a better site for the battle, and, despite his affection for him, declared him responsible for the defeat.

But Chingis-khan arrived at Ghazni to find Jalal ed-Din departed. The latter's troops, in fact, after their unexpected victory at Parvan, had dispersed on account of a misunderstanding between Afghans and Turks. Jalal ed-Din, knowing he could not defend Ghazni against the great Mongol army, had made for the Indo-Afghan frontier to take refuge in the Punjab. Chingis-khan, forcing his marches again, came up with him in the middle of the night on the banks of the Indus as the Khwarezmian prince was making his preparations to cross in the morning (November 24, 1221). "The little army of Jalal ed-Din was at once surrounded by the Mongol forces in a semicircle several lines deep with each of its ends on the Indus. At daybreak, the signal was given to attack. The Mongols bore down on the enemy troops, drove in on them and cut to pieces the two wings. Jalal ed-Din was left in the center with seven hundred men and fought the fight of the desperate. The half-circle of the Mongols closed in steadily on him, but, curiously, without shooting at him: Chingis-khan wanted to take him alive. The Khwarezmian prince fought till midday. At last, seeing that he could not pierce the enemy lines, he jumped on a fresh horse, and, to get himself clearance, made a last furious charge; the Mongols drew back just a little. It was what he wanted. Turning at once, he galloped to the Indus, jumped his horse into it from a height of twenty feet, and, shield on back, standard in hand, swam across. At this Chingis-khan ran to the bank. He stopped his troops who wanted to plunge into the water after Jalal ed-Din, and, pointing out the latter to his sons, told them this was a man on whom they should model themselves."

Notwithstanding this display of generosity, or rather of chivalrous admiration, toward the one adversary in this campaign who had stood up to him, Chingis-khan so far as Jalal ed-Din's followers were concerned made no departure from his usual harshness. He riddled with arrows those of the prince's soldiers who had thrown themselves in the river after him, and meted out a like fate to the rest of his army that had stayed on the bank. Jalal ed-Din's two sons, who had fallen into Mongol hands, were ruthlessly executed.

66

From the Destruction of Towns to the Revelation of Urban Civilization

Chingis-khan did not pursue on to Indian soil the heir to the Khwarez-mian throne. Not until the following year did a Mongol detachment, under Balanoyan, of the Jalairs, make an incursion on the eastern bank of the Indus, near Multan. This was a simple reconnaissance raid, of no serious military significance. The heat of the Punjab summer, hard on these folk of the Mongol steppe or Siberian *tayga,* was enough to make them raise the siege of Multan. They contented themselves with looting in the provinces of Multan and Lahore, and returned to join the main army in Afghanistan.

On the other hand, Chingis-khan made his vengeance felt on those unfortunate Afghan or Khorassanian towns that had associated them-selves, in whatever degree, with the attempted counterattack of Jalal ed-Din. In the spring of 1222, Ögödei went to punish Ghazni, which might serve as base for a renewed offensive if the exiled prince came back. He brought the inhabitants out on the pretext of counting them, then slaughtered them to a man, with the exception of the skilled craftsmen who, as usual, were taken to practice their trade in Mongolia. Ghazni was systematically razed.

Then the Mongols turned to Herat. At the news of the victory of Jalal ed-Din at Parvan, the inhabitants of Herat had revolted against Mongol overlordship. Chingis-khan sent against them an army commanded by Eljigidei, with additional reinforcements of some fifty thousand men of the neighboring militias, conscripted for the siege. The defenders, know-ing they could hope for no mercy, vigorously repelled the first assaults.

Then dissension arose among them, and Eljigidei profited by it to take the place (June 14, 1222). The entire population was put to the sword. "The Mongols did nothing for a week but kill, pillage, burn and demolish." When the Mongol army had gone, those of the inhabitants who had managed to survive the slaughter, hidden in the gorges and caves round about, returned to the ruins. The Mongols, who suspected this would happen, shortly afterward sent a squad of horsemen to Herat to exterminate these "returning ones."

At Merv, the sacking of the town by Toluy, systematic as it had seemed, had left certain quarters standing. Moreover, so fertile was the valley of the Murghab that after Toluy's departure the site had been rapidly peopled again. The news of the Battle of Parvan caused an explosion of joy among these unfortunate folk. They also believed that the hour of Khwarezmian revenge was come. Aided by former officers of Jalal ed-Din, they hastily rebuilt the wall, and the dam on the Murghab that assured the town water. The prefect the Mongols had left there (a Persian) was of course put to death. But here also in its own good time Mongol vengeance struck. A force of five thousand, under Dörbey, massacred the entire population and razed the last vestiges to rubble. The town of Balkh likewise was visited by a second and more total devastation, a new and more wholesale massacre.

Afghanistan, like Khorassan, was beyond participation now in any revolt. Towns were destroyed from pinnacle to cellar, as by an earthquake. Dams were similarly destroyed, irrigation channels cut and turned to swamp, seed burned, fruit trees sawn-off stumps. The screens of trees that had stood between the crops and invasion by the desert sands were down. The handiwork of thousands of years was leveled to steppe again; orchards were laid defenseless to the driving, all-penetrating sandstorms from steppe or desert. These oases of the singing names, in which had arisen the cities of the Arabian Nights, flower of the delicately wrought Arabo-Persian civilization, marvels of the ancient Orient, were nothing now but arid steppe, this by the nomads' aid making all once again its own. This was indeed, as after some cosmic catastrophe, "the death of the earth," and eastern Iran was never wholly to recover.

In the autumn of 1222, Chingis-khan, turning his back on these regions now forever laid waste, recrossed the Amu-darya and returned again to Transoxania, country relatively spared by comparison with

Khorassan. As he passed through Bukhara, he had the curiosity to have outlined to him the Moslem religion. A strange idea, it might seem, for a man at whose hands Islam had just suffered one of the most dire cataclysms in history. But Chingis-khan had never had the intention, or even the sense, of making war on Islam. As he saw it, as his soldiers saw it, he was punishing the Khwarezmians for the slaughter of his caravan and his ambassadors, chastising them for this crime against what we would call the freedom of trade, a violation of the law between nations. In the course of operations, he had punished them also for the deaths of his son-in-law and his favorite grandson. He had punished them after the Mongol fashion, which was primitive, after the only fashion known to his Mongols, the soldiery of a primitive people. Hence the astonishing contrast we have so continually stressed, between the horrifying butchery perpetrated by Chingis-khan's soldiers and the basic moderation, the rooted morality, the generosity within his own circle, of the Conqueror.

Now, then, he wished to learn about Islam. He caused to be expounded to him the principles of the Koran. He found them good, the Allah of the "believers" differing in fact, at bottom, not so very profoundly from the Turco-Mongol *Tengri*. He criticized the pilgrimage to Mecca, however, "seeing that the *Tengri* is everywhere." At Samarkand, he ordered the Koranic prayer, the *khotba*, to be said in his name, since he had taken the Sultan Mohammed's place as sovereign. Islam thus became one of his state religions, on a par with the shamanism of the Mongol sorcerers or the Nestorian Christianity of his Kereit daughter-in-law. The man whom the Islamic world, in horror at the destruction of Khorassan and Afghanistan, called now only "the Reprobate" or "the Accursed," proposed to be looked on by his new Moslem subjects as a sort of emperor of Islam and lawful sultan. He had, it is true, destroyed —with what root and branch fervor!—the urban civilization of Khorassan: but that did not mean he was sworn enemy to the regime of cities as such; the less so indeed in that he even now grasped in fact only imperfectly what this was, and had at first simply not conceived of it at all. He asked only to be instructed.

And indeed two Moslems who had come to Khwarezm from Urgenj, two Transoxanian Turks, products of the settled civilization, scholarly, Iranized men of law and government in the old Arabo-Persian tradition, Mahmud Yalavach and his son Mas'ud Yalavach, came forward as instructors prepared "to teach him the meaning of the towns"—for which read: the advantages inherent in urban agglomeration from the point of view of a nomad conqueror, and how to administer them so as to derive full benefit. The lesson interested him greatly—we have seen how one of his great qualities was this ability to listen—and he there and then took the two Moslems into his service. With acumen, he appointed them to administer, in conjunction with the *darughas* or Mongol prefects, the old cities of the two Turkestans, Bukhara, Samarkand, Kashghar, and Khotan.

The task thus assigned to the two Moslem men of learning marks a major juncture in the life of the Mongol conqueror: the point at which the nomad chief, hitherto completely ignorant of the conditions of urban civilization, begins to adapt himself to the consequences of his victory, to go to school with the old civilized empires of which he is now unexpectedly the heir, and of which he is to become, by force of circumstance, the perpetuator.

His friendship for the Chinese philosopher Ch'ang-ch'un is another, no less remarkable, aspect of his character, and, if one may put it so, of the trueness of his cultural ear.

Chingis-khan and the Problem of Death: The Summoning of the Alchemist

We have seen Chingis-khan, on the eve of his great expedition against the Khwarezmian empire, envisage the possibility of his death and the terms of his testament, though at the time he was still in full health and vigor. This idea of death seems, from that moment on, to have haunted him. In China he had heard tell of the "elixir of perpetual life," that mysterious draught the secret of which the Taoist thaumaturges possessed, and by which the lives of initiates might be indefinitely prolonged. Just at this, Chingis-khan's, time, also, North China was full of the extraordinary saintliness of a Taoist monk called K'ien Ch'ang-ch'un. Resolved to attach to his service so renowned a personage— whom he thought of doubtless as a kind of superior shaman—the Conqueror in 1219 sent for him to come to him at his camp, then in Nayman country.

In reality, Ch'ang-ch'un was something quite other than a common soothsayer. He was a thinker and a poet. Alchemical prescriptions in ancient Taoism were adjuncts of a philosophical system of astonishing power, a body of meditative metaphysical tradition of rarely equaled range and elevation.

"There was something formless yet complete," declares the *Book of Lao-tzu,* the Bible of the doctrine, "that existed before heaven and earth; without sound, without substance, dependent on nothing, unchanging, all pervading, unfailing. One may think of it as the mother of all things under heaven. Its true name we do not know; 'Way' is the by-name that we give it. Were I forced to say to what class of things it belongs I should call it Great." [1] The sage who, by meditation, has become one with it, has associated himself with the unnamed force that moves the worlds. He has made himself one with the universe. "Let the thunderbolt crash from the mountains, the hurricane tear up the ocean, the sage does not become anxious. He rides on the air and the clouds, bestrides the sun and the moon, he soars beyond space."

For Ch'ang-ch'un, of course, such images were self-evidently symbolic. For our good Mongols, however, as they heard tell of them, here were literal signs of those magic "powers" to which they sought the key. Chingis-khan was already, as his Persian historian was to write, "the Conqueror of the World." Now he would conquer the ancient secrets that would bend to his will the forces of heaven. And accordingly he sent for Ch'ang-ch'un.

[1] [Arthur Waley's translation of Chapter XXV, on p. 174 of *The Way and its Power, A Study of the Tao tê Ching and its Place in Chinese Thought.* (Grove Press, New York n.d.)]

To Join Chingis-khan:
Across Mongolia in 1221

The Taoist philosopher was seventy-two. Despite his age, he did not hesitate. When the Mongol officers appointed to organize the journey wished
him to travel, however, with a convoy of women intended for the pleasures of Chingis-khan, he found the company inappropriate and refused
point-blank. "I am a mere mountain savage. But I am not to be expected
to travel with harem girls." [1] His stipulation was complied with.

In March 1221 Ch'ang-ch'un left the province of Peking and plunged
into the steppes of what is now Inner Mongolia by the route that runs
along the western promontories of the Great Khingan from the Dolon-
nor to Lake Buyur. This is more or less desert steppe, with poor grass
and just a thin scattering of elm thickets, country unchanged in appearance since the description in the life of our traveler: "In the far distance
on every side we could see smoke rising from groups of black wagons
and white tents. The owners move from place to place in search of water
and pasturing-grounds. The country is here flat, marshy, and quite un-
wooded. Whichever way one looks, there is nothing to be seen but dark
clouds and pale grass." [2] Moving always directly north, the caravan
came, a little east of Lake Buyur, to the River Khalkha beside which
Chingis-khan, ten years before, had fought the Kereits. It was a sandy
river, its waters reaching only to the horses' girths, its banks willow-
covered. On April 24, the monk and his companions reached the camp,

---

[1] [No. 12, p. 54. All the passages so marked and taken from Ch'ang-ch'un's work
are reproduced here in Arthur Waley's translation.]
[2] [*Op. cit.*, p. 64.]

near the north bank of the Khalkha, of Temüge, Chingis-khan's youngest brother, entrusted by him with government in Mongolia. "By now the ice was beginning to melt and there was a faint touch of color in the grass. When we arrived a marriage was being celebrated in the camp. From five hundred *li* around the headmen of the tribes had come, with presents of mares' milk, to join in the feast. The black wagons and felt tents stood in rows; there must have been several thousand of them." ³ On April 30, Ch'ang-ch'un was presented to Temüge, who put a hundred horses and oxen at his disposal for the journey to Chingis-khan, in Afghanistan.

It may seem strange that, to go from Peking to Afghanistan, the Chinese monk should have had to make this vast and laborious circuit. Would it not have been infinitely more direct to follow the caravan trail from the Tarim basin, the ancient Silk Road, through the Tangut country of Kansu, then the Uyghur country of Turfan and Kucha? But while the *iduq-qut* of the Uyghurs fought in the Mongol armies, the Tanguts had recently fallen out with Chingis-khan, to whom they had refused to send their military contingents. So our traveler was obliged to traverse the whole of the Mongol country to reach eastern Iran. He made his way up the Kerülen valley, Chingis-khan's birthplace, and thence to the Tula, former territory of the Kereit Ong-khan. The account of his journey notes the characteristics of the Mongol climate, very cold in the morning, hot, by this season, in the late afternoon, and the charm of the flowers then dotting the gramineal carpet of the steppe. Moving along the southern foothills of the Kentey—the Mongols' sacred mountain—the caravan passed into the valley of the upper Tula and its tributary, the Kharuka, which gave on to the upper Orkhon. This was the heart of Mongol country. "The people live in black wagons and white tents; they are all herdsmen and hunters. Their clothes are made of hides and fur; they live on meat and curdled milk. The men wear their hair in two plaits that hang behind the ears. The married women wear a head-dress of birch-bark, some two feet high. This they generally cover with a black woolen stuff; but some of the richer women use red silk. The end [of this head-dress] is like a duck." ⁴ The Mongols, the account adds, could not write; all was done by verbal covenant, reinforced, if need be, by notches on planks. "They are obedient to orders and unfailing in their performance

³ [*Op. cit.*, pp. 64-5.]
⁴ [*Op. cit.*, p. 67.]

of a promise" [5]—high testimony indeed to the power of *yassaq,* the discipline Chingis-khan had established in all the domains, and which contrasted so markedly with the anarchy earlier prevailing.

The Chinese traveler now found himself in the Khangay mountains. His biographer notes in passing the beauty of these precipitous peaks, "thickly wooded with pines and firs, so lofty as to defy the clouds and hide the sun," [6] in country snow-covered six months of the year. The caravan crossed the upper Orkhon, then the Borgatay River, skirted Lake Chagan-po, and, crossing the Chagan-olon on July 19, came to the *ordu,* the palace of tents in which the wives of Chingis-khan awaited the hero's return. On the morning of July 29, the Chinese traveler and his companions left the *ordu,* setting out southwest, toward the former Nayman country. On August 14, southwest of what is now Uliassutay, south of the Dzapkhunghol, they passed close by a town in which Chinqay, Chingis-khan's chancellor, had set up grain stores and a colony of Chinese craftsmen and art workers deported to these mountains. The Conqueror had also left there two concubines of the King of Gold, taken at the fall of Peking. All these exiles welcomed the Chinese monk with tears of joy.

Chancellor Chinqay had been charged to tell our monk how eagerly Chingis-khan awaited his coming. To speed the progress of the caravan, he joined it. They were now in the wild tortuous region between the Khangay and the Altay. "Most of the mountains had snow at their peaks; lower down were often *tumuli,* and climbing to the grave-mound on the top of one of these were found remains of offerings to the Spirits."[7] The passes of the Nayman country were so difficult, and Chingis-khan had professed himself so impatient to welcome the Taoist monk, that the caravan abandoned a great many of the wagons to continue the journey on horseback. These mountains were haunted by demons. The Chinese were told that "once not far from here the King of the Nayman tribe was also bewitched by a mountain spirit, the creature inducing him to part with his choicest provisions." [8]

On September 2 they reached the northeast slope of the Altay.

[5] [*Op. cit.,* pp. 67-8.]
[6] [*Op. cit.,* p. 69.]
[7] [*Op. cit.,* p. 71-2.]
[8] [*Op. cit.,* p. 76.]

To cross the Altay range, there was but one narrow trail once blazed by Ögödei. And on this the escort had alternately to push the wagon up the inclines and hold them back going down. "We thus proceeded four stages and negotiated five successive ranges and came out at last on the south side of the mountains." [9] Once on the southern slope of the last range, the caravan came down—doubtless by the col of Dabistan-daban —into the valley of the Bulgun, which is one of the sources of the Urungu, or, to be more precise, a little east of it, into the valley of the little Narun. They then crossed a desert of sand dunes, also haunted by demons, which were scared away by daubing the horses' heads with blood. To the south, they could see rising, in an unreal line of silver, the first foothills of the T'ien-shans.

At the end of September, the caravan reached the Uyghur town of Beshbaliq, the present-day Dzimsa, about eighteen miles east of what is now Urumchi. Uyghur prince, populace, Buddhist monks, others, all came to greet the famous Chinese monk. After so much journeying through mountains and desert, these Uyghur oases, patiently fertilized by their ingenious irrigation channels, seemed to the travelers a paradise. At Jambaliq, Ch'ang-ch'un was feasted on a terrace with excellent wine and delicious melons. It was the last Buddhist town. West of it Moslem country began. Passing along the edge of the Dzungaria Desert, the travelers came to the beautiful Lake Sairam, its waters reflecting the peaks of the T'ien-shans with their thick forests of birch and pine. Chingis-khan's second son, Jaghatay, had in 1219 made a way here through the mountains, between the lake and the valley of the Ili, by the pass of Talki, throwing wooden bridges across the torrents with their boiling waterfalls. These bridges were wide enough for two wagons to cross on them abreast. South of the Talki, the caravan went down into the valley of the Ili, with its meadows and mulberry and jujube trees.

[9] [*Op. cit.*]

Conversations of Chingis-khan
with the Chinese Sage

On October 14, 1221, the Ch'ang-ch'un caravan came to the town of Almaliq, near the present-day Khuldja, in the heart of the beautiful valley of the Ili. The local prince came to meet the travelers with the Mongol *darugha* or prefect. The caravan here completed the restoration of its strength. The country was famous for its fruit (Almaliq means in Turkish "the Apple Orchard"). Our travelers' account sings the praises of the irrigation works which made the whole district a veritable garden, and of the famous cotton plantations.

Continuing in line westward, the caravan passed in the second fortnight in October through the fertile region of the sources of the Chu, the Talas, and their tributaries, and, by way of Chimkent and Tashkent, came to the Sir-darya which it crossed on November 22. On the other side, they were in Transoxania. On December 3, Ch'ang-ch'un arrived at Samarkand. By agreement with the Mongol authorities, he passed here the rest of the winter: Chingis-khan, busy putting an end to the last revolts in the Afghan towns, had more pressing concerns than the philosopher. In mid-April of the following year his thoughts turned again to Ch'ang-ch'un and he sent him a message: "Adept! You have spared yourself no pains in coming to me across hill and stream, all the way from the lands of sunrise. Now I am on my way home and am impatient to hear your teaching. I hope you are not too tired to come and meet me." [1] Ch'ang-ch'un set out at once. He went through the Iron Gates, crossed the Oxus, passed through Balkh and came at last on May 15, 1222, to the camp of Chingis-khan.

[1] [No. 7, pp. 97-8.]

The Conqueror had the warmest of welcomes for the monk come so far to bring him the words of wisdom. He was flattered, too, for Ch'ang-ch'un, invited on earlier occasions, in China itself, to the court of the King of Gold or that of the emperor of Hang-chou, had declined to go: "Other rulers summoned you, but you would not go to them. And now you have come ten thousand *lis* to see me. I take this as a high compliment." [2] Ch'ang-ch'un answered: "That I, a hermit of the mountains, should come at your Majesty's bidding was the will of Heaven." Chingis-khan invited him to be seated, and at once put the question: "Adept, what medicine of long life have you brought me from afar?" Honestly, the monk answered him, not as alchemist or thaumaturge, but as a philosopher: "I have means of protecting life, but no elixir that will prolong it." [3]

Chingis-khan was, we may be certain, profoundly disappointed. His whole object, we know, in having had the Chinese monk come all this immense way to him, had been to learn from him this purported Taoist master's secret, of a mysterious draught that would let him cheat death forever. Nevertheless—and here we get an authentic glimpse of his self-mastery, of the nobility of character, the natural generosity that, in this semi-barbarian chieftain, bespeaks the man of breeding—he betrayed no dissatisfaction, but, on the contrary, congratulated Ch'ang-ch'un for his frankness and sincerity. He conferred on the excellent monk a title of honor and had two tents set up for him not far from the imperial tent.

But it must be admitted that, if Chingis-khan betrayed no disappointment in the Chinese sage, if he showed him but greater esteem, soon indeed conceived an affection for him, he no longer manifested the same eagerness for conversations that tended now to the philosophic, and of which truth to tell, highly intelligent as he was, he could make not a great deal. . . . And the Conqueror was engaged in his final wiping-out of last pockets of resistance in Afghanistan and Khorassan—in the final destruction, alas, of those countries. Ch'ang-ch'un, whose place was emphatically not among such horrors, asked his permission to return to wait for him at Samarkand. Chingis-khan gave it, together with instructions for him to be especially well treated. The Mongol governor of Samarkand, a Khitay named Ye-lü A-hai, welcomed him accordingly with much care for his comfort; we know he presented him with a melon field.

2 [No. 12, p. 100.]
3 [*Op. cit.*, p. 101.]

At Samarkand, the Chinese Taoist, who seems to have been one of the most inquiring minds of his time, made friends with the Moslem scholars of the country, the *danishmands,* as they were called.

In September of this year 1222, Chingis-khan, who had put his end to the Afghan insurrections, sent for Ch'ang-ch'un to be with him again. The monk arrived on September 28 at the imperial camp, south of Balkh, at the foot of the Hindu-kush. Ch'ang-ch'un with the independence of character that was the mark of the Taoist sages, explained firmly that in China the masters of his religion were privileged not to kneel in prostration before sovereigns, and that all that was required of them was to bow their heads, with clasped hands. Chingis-khan accepted with a good grace this mark of philosophic independence. It is piquant to see the barbarian conqueror here proving himself once again more liberal than Alexander the Great: it was, it will be remembered, for having refused to "adore" the Macedonian by Asiatic-style prostration that the philosopher Callisthenes, nephew of Aristotle, had been disgraced and finally executed. Wishing, on the contrary, to honor his guest, Chingis-khan courteously offered him *qumiz,* but Ch'ang-ch'un, for religious reasons, firmly declined to drink of it. Ch'ang-ch'un was next invited to dine daily with the Conqueror. This invitation in turn he declined, stating, with the same philosophic dignity, that solitude better befitted a man such as himself than the tumult of the camps. Again Chingis-khan had heart and intelligence enough to respect his preferences.

Ch'ang-ch'un nevertheless followed the nomad court when in the autumn of 1222 it began its return north. On the way, Chingis-khan had brought to his friend the philosopher grape and melon juice, and other delicacies. On October 21, between the Amu-darya and Samarkand, he had a tent made ready to have Taoism expounded to him. The chancellor Chinqay was present and the Khitay Ye-lü A-hai interpreted. The emperor was greatly edified and the sage's words charmed his heart. On October 25, a fine night, the colloquy was continued. The Conqueror was so impressed by Ch'ang-ch'un's teaching that he ordered the latter's words to be set down in Chinese and Uyghur. What his informant revealed to him must have been the maxims of Lao-tzu and Lieh-tzu, the two legendary founders of Taoism of the fourth and fifth centuries B.C., or perhaps the words of Chuang-tzu, the third of the great sages, a contemporary of Aristotle. Perhaps the Conqueror heard recited the famous invocation in the *Book of Lao-tzu* of the unnamed Force that animates and moves the worlds:[4]

> The largest square has no corners,
> The greatest vessel takes the longest to finish,
> Great music has the faintest notes,
> The Great Form is without shape.

Perhaps the master taught his imperial disciple the asceticism of the *Book of Lieh-tzu*: "My heart is concentrated, my body dispersed. All my sensations are become alike. I no longer feel what my body is held up by or my feet rest on. At the will of the wind I go east and west like a dried-up leaf, so that in the end I know not whether it is the wind carries me or I the wind."

On that beautiful night of October 25, 1222, by Samarkand, perhaps the anchorite repeated to the Conqueror the charming, profound image of Chuang-tzu: "How to know whether the self is what we call the self? Once I, Chuang-tzu, dreamt that I was a butterfly, a butterfly fluttering, and I was happy. I did not know I was Chuang-tzu. Suddenly I woke up and I was myself, the real Chuang-tzu. And I no longer knew whether I was Chuang-tzu dreaming that he was a butterfly or a butterfly dreaming that it was Chuang-tzu." Perhaps the two speakers recalled the Shakespeare-like scene in which Lieh-tzu, showing a skull picked up by the roadside, murmurs, the Chinese Hamlet: "This skull and I know that there is really no life, really no death." Perhaps, finally, the Chinese philosopher initiated the Mongol emperor into the Platonic myth of the great celestial bird, as it is recounted at the beginning of the *Book of Chuang-tzu*: "The great bird mounts on the wind to a height of ninety thousand *lis*. Looking down from up there in the blue, are these horses he sees, galloping? Is it primordial matter flying in a dust of atoms? Are they the breaths that give birth to beings? Is the blue the sky itself or but the color of infinite distance?"

No doubt but that such words, blurred as their metaphysical import may have been for him, made on the Conqueror a profound impression. When, on November 10,[5] the monk presented himself before him again,

---

[4] [Arthur Waley's translation, *The Way and its Power*, p. 193.]

[5] [In fact it was November 5. In this description Grousset wandered very far from his original source. Cf. No. 12, pp. 13-14.]

Chingis-khan, who lived still in a mental climate of esotericism and magic, asked if he ought not to ask others present to withdraw. Ch'ang-ch'un dissuaded him. "The wild man of the mountains," he answered, referring to himself, "has dedicated himself for a long time to the seeking of the Tao and the life of solitude. In the camp of Your Majesty I hear only tumult and cannot collect myself. I beg the favor to be allowed to return home." Graciously, Chingis-khan once again gave his consent. Ch'ang-ch'un distributed what he had among the poor of Samarkand— God knows what destitution the town harbored since its storming two years before—and was preparing to set out for China, when rain and snow beginning to fall brought home to him how difficult it would be at this season to cross the T'ien-shans. Chingis-khan took advantage of it to ask him affectionately to put off his departure: "I am myself on my way to the east. Will you not travel with me? My sons," he said, "are soon arriving. There are still one or two points in your previous discourses which are not clear to me. When they have been explained, you may start on your journey." [6]

The monk, then, in view of the unfavorableness of the season and to please the Conqueror who showed him so much affection, spent the winter of 1222-23 at the latter's side, in Transoxania. On March 10, in the region of Tashkent, on a hunting expedition, Chingis-khan, chasing a wounded boar,[7] fell from his horse. The raging boar turned, and for a moment the Conqueror was in danger. Ch'ang-ch'un took the opportunity to point out to him the unwiseness of hunting at his age, making what was a point of pure Taoist doctrine: "His fall, the Master pointed out, had been a warning, just as the failure of the boar to advance and gore him had been due to the intervention of heaven. 'I know well,' replied the Emperor, 'that your advice is sound indeed. But alas we Mongols are brought up from childhood to shoot arrows and ride. Such a habit is not easy to lay aside.' "

On April 8, 1223, Ch'ang-ch'un finally took his leave of Chingis-khan. The latter, as a farewell present, gave him a decree bearing the imperial seal, exempting from tax the masters of Taoism. He sent one of his officers to accompany the sage.

[6] [No. 12, p. 117.]
[7] [Grousset's original French text has *ours, i.e.* bear. He probably relied on an English source (Waley or Bretschneider) and must have misread his own notes. Ch'ang-ch'un speaks of a "boar." Cf. No. 7, p. 118.]

Ch'ang-ch'un made his way back by the Chu, the Ili, and Almaliq. He recrossed the desert of Dzungaria, its landscape of dunes yearly altering with the sandstorms—not without spirit intervention, so the inhabitants told him. He threaded once more, in the opposite direction, the pass of Dabistan-daban or another further east; then, over the waterless, barren Gobi, avoiding the hostile Tangut, he took again the direct road to China. A last stage through the Öngüt country of Kuku-khoto, and he reached the Chinese province of Shan-si in July 1223. He was to die four years later, in 1227.

The interest and sympathy evinced by Chingis-khan in respect of Chinese Taoism stirred great hopes in Taoist breasts in China. For proof we have a stele engraved in 1219, two years, that is, before the Conqueror's meeting with Ch'ang-ch'un, but composed at the instigation of the monk who then accompanied the latter to Afghanistan. The stele, which has Chingis-khan speaking, presents a curious picture of him, a perfect embodiment of the Taoist ideal. "Heaven," the Conqueror is made to say, "has wearied of the sentiments of arrogance and luxury carried to their extreme in China. I, I live in the wild region of the North, where covetousness cannot arise. I return to simplicity, I turn again to purity, I observe moderation [all ideals of the Taoist good life]. In the clothes I wear or the meats I eat, I have the same rags and the same food as cowherd or groom in the stables. I have for the common people the solicitude I would have for a little child, and the soldiers I treat as my brothers. Present at a hundred battles, I have ever ridden personally in the forefront. In the space of seven years I have accomplished a great work, and in the six directions of space all is subject to a single law."

Doubtless we have in this famous text the habitual phraseology of the Taoist philosophers. The last phrase is indeed copied from the bulletins of victory of the former Chinese emperors, but it is difficult not to see in it also a reflection of the character of the Mongol chief, or at any rate the image of himself he projected among his contemporaries.

It is interesting to compare the respectful attention with which Chingis-khan listened to the counsels of wisdom of the Taoist monk, and the horror in which he held the spinners of rhetoric and phrasemakers. Showing a steadfast disdain for the pomposities of Persian or Chinese protocol, he adjured the princes of his family to do likewise. "The princes of the blood called him by his own name—Temüjin—and in official documents issued by him, his name was accompanied by no honorific title." He had taken into his service for his correspondence in Persian or Arabic one of the former secretaries of the Sultan Mohammed of Khwarezm. He instructed this secretary one day to draft a threatening letter to the *atabeg* of Mossul. The scribe, Persian fashion, wound the threat round with so many flowers of rhetoric that Chingis-khan was in two minds whether he was being made mock of. And as he took mocking ill, he forthwith had the overpompous writer executed.

Surfeited with Conquest, the Great Army Returns to Its Native Land

Chingis-khan, as we have seen, had spent in the province of Samarkand the winter of 1222-23. When, in the spring of 1223, he left this country to cross back to the northern bank of the Sir-darya, into the region of Tashkent, he gave orders that as the army marched out, the mother of the late Sultan Mohammed, the proud Turkhan-khatun, and with her the wives and all the relatives of the dead sovereign the Mongols had taken prisoner, "should line the roadside and cry aloud, with long wailing lamentations, their farewells to the former Khwarezmian empire."

The episode fits with the answer Chingis-khan had once made his friend Bo'orchu concerning "the greatest pleasure of man." "It is," the good Bo'orchu had declared, "to go hunting on a day in springtime, mounted on a fine horse, hawk or falcon at wrist, and see one's prey brought down." "No," the Conqueror answered, "the greatest delight for man, is to inflict defeat on his enemies, to drive them before him, to see those dear to them with their faces bathed in tears, to bestride their horses, to crush in his arms their daughters and wives."

Now, all the enemies of the Mongol chief were brought low. He passed the spring of 1223 north of Sir-darya. In the valley of the Chirchik, a small northern tributary of the river, south of Tashkent, he held a solemn "court," seated on a throne of gold, among his followers, *noyats,* and *ba'atuts;*[1] then, through that spring and into the summer of 1223, he disported himself in great hunting forays over the steppes of Qulan-bashi, in the region, that is, of what are now Aulie-Ata and Frunze,

[1] Mongol honorific titles.

south of the upper Chu and north of the Alexander mountains. His youngest son Toluy was still with him. Jaghatay and Ogödei, who had spent the winter hunting in the region of Bukhara, whence they sent him each week fifty loads of game, had now also rejoined him. As for the eldest of his sons, Jöchi, he had stayed further north, toward the steppes of the lower Chu, but by his orders an immense quantity of game, especially wild asses, was driven down into the neighborhood of Qulan-bashi, where the Conqueror could hunt his fill. "After Chingis-khan, his soldiers amused themselves shooting at these animals which were so tired by long traveling they could be taken in the hand. When everyone tired of this sport, the wild asses remaining were set free, but before unloosing them their captors made their personal marks on their coats."

Then, by short stages, the Great Army that now knew no more enemies took its way again north. Two of the Conqueror's grandsons, Qubilay and Hülegü, both sons of Toluy—the future emperor of China and the future khan of Persia—came to meet him by the River Imil, at Tarbagatay. Qubilay, then eleven, had killed a hare on the way; Hülegü, nine, had brought down a stag, and as it was the custom of the Mongols to rub a child's middle finger with meat and fat the first time he went hunting, Chingis-khan himself performed this office—this "consecration"—for his two grandsons. The Conqueror then spent the summer of 1224 on the banks of the upper Irtysh or Black Irtysh. He lingered a long while in Nayman country, and it was not until the spring of 1225 that he came again to his camping grounds in the Black Forest on the banks of the Tula. He had been away six years.

Of the return of the Conqueror to his native land, Mongol legend has more to say than history. Sogang-sechen, in the seventeenth century, recorded traditions having to do with action taken by the Empress Börte. Throughout his six years' campaigning, Chingis-khan had had with him only one of his secondary wives, his Merkit favorite, the fair Qulan, "Madam Wild Ass." Börte, though she was not jealous, finally, tradition would have it, decided the absence was lasting too long. She is said to have pretended to fear harm might come to a Mongolia left without defenders. "The eagle," she sent word to Chingis-khan, "makes its nest at the top of a high tree, but while it lingers abroad, much lower birds may come and devour its eggs or its eaglets." Chingis-khan made up his mind then to return to Mongolia, not without a certain unease as to how Börte would greet him. . . . He hastened to her, to make sure of her intentions. But Börte, levelheaded woman that she was, hastened to make it clear she found her husband's conduct quite natural: "On the reedy-shored lake, there are many wild geese and swans. The master may take at his will. Among the tribes there are many girls and young women. It is for the master at his pleasure to indicate the favored ones he chooses. He may take a new wife, he may saddle a steed till now unbroken." At which the hero, reassurred, stepped again into his *ordu*.[2]

Vanity of human grandeur! Four centuries after the Hero's death this domestic contretemps—probably fictitious—is all his descendants recall of the prodigious campaign that had placed at his feet the greatest empire of the Moslem world.

[2] [In this passage Grousset follows the original text of Sogang-sechen very loosely. He bases his version on I. J. Schmidt's old translation (No. 32), omits certain lines and adapts the text to his own needs. The original Mongol text is written in alliterating verse of considerable beauty. For a more accurate translation of the original cf. John R. Krueger, No. 33, p. 52.]

Persia, the Caucasus and Russia: The Fantastic Ride of Jebe the Arrow and Sübötei the Bold

Before setting out with Chingis-khan on his last incursion into China, we have to switch back to his two officers, Jebe and Sübötei, pounding through northwest Persia, the Caucasus, and southern Russia. This their fantastic reconnaissance ride did more perhaps than even the massive expeditions the Conqueror led in person, to establish the legend of the ubiquity, the invincibility of the Mongol horsemen.

We have seen how Jebe and Sübötei, the Mongol army's two best strategists, had been dispatched with twenty thousand horsemen in pursuit of the Sultan Mohammed of Khwarezm through Iran. Level with Hamadan, the sultan had slipped through their clutches to die on an islet in the Caspian. Realizing this shifted their sights for them, they continued their ride east, but now as a reconnaissance sortie for the benefit of future Mongol expeditions.

As they rode, they extracted ransom from towns that submitted, sacked any that resisted. Thus they took by storm the important Persian city of Qazwin, eighty-seven miles west of the present Teheran, a town famous for its carpets and as warehouse for the silks of Ghilan. "The inhabitants fought back in the streets, knife in hand, killing many Mongols, but their desperate resistance could not fend off a general massacre in which there perished more than forty thousand people."

From here, Jebe and Sübötei galloped over the high steppes that constitute the greater part of northwest Persia, and drove into the province of Azerbaijan—a province always wealthy by reason of the irrigation oases studding it at its center, chief among them Tabriz, and also of the double forest strip bordering it on the east, towards Ardebil, in the direction of the Caspian, and on the west, towards Urmiya, in the direction of Kurdistan. The Mongols made straight for Tabriz, a fine town set in a well-watered alluvial plain, healthy of climate, surrounded by gardens. The Turkish governor or *atabeg* of Azerbaijan, Özbeg, who lived in Tabriz, bought their agreement to leave him in peace with a heavy payment of silver, apparel, and horses.

Jebe and Sübötei went then to take up winter quarters (for the winter of 1220-21) on the shores of the Caspian, near the mouths of the Arax and the Kura. They built up the strength of their horses in the steppes of Moghan, where January is a particularly mild month, with vegetation already sprouting. But they did not stay long there. January-February 1221 saw them moving up the Kura valley and into Georgia, a Christian kingdom, then at the height of its power. To protect Tiflis, the brilliant Georgian cavalry, with King George III at its head, came out to meet them. The encounter took place in the plain of Khunan, near where the River Berduj, known also as the Borchala or Debeda, joins the Kura, south of Tiflis. In the early stages of the action, the Mongols, as their custom was, let their opponents exhaust themselves in fruitless attacks, then attacked suddenly themselves and cut them in pieces. In this lovely Georgian countryside, with its rich crops, its pretty villages full of ancient churches, the destruction they wrought was terrible, but too hasty really to ruin the country.

In the spring, Jebe and Sübötei moved down again into Persia, into the province of Azerbaijan, to attack Maragha. This was one of the finest cities of the region, with famous orchards and innumerable gardens, sheltered behind screens of poplars, walnuts, and willows. As usual, the Mongols pushed to the forefront of the assault Moslem inhabitants of the surrounding country, killing those who held back. On March 30 they took the town, slaughtered the population and burned all they could not carry away.

The two Mongol captains then remembered that the year before they had contented themselves with extracting a ransom from Hamadan. The town was surely prosperous with its gardens and fountains, its meadows and screens of willows watered by streams bounding down from the Elvend. They went back there again, and, when the townspeople refused to pay a second ransom, laid siege to the place. The inhabitants put up a good defense: this rich Persian bourgeoisie, knowing it could expect no mercy, showed the courage of despair. The day of the final assault, they fought it out street by street, knife in hand. Of course, the Mongols responded with wholesale massacre, and fired the city. From here, Jebe and Sübötei made their way back in the autumn of 1221 to Georgia. Sübötei lured the Georgian cavalry into an ambush where Jebe awaited them. Once more the Georgians were cut to pieces.

The two Mongol captains then conceived a plan of singular audacity. From the pillaged Transcaucasia they resolved to press on, with their twenty thousand horsemen, into that unknown world: Europe. By the Pass of Derbend, the "gateway" between the ranges of Daghestan, last foothills of the Caucasus barrier, and the shore of the Caspian, they moved into the steppes watered by the Terek, the Kuma, and their tributaries, which merge northward into the immensity of the steppes of Russia: "grey steppes" to the northwest, domain of horse and sheep raising, stretching the length of the northern coast of the Black Sea, from the foot of the Caucasus and the Kuban basin to the mouth of the Danube; "white steppe" to the northeast, covering the depression of the salt marshes around the Caspian.

Here the Mongols felt at home. Out of their element in the countries of long agricultural tradition, in Iran or China, here they found again the unbounded horizons of their native territory, immense stretching plains, scorching or freezing by turns as the steppe they came from, grasslands unending where their horses might recoup their strength. But as they emerged from the Caucasus passes, just as they reached the open steppe, a combined force fell on them of the different peoples of the country: a coalition of the mountain folk of the Caucasus, Lesghiens, and Cherkesses, the Alans or Ases, an ancient people of Iranian-Scythian stock, Orthodox Christians, who dwelt in the steppes of the Terek and Kuma, and lastly the Qipchaqs or Comans, Turkish tribes still "pagan"—not turned Moslem, that is—who led a nomad existence in the south Russian steppe, from the lower Danube to the Volga. Together these represented a sizable force. Jebe and Sübötei were nimble enough to split it by persuading the Qipchaqs to desert. Were these latter not, like them, Turko-Mongols, leading the same life of the nomad stock raiser? Why were they joining forces with their natural enemies, Christian or Moslem, against their brothers of Upper Asia? The two Mongol leaders knew how to reinforce these ethnic arguments with a more persuasive one: the Qipchaqs saw tangible return for their neutrality, in the shape of a share of Mongol booty. Left on their own, the Alans and the mountain peoples were defeated. Which accomplished, Jebe and Sübötei turned again, naturally, on the Qipchaqs, hastened in pursuit of them, cut them to pieces, and retrieved—with interest—all the booty they had paid over.

The land of Russia, then divided into a great many principalities, extended southward very little beyond Kharkov and Kiev, or at most Kanev. The Russian princes, who had found little to be happy about in having as neighbors the incessantly pillaging Qipchaqs, were aloof from the fray, and it was unlikely Jebe and Sübötei would want to come probing after them into their dark country or the depths of their forest clearings. But the most powerful of these princes, the Grand Duke of Susdal and of Vladimir, northeast of Moscow, had married the daughter of a Qipchaq chief. Thanks to these family ties, the Qipchaqs contrived to secure the intervention of the three nearest Russian princes, of Kiev, of Chernigov, and of Galich. The three princes having joined forces on the Dnieper, Jebe and Sübötei sent ten envoys to them with proposals for keeping the peace. The Russians, the envoys said, should take the excellent opportunity to have their revenge for the former ravages of the Qipchaqs. They had only to ally against them with the Mongols, with whom they would share the booty. Even from the religious point of view, the Mongols should be preferable to them as allies, as worshipers of a single god, rather than the idolatrous Qipchaqs. Was the reference in this last argument to the Mongol Sky-god, the *Tengri,* or to Nestorian beliefs? Whichever was the case, the Russians, far from entertaining the suggestions, put the envoys to death. By such action four years before had the Sultan of Khwarezm brought the thunder down about his empire.

The Russian army, eighty thousand strong it is said, moved down the Dnieper valley opposite what is now Alexandrovsk. Advantage at first was with the Russians. In fact, Jebe and Sübötei were making a strategic withdrawal intended to tire the Ukranian cavalry and draw it into some trap. Nine days the Russians pursued the Mongols. Suddenly, by the Kalka, Kalak, or Kalmius, a little coastal river that runs into the Sea of Azov near Mariupol, Jebe and Sübötei checked and turned. The

Russians, taken by surprise by this *volte-face,* put themselves at a further disadvantage through poor co-ordination. The Prince of Galich, then the contingents of Chernigov, and likewise the Qipchaq auxiliaries, charged without giving those of Kiev time to fall in with their move. Jebe and Sübötei, fighting on ground they had apparently deliberately picked for the confrontation, threw them into disarray, and the Prince of Galich fled (May 31, 1222). The Prince of Kiev, Mstislav Romanovich, whose force was still intact, drew back into his fortified camp, where he held out for three days, then opened negotiations, and offered a price for his safe passage home that the Mongols accepted. But they had not forgotten the murder of their envoys. When they had the prince at their mercy, they put him to death and slaughtered his men. For the record: he was suffocated under planks or carpets, a death the Russian chroniclers do not fail to wax indignant over, but which, among the Mongols, nevertheless represented a death "of honor," reserved for royal personages whose blood, out of respect, they did not want to shed.

After this resounding success, Jebe and Sübötei might have been expected to drive against the Russians in Kiev and Chernigov. They did not. Satisfied with the lesson they had inflicted, they were content to destroy a few Russian towns on the Russo-Coman frontier. A Mongol detachment crossed into the Crimea, a country then enriched by trade with Genoa and Venice. The principal port of the region was Soldaia, the present-day Sudak, where the Genoese came to ship the furs of the north, squirrel and black fox, and the slaves of both sexes they exported as far afield as Egypt. The Mongols sacked this trade center, and this was, for the time being, their one act of hostility to the "Latin" world.

At the end of 1222, Jebe and Sübötei sallied northeast to attack the "Bulgars of the Kama." This people, Turkish in origin, Moslem by creed, inhabited the forest zone of what is now the country of Kazan, near the junction of the Kama with the upper Volga, where they grew rich exporting to Persia and Khwarezm the products of the north, furs, wax, and honey. At the approach of the Mongols, the Bulgars ran to arms, but they were drawn into an ambush, surrounded, and slaughtered in great numbers. And now Jebe and Sübötei began thinking of return to Asia. They crossed the lower Volga, the Ural, finally subjugated east of this river the Qangli, nomad Turks living in the region of the present-day Uralsk and Aktyubinsk; then, by the Emil, in the Tarbagatay, they returned to Mongolia.

Chingis-khan might well be pleased with them. In the course of their immense reconnaissance they had covered, as the crow flies, over five thousand miles, they had vanquished Persians, Caucasians, Turks, and Russians, and above all they brought back invaluable information as to the weaknesses of the countries they had traveled. It was knowledge Sübötei was to draw on again when, twenty years later, the sons of Chingis-khan charged him to conquer Europe.[1]

---

[1] [This statement is misleading. The 1237-42 European campaign of the Mongols stood under the commandment of Batu.]

The Conqueror's Years of Repose

While his two faithful officers carried out this trial run for his successors' conquest of Russia, Chingis-khan had made his way back by short stages to Mongolia from Turkestan. As we have seen, he was back on the Tula, in the region of what is now Ulan Bator, in the autumn of 1225.

These were the Conqueror's years of relaxation. His writ ran from Samarkand to Peking. On the never static frontiers of the immense empire, loyal generals warred for him against the last Khwarezmians or last Kings of Gold. He who had had such difficult beginnings could now have a mind at ease about the creation he had wrought. And not yet an old man—he was still only fifty-eight—he could contemplate a period of relative repose. Or so at least his distant descendant, the Mongol historian Sogang-sechen, was to have it four centuries later. He shows us the Conqueror filled one day, as he stood looking over some green meadows, with a strange melancholy, a desire for quietness inexplicable in this man of iron. "Behold," the Ordos writer has Chingis-khan say, "behold a fair place for gatherings of tranquil people, a fine grazing ground for stags and roe deer, an old man's perfect haven of repose."

In fact, the relaxations Chingis-khan favored had certainly nothing about them of this Buddhist pastoral aura. We know what they were. First and foremost came hunting—the gigantic expeditions we have seen him making in 1223 in the Tashkent region, which gave him still something of the taste of war. Then also he liked gaming and of course drinking.

Chingis-khan's round of pleasures is evoked in the account of the Chinese Chao Hung, Hang-chou's ambassador to the Mongol officer Muqali. One day, Muqali sent for the ambassador and asked him:

"We played ball today. Why did you not come?" The Chinese answered that, not having been specially invited, he had not presumed to join in the game. To which Muqali replied with jovial friendliness: "Since you have been in our empire, I have thought of you as one of my intimates. Whenever there is a feast, or a game, or a hunting expedition, I mean you to come and amuse yourself with us without waiting for an invitation." Laughing, he then made the ambassador drink, by way of penalty, six large cups of wine, and let him depart that evening only in a state of total inebriation. Muqali had indeed conceived a real affection for this Chinese who in the war the Sung court was waging on its own account with the King of Gold had displayed such remarkable strategic capacities. When the time came for the ambassador to take his leave, the Mongol chief gave orders for him to be treated right up to the end with especial care for his comfort: "Stay several days in each important town. Let him be served the fullest-bodied wines, the most scented tea, the tastiest dishes. In his honor, let handsome youths excel themselves on the flute, sweet-faced young women musicians make their instruments resound." [1]

The last detail should not surprise us. We know, in fact, that Muqali took with him on his campaigns a score or so accomplished female musicians. The Chinese diplomats have high praise for his taste in women. "When the ambassador presented himself before the Mongol captain," notes one of them, "he was invited, the introductions protocol required completed, to sit down and drink some wine in company with one of the wives of Muqali and eight of his concubines who were present at the feast. The whiteness of face of these women is dazzling, and their appearance highly attractive. Four of them are *Kin* princesses, the other four Tatar women. They are very beautiful and the general loves them greatly."

The supreme delight of these feasts was of course the drinking. Chingis-khan declared that it was seemly to get drunk only up to three times a month; he added that it would be preferable, clearly, to make it only twice or even only once. "It would be even perfectly good never to get drunk. But where is the man who could observe such a rule of conduct?"

[1] [The whole episode is reported in almost identical words by Grousset on pp. 522-523 of No. 35, where he ascribes the words to Chingis. The story is probably apocryphal, cf. No. 36, vol. V, p. 148.]

We have already stressed the curious contrast between the horrors perpetrated by the Mongol armies and the bonhomie of the Conqueror's relationships with his own circle. Nay, odd as the expressions may seem used of a barbarian, Chingis-khan gave proof when occasion arose of a nobility of soul, a gentlemanly chivalry, quite unlooked-for in his milieu.

One of his former vassals, the Khitay chief Ye-lü Liu-ko, who had been able to re-establish, with Mongol aid, a little principality in Liao-Tung, in the south of Manchuria, died in 1220. Chingis-khan was then in Transoxania. The widow, the lady Yao-li-szu, assumed the regency, by consent of Prince Temüge-otchigin, brother of the Conqueror, charged by the latter in his absence to administer Mongolia. On Chingis-khan's return, she came with her sons to the imperial *ordu*. "When she appeared before her suzerain, she went on her knees according to etiquette. Chingis-khan welcomed her with particular distinction and did her the honor —the most sought after—to 'proffer her the cup.'" She proposed that the Khitay kingdom should go to the late king's eldest son, a young man who had accompanied Chingis-khan in the war in Khwarezm and with whom he had been well pleased. Chingis-khan gave his consent to the regent's wishes, and greatly praised her wisdom and fairness. "When she took her leave, he gave her nine Chinese prisoners, nine valuable horses, nine ingots of silver, nine lengths of silk, nine precious jewels" (the number nine was sacred for the Mongols). As for the young Khitay prince, he rewarded him no less magnificently for his services. "Your father," he told him, "once placed you in my keeping as pledge of his loyalty. I always acted toward him as if he had been my younger brother and I love you as a son. Command my troops [in Liao-Tung] with my brother Belgütei and live together in close unity."

Chingis-khan showed a like generosity to the heir of the Öngüt princes, the Nestorian Christian Po-yao-ho. This young man—he was only seventeen—had also been with him on the Khwarezm campaign. On their return Chingis-khan gave him in marriage his own daughter, the wise Alaghay-beki. Po-yao-ho and Alaghay reigned peaceably together in the hereditary domain—in the region of Kuei-hua-ch'eng, in the north-west Shan-si—over the Turko-Öngüt people so interesting to us by reason of their loyalty to the Nestorian faith. The couple were to have no children, but Alaghay, like her father a forceful personality, was also great-hearted. She brought up "as if they were her own," the sons her husband had by a concubine, and prepared them for kingship. These adopted sons of the valiant *qatun* Alaghay were in their turn to marry Chingiskhanid princesses and perpetuate the close alliance of the two houses, the alliance that brought Christianity to the very steps of the Mongol throne.

Return to China

Chingis-khan's rest on his return to Mongolia did not last the year. Once more, events in China claimed his attention.

Since his departure, the struggle against the King of Gold had gone on without pause. His officer Muqali, whom he had left in charge, had a difficult task. A noble figure, and all in all a likable one, this Mongol warrior, his master's companion in the early days of obscurity, was now raised by the Conqueror to the highest eminence. Chingis-khan, to assure his officer authority over the Chinese population, had indeed conferred on him, as we have seen, the royal title of *go-ong* or, in Chinese, *kuo-wang,* king of the country. Living himself on practically nothing, like all the Mongol generals, Muqali when the prestige of the "Banner" was involved knew how to cut the figure of a king. Generals of contingents sent by vassal princes to serve in his command were required on arrival to walk holding his horse's rein as their lords held the rein of the horse of Chingis-khan. Yet like the master he served, he also knew how to listen, and was far from deaf to the counsels of civilization. One of the captains of the King of Gold come over into the Mongols' service one day proffered some courageous observations on the barbarity with which their troops behaved in conquered country. "He explained to Muqali that, in the interests of the very success of Mongol conquest, it was important to calm populations already subjected and inspire confidence in those not yet so." Far from being angry, Muqali saw that the point was a good one. "He gave orders immediately that plundering should cease and captives be released. The strict discipline he thereafter enforced in his army in this respect greatly furthered the subjection of the country."

This humanization of the war was in fact good policy. Muqali at the same time made a change in the character of Mongol conquest, which had hitherto gone no further than horseback raids, destruction, and slaughter, not followed up by any effective occupation. Effective occupation of conquered territory now became with him a definite objective. To this end, he employed an increasing number of Chinese, Khitays, and even Jürchets who had rallied to his side, who could remedy the deficiencies the Mongols were most constantly aware of, by providing them with infantry and siege engines. Several generals of the King of Gold who had come over to the Mongols were of service to him here: Ming Ngan, for instance, Chang-chou, and the already mentioned Shi T'ien-yi. Those who had come over brought others. This was the case with Ming Ngan and Chang-chou. The former, who had come over several years earlier, took the latter prisoner when his horse was brought down at the height of a battle. "Whoever fell into the hands of the Mongols must make submission to Chingis-khan or resign himself to death. Chang-chou nevertheless refused to bow the knee before the Chinghiskanid general, saying that he was of equal rank in the armies of the King of Gold and that he would not humiliate himself to save his life." Nobly—and cleverly—Ming Ngan respected his courage and set him free. He also however then made arrangements to hold Chang-chou's parents as hostages. "Chang-chou hesitated a long while between filial piety and his duty to his sovereign," and, as he was a good Chinese, filial piety won: he brought himself to pay homage to Chingis-khan, and was at once appointed to a command under Muqali.

Desperate fighting went on in fact unremittingly. The armies of the King of Gold, who had previously defended for more than five years the approaches to Peking, showed more stubborn still from where they had fallen back to in Honan, behind the barrier of the Yellow River. In seven years (1217-23), Muqali had little by little driven them back into this province, but only by bitter effort, most districts having been conquered, lost again, and then again reconquered, several times. As early as 1217, in the south of what is now Ho-pei, the Mongol general had taken the important town of Ta-ming, which controlled the approaches to the Great Plain, but cannot have been able to hold it, since he had to capture it again in 1220. In 1218 he took, or rather, retook from the King of Gold the capitals of Shan-si, T'ai-yuan, and P'ing-yang, and in 1220 that of Shan-tong, the present Tsi-nan. In 1222, we find him holding the ancient capital of Shen-si, Ch'ang-ngan or Si-ngan-fu. In 1223, he had just snatched from the King of Gold the important P'u-cheu or Ho-chong, in the southwest corner of Shan-si, in the bend of the Yellow River, when he died, exhausted. Feeling his end at hand, he told his younger brother who had hastened to his side: "Forty years I have made war to serve the khan my master in his great enterprises, and I have never spared myself. My only regret, in my dying hour, is not to have been able to take K'ai-feng to offer it to him. Try to take it." So he spoke, and died. He was only fifty-four (April 1223).

Even as the court of K'ai-feng put up its desperate defense, it also had its feelers out for peace. As early as August 1220 the King of Gold had sent an ambassador to Chingis-khan—Wu-ku-sun Chung-tuan, vice president of the Court of Rites—in an effort to move him to consider terms. The Conqueror was then deep in the "West," in Afghanistan. The ambassador came to him via the Ili, in the autumn of 1221. To the request to conclude peace, Chingis-khan replied: "I earlier asked your master to give up to me all territory north of the Yellow River and to be content to keep for himself the district south of it, with the simple title of king [*wang*]. This was the condition on which I was prepared to suspend hostilities, but now Muqali has conquered all the territory I claimed then, and you have no choice but to sue for peace." Wu-ku-sun implored him to have pity on the King of Gold. Chingis-khan answered: "Only in view of the distance you have traveled yourself to come here, I show leniency to you personally. Here is my decision. The country north of the Yellow River is now in my hands, but your master controls still a few places to the west of T'ung-kuan [in Shen-si]. He must deliver them up to me!" There was nothing for the ambassador but to bring back these conditions. The court of K'ai-feng dared not accept: the fortresses around T'ung-kuan constituted—as a glance at the map will confirm—the only defense of Honan on the west, and to relinquish them would have been for the King of Gold to hand over the keys of his kingdom. Right up to 1227, nevertheless, the King went on unremittingly attempting to appease the inflexible Conqueror by protestations of vassalhood.

In 1216, one of the King of Gold's generals named P'u-hsien Wan-nu had taken advantage of the general disorder to carve for himself in the former Jürchet country, in southern Manchuria, a kingdom of his own, which he called by the Chinese name "the kingdom of Tung-hsia." In 1221, this individual had sent his conciliatory ambassador to Chingis-khan in Transoxania or Afghanistan. But the Mongols could not leave long in existence this sprig of an enemy tree: between 1224 and 1227 "Tung-hsia" disappeared from the map.

What irked Chingis-khan, even more than the last-ditch resistance of the King of Gold, was the defection of the Tanguts, of the "kingdom of Hsi-hsia," as it was called.

As we know, the Tanguts, a people of Tibetan affinities partly sinicized (they had even invented a script for their own use with characters derived from the Chinese), had been for two centuries masters of the Chinese province of Kansu, and of the steppes of the Ordos and the Alashan. After several campaigns, Chingis-khan had in 1209 forced their king to acknowledge himself a vassal. But the relation thus established required the vassal, in time of war, to furnish his contingent for the suzerain. When, in 1219, the Conqueror was making ready for his expedition against the Sultan of Khwarezm, he sent accordingly for the auxiliaries owed him by the Tangut sovereign: "You have promised to be my right hand. Now, I have broken with the Sarta'ul [the Sultan of Khwarezm] and I am setting out to war. Set out to war with me, be my right hand!" But the Tangut sovereign was dominated, it appears, by an all-powerful minister, who hated the Mongols. This minister—Asha-gambu—himself, before his master had had time to say where he stood, gave Chingis-khan's request the most insolent of answers: "If Chingis-khan has not sufficient forces to do for himself what he proposes, why does he assume the role of emperor?" And with final presumptuousness he refused to dispatch any contingent.

Such a refusal, at such a moment, had stung Chingis-khan deep. This was insolence of a kind he was not accustomed to overlook. But the campaign against the Sultan of Khwarezm had been decided on, the measures required for it had in fact already been taken. It was impossible, without completely upsetting these arrangements, to mount a punitive expedition against the Tanguts. He had had therefore, so far as the latter were concerned, to contain himself for the time being. But it had been only for the time being, as he had himself declared: "If by the protection of the eternal *Tengri* I return victorious, Khwarezm obedient to my reins of gold, then the hour of vengeance will strike for the Tanguts!"

And now he was back, the Khwarezm empire in its length and breadth in ruins, and the vengeance hour was come.

"If It Means My Death I Will Exterminate Them!"

Chingis-khan set out against the Tanguts in the spring of 1226.[1] Two of his sons, Ögödei and Toluy, went with him. And as on his campaign against the Sultan of Khwarezm he had taken one of his secondary wives, the Lady Qulan, he took as companion on this new expedition his Tatar favorite, the Lady Yesüi.

The campaign began inauspiciously. The invasion army was crossing Alashan, a desert "esplanade," broken by long sand dunes, with a narrow fringe of oases and grassland, dominated on the east by a chain of mountains rising to 10,000 feet and more, the wooded slopes of which are the haunt of the wild ass and the musk stag. Chingis-khan, despite the exhortings to prudence he had heard from the Chinese sage, plunged with his usual enthusiasm into the pleasures of the chase. A band of wild asses, driven from the bushes by the beaters, ran out in front of him. His horse—a reddish animal—reared and threw him.

When the Conqueror was picked up, he complained of sharp internal pains. They pitched camp on the spot, at Cho'orqat. Next morning, Chingis-khan's companion, the lady Yesüi, called the princes and principal lords to tell them he had passed a troubled night, with a high fever. One of the assembled generals, Tolun-cherbi, of the Qongqotat tribe, at once suggested they defer the expedition. "The Tanguts are a sedentary people, with walled towns and fixed camps. They will not pick up and carry away their towns. When we come back, they will still be there."

[1] [A more detailed but still not very well documented description of this campaign can be found in No. 42.]

Tolun-cherbi counseled, then, a return to Mongolia, there to await Chingis-khan's recovery before re-embarking on the campaign.

All the princes and all the Mongol lords approved his suggestion, but Chingis-khan would hear none of it: "If we withdraw, the Tanguts will not fail to claim that it was because courage failed us. Let us send them first a messenger and wait here for their answer." So it was done. What amounted to an ultimatum was sent to the Tangut sovereign: "You had sworn to be my right hand. When I set out to war against the Moslems, I reminded you of your commitment, but you were untrue to your word, you did not send me your contingent. Indeed, instead you sent insulting word to me. I postponed my vengeance, but the hour is come. I come to settle your account!" Receiving this ominous message, the Tangut king was irresolute: "The insults, it was not I pronounced them." But the ill-sent minister Asha-gambu took full responsibility for that old defiance: "The mockery, yes, it was I who spoke it. Now, if the Mongols want to fight, let them come into Alashan where I have my camp with my *yurts* and my camels and their loads, and we will measure our strengths. If they must have gold, silver, silk, other treasures, let them come and get them from our towns, from Eriqaya and Erije'ü," that is, from Ning-hsia and Liang-chou.

Such a gauntlet Chingis-khan, fevered as he was still, in pain still from the fall from his horse, was adamant they were not going to leave even temporarily lying. "After such words, we can no longer draw back. If it means my death, I will take them at their word, I will go to them!" And he bound himself by a great oath, calling to witness his decision the Eternal Heaven, supreme god of the Mongols.

The Mongol army in March 1226 advanced on the Tangut kingdom by way of the Etzin-gol, a river rising from the Nanshan mountains and flowing south to north into the Gobi, where it peters out, it and its thin strip of vegetation—reeds, tamaris, and toghraq—in a desert of stones and sand. The Mongols took the town of Etzina which stands guard in the north, at the edge of the Gobi, over the entry to the valley. Country famous, writes Marco Polo, for the quality of its camels, sought after for Gobi caravans, and also of its gerfalcons, used in great hunts. Moving up the valley, the Mongols came into the "Kansu corridor," a band of loess running southeast-northwest, on the northern edge of the Nanshans, between this range and the Gobi, and fertilized in places by rivers running down from the mountains to form the Etzin-gol. The oases thus strung along it, the most considerable Kan-chou and Su-chou, are surrounded by screens of willow and poplar, by gardens and even meadows, by corn and millet fields, that make them places of delight for caravans arriving from the desert. From earliest days, indeed, Kan-chou and Su-chou were famous as caravan cities, termini of the routes of central Asia, "ports" of the Silk Road. Trade, as Marco Polo attests, had given rise there to a flourishing Nestorian Christian community among the preponderantly Buddhist population. Marco Polo, some forty-seven years later, was to note in Kan-chou marvelous Buddhist statues in Buddhist monasteries, whose rule had his admiration, and the existence of three Nestorian churches. In the summer of 1226, the Mongols seized both these towns, while Chingis-khan, who found heat debilitating, went to camp in the nearby perpetually snow-capped mountains. In the autumn, the Mongols, driving eastward, took possession of Liang-chou, and came to the Yellow River at Ying-li, some sixty-two miles south of Ning-hsia, the enemy capital.

In this country of caravan-stage oases, the depredations of the Mongols were, as usual, ghastly. "To escape the Mongol sword, the inhabitants in vain hid in the mountains—in the west in the Richthofens, in the east on Alashan and Lo-chan—or, if that were not possible, in caves. Scarcely one or two in a hundred succeeded. The fields were covered with human bones." The Mongol bard specifies that Chingis-khan, following up the Tangut chief Asha-gambu's defiant challenge, defeated him and forced him to take refuge in the Alashan mountains. "He seized from him his tents, his treasure-laden camels, all his people, till all this was scattered as so much ash. Tanguts of an age to bear arms he had slaughtered, the lords being first to die." He had issued standing orders unleashing his soldiers to savage as they wished a people he considered had faults to answer for: "As many Tanguts as you can take are yours to do as you please with!"

The Mongol generals were right behind Chingis-khan in this. Sons of *tayga* or steppe, understanding only the life of hunter or shepherd, it was beyond them to imagine what useful purpose these agricultural populations they had conquered might serve, or this tilled land they were annexing. Better to kill off all these useless folk who could neither tend a herd nor travel with them on their nomad migrations, better burn the harvest as they were destroying the towns, let the land lie untilled and be restored to its dignity as steppe. The policy was quite seriously considered: "Chingis-khan's generals pointed out to him that his Chinese subjects were of no possible use to him, and that it would be better to slay them down to the last inhabitant, and so at least have the benefit of the soil which would be converted to grazing." The terrifying program was on the point of being adopted when one man weighed in against it with everything he knew: Ye-lü Ch'u-ts'ai, the Khitay scholar, the conquered Chinese "counselor." He cried out against this barbarian proposal. He recounted the advantages to be derived from the fertile countryside and its hard-working inhabitants. He showed how by making reasonable dues payable on land, tariffs on merchandise, taxes on wine, vinegar, salt, iron, and the produce of waters and mountains, they could garner some five hundred thousand ounces of silver, eighty thousand lengths of silk, four hundred thousand sacks of grain, and declared his astonishment that the settled peoples could still despite all this be accounted useless.

What in Chingis-khan could be counted on to prevail was his intelligence and sturdy good sense. He committed or allowed to be committed terrible atrocities because in the Mongol *ambiance* of his day there was no notion war might be fought otherwise, as there was no conception of a way of life other than the nomadic, the lands of the settled communities being looked on as no more than raiding grounds, good for pillage and man-hunting. From the moment someone explained to him that matters were not thus, the Conqueror asked nothing better than to reap the fruits of knowledge. Then and there he asked Ye-lü Ch'u-ts'ai to draw up a plan for regular administration of the settled lands, with fixed taxes—in short, with all his Chinese counselor had just told him of.

While Chingis-khan was making his systematic conquest of Tangut territory, his third son, Ögödei, accompanied by the Mongol general Chaghan, had, in this same year of 1226, led a mounted raiding force across the states of the King of Gold. Riding down the Wei valley to Hsi-ngan-fu, he made his way thence into the heart of Honan, to right under the walls of K'ai-feng. The Conqueror's hatred of these accursed Jürchets was fueled by memories as vivid as ever of the injuries they had once done him: "These people of the Kings of Gold, it was they who brought our fathers to their death. Share them out among you. Make their sons your servants to carry your falcons. Let your wives make the

fairest of their daughters sewing maids to wash and mend your clothes!"
Nevertheless, the King of Gold sent embassy after embassy to seek
peace. The one dispatched to Chingis-khan in June–July 1227 met, apparently, with a kinder reception than its predecessors. The Conqueror,
increasingly a sick man since his hunting accident, seems then, according
to the Chinese chroniclers, to have shown an unexpected desire for
peace. He is said to have told his entourage that already the preceding
winter, "when the Five Planets were in conjunction," he had vowed to
himself he would put an end to the massacre and pillage, and that now
the time was come to realize his desire. The presents the King of Gold
sent as tribute were also not without their effect in disposing the terrible
Mongols to be charitable. Among these were some great pearls that
Chingis-khan ordered to be distributed among those of his officers who
wore ear pendants. To be among the recipients, every one of them at
once had his ears pierced.

"My Children,
the End Is Near for Me . . ."[1]

The year 1227 was dawning, the last year of Chingis-khan's life. Toward the end of 1226—between November 21 and December 21—he had laid siege to the town of Ling-chou (or Ling-wu), the Mongol chroniclers' Dörmegei, lying some eighteen miles from Ning-hsia, the Tangut capital, but with the Yellow River between. The Tangut sovereign sent out a relieving army from Ning-hsia to try to raise the siege. Chingis-khan came out to meet this force in a plain studded by pools left by flooding of the river, and at this time of year frozen over. Once again, the Tanguts suffered crushing defeat. The Mongols took and sacked Ling-wu.

It remained to take the capital itself, the city of Ning-hsia, or, as it is called in the Mongol chronicles, Eriqaya, Marco Polo's Egrigaia. Standing four miles or thereabouts back from the Yellow River, in a part where the Great Wall takes to the latter's right bank instead of its left, Ning-hsia nevertheless lives by the river. Its waters are brought to it piecemeal through a complex network of diversions and artificial canals which dates back to the beginning of the Christian era, and testifies to the science of the ancient Chinese engineers who contrived thus to transform into a fertile oasis a tongue of land between two deserts. Ning-hsia was also, as has been seen, an industrial and commercial center of great importance, famous especially for its cloths of white camel hair, declared by Marco Polo "the finest in the world." Commercial activity at Ning-hsia was attested by the existence of a rich Nestorian community, with three churches, within the preponderantly Buddhist population.

[1] [On the last campaign and the death of Chingis see No. 43.]

Chingis-khan, at the beginning of 1227, threw a contingent around Ning-hsia to blockade the city. He himself, with another division, went off to conquer the upper basin of the Yellow River, where he attacked first, in February, the town of Ho-chou, sixty miles southwest of Lan-chou. This is forbidding country. On the Sino-Tibetan border, the river's course is simply a series of canyons carving their way sixteen hundred feet deep through loess or granite and zigzagging in the depths of steppe valleys through marshes and torrents. Farther to the west, around Hsi-ning, toward the Kökö-na'ur—the "blue lake" that here marks the frontier of Chinese and Tibetan territory—the country is wilder still, with plateaus 6,600 to 10,000 feet above sea level, slashed with gorges and divided up by the southern foothills of the Nanshans. The Hsi-ning market there commands the caravan route that climbs toward the high Tibetan plateaus and Lhasa.

In March 1227, Chingis-khan pushed on to Hsi-ning and captured it. In April, he moved across from the western limits of Kansu to that province's eastern frontiers, by the Lin-pan-shan mountains, source of the Ching-ho River that flows southwest toward the Wei valley and the rich plain of Ch'ang-un. He spent the rest of the spring in this district, around Lung-to, by the headwaters of the Ching-ho. At the end of May or in the first two weeks of June he went to take up summer quarters in the Lin-pan-shans, which, rising in places to ten thousand feet, offered him refuge from the heat. Then he came down some thirty-seven miles farther south, in the district of Ch'ing-shui, where the last outlying southern Lin-pan-shan foothills overhang the upper valley of the Wei. The Conqueror, who, it seems, had never fully recovered from his accident the year before, was feeling himself borne down by an increasing weariness. Under no illusions about his condition, he called the more insistently on his officers to press on with the siege of the Tangut capital, Ning-hsia.

Ning-hsia's defenders were at the end of their tether, but the Tangut king, Li Hsien, who had stayed with them, still sought to gain time. He asked for a stay of a month to surrender the town. The same month, in about the first fortnight of June, he resigned himself to capitulation. He came in great pomp to the Mongol camp with magnificent gifts the Chingiskhanid bard lists admiringly: images of Buddhas resplendent with gold, cups and bowls of gold and silver, youths and maidens, horses and camels, all in multiples of nine, in accordance with Mongol protocol.

But notwithstanding the somewhat belated tribute and despite his profession of submission, Li Hsien did not obtain from Chingis-khan the audience he sought, or at least, he was permitted only to make obeisance to the Conqueror "through a closed door." In fact, even this meeting must have been faked: Chingis-khan, now seriously ill, was undoubtedly not present at the audience he was supposed to have given the defeated king. Not that the latter's fortunes fared any the better in consequence. The Conqueror had already given orders to Tolun-cherbi to put to death the last Tangut sovereign, orders that we may imagine were executed with blithe dispatch.

While his generals were taking the enemy capital, in the mountains of eastern Kansu, the Conqueror of the world was living his last weeks on earth. The time had come for him to think seriously of his successor. Among his sons the eldest, Jöchi—if he was indeed his son, and most men doubted it—had never, it seems, been for him the object of more than constrained affection. Of latter years, moreover, Jöchi had behaved strangely. After the destruction of the Khwarezmian empire, instead of rejoining his father in the spring of 1223, when he was making his great hunting expeditions north of Tashkent, he stayed sullenly away in his province in the Sibero-Turkestan steppes, and he had not put in an appearance since. Hurt by the unvoiced imputation of bastardy he sensed around him, angered perhaps also at having his younger brother Ögödei set above him, was he contemplating secession? Chingis-khan had for a moment suspected this might be the case, and it is said that in this same year, 1227, father had had in mind a punitive expedition against son; but it was soon learned that Jöchi's non-response to paternal invitations had been due to illness: the "eldest son" had died in his province north of the Aral in or about February 1227.

Of the hero's three surviving sons, Jaghatay was away, commanding a reserve army. "Warned by a dream," Chingis-khan summoned his two other sons, Ögödei and Toluy, who were campaigning in the area. First asking the officers who filled his *yurt* to step aside a moment, he made to these two princes (ever, indeed, his two favorite sons) his last recommendations: "My children," he told them, "the end is near for me. Aided by the Eternal Heaven, I have conquered for you an empire so vast, that from its center to its bounds is a year's riding. If you would retain it, hold together, act in unison against your enemies, concert to further the fortunes of your followers. One of you must occupy the throne. Ögödei shall be my successor. Respect this choice after my death, and let Jaghatay, who is not here, make no trouble."

His sickness gaining on him, his mind ran on the war against the King of Gold. For if the fall of the Tangut capital was no longer more than a matter of days, the King of Gold, the Mongols' hereditary enemy, still held his stronghold retreat of Honan, with at its center the great capital K'ai-feng, seemingly impregnable. The thoughts of the dying man were on this—the unfinished—part of his handiwork, and he confided to his son Toluy how he might complete it. "The best of the King of Gold's troops," he told him, "are manning the fortress of T'ung-kuan [which controlled access to Honan from Shen-si]. Now, this fortress has the protection on the south of steep mountains, and on the north, of the Yellow River. It is difficult to rush the enemy there. You must ask the Chinese of the Sung empire to be allowed to pass through their territory; as they too are enemies of the King of Gold, they will consent. Then our army will make its way through that territory to south Honan, and from there drive directly on K'ai-feng. The King of Gold will be forced to call to his aid the troops massed on the Pass of T'ung-kuan, but they will arrive too late, worn out by the long march, and it will be easy to defeat them."

So the great Mongol even on his deathbed outlined for his sons and generals a last plan of campaign—one they executed in fact under Toluy six years later. The fall of K'ai-feng to the Mongols in May 1233 was in a very real sense the inflexible Emperor's personal, if posthumous, victory.

The dying Conqueror was intent also on exacting his full tithe of vengeance—this too posthumously—from the last Tanguts. Their capital, Ning-hsia, was falling, but the thought rankled that by bringing him to make war in the state of health he was in, these recalcitrant vassals had led him to his death. He gave orders therefore to exterminate all the defenders of Ning-hsia, men and women, "fathers and mothers," to the last generation. After his death, at the offering of the funeral sacrifices to his corpse, it was to be announced to him—these were his last instructions—that he was truly avenged, that the Tangut kingdom had been wiped from the face of the earth: "During my repast, declare to me: to the last man they have been exterminated! The khan has annihilated their race!" The Conqueror of the world had for his funeral rites the massacre of an entire people. The elimination cannot, however, have been quite total, since a considerable number of Tangut subjects were allotted to the Lady Yesüi who had accompanied her master in the last campaign.

Chingis-khan had an affectionate word for the faithful Tolun-cherbi, who the year before, after his fall from his horse, had tried to persuade him to defer the expedition. "It was you, Tolun, who after my hunting accident at Arbuqu were concerned about my condition, you who wanted me to get proper care taken in time. . . . I did not listen to you, I came to punish the Tanguts for their venomous words. . . . All the king of the Tanguts has brought us, his movable palace, his dishes of gold and silver, take it, I give it to you."

Perhaps, in the final hour, the Conqueror reflected with the melancholy attributed to him by a chronicler: "My descendants will go clothed in gold-embroidered stuffs; they will feed on the choicest meats, they will bestride superb steeds and press in their arms the most beautiful of young women. And they will have forgotten to whom they owe all that. . . ."

Chingis-khan died on August 18, 1227,[2] near Chung-shui, north of the River Wei, in the mountains of eastern Kansu, where he had gone to have cooler air, at least, about him in his pain. He was barely sixty.

[2] [This is the date given by Juvaini. According to Chinese sources the day of Chingis' death was August 23, whereas Rashid ed-Din has August 28. The problem is discussed at length by Pelliot, No. 18, pp. 305–9.]

"As a Falcon Soars Circling in the Heavens . . ."

The last journey of him who had been Conqueror of the world, from Kansu to the sacred mountain of Kentey, has been made the theme of one of the most magnificent poems in Mongol literature—a poem already crystallized in its essentials in the first half of the seventeenth century, since we find it in both the *Golden History, the Altan-Tobchi,* of 1604, and in Sogang-sechen, of about 1662. The khan has just died. His body is laid in a wagon to be brought back to the homeland. Amid the lamentations of the army, one of the Mongol generals, Kelegütei, also known as Kilügen, addresses the dead man: "Have you gone, my Lord, soaring like a falcon? Have you gone, my Lord, becoming ill [because] of a creaking wagon? Have you in truth abandoned, my Lord, your own wife and sons? Have you in truth left behind, my Lord, your own massed subject peoples? Did you get lost, my Lord, like a chattering falcon? Did you fly in the wind like the gently waving grass? At your age of sixty-six, did you, my Lord, Arise to render happiness to your nine-colored peoples?" [1]

Amid the lamentations, the funeral chariot has moved off, but suddenly the wheels sink bogged in the clayey soil. The strongest horses and the crowd around strive in vain to free it from the mud; they cannot budge it. Then Kilügen the Valiant calls again on the soul of Chingiskhan: "My heavenly Boghda Lord, Lion of Men, Born with a destiny from Eternal Blue Heaven! Have you reached the point of completely abandoning all your extensive and great people, in your elevated rebirth? Your wife whom you met and with whom you multiplied, your

[1] [Translation by John R. Krueger, No. 33, p. 71.]

evenly established kingdom, your administration arranged as you desired, your people united by the myriads, they are here. Your queen whom you met and greatly loved, your golden *yurt,* palace and dwelling, your realm established in purity, your people, gathered and amiable, they are here. The land you have ridden upon, the water you washed in, your subject Mongol people, vast as growing things, your many functionaries, princes, and ministers, your camp where you were born, Deli'ünboldaq on the Onon, they are here. Your [banner] of protective-genius, made from the forelocks of bay stallions, your tambourines, cymbals, trumpets, flutes, piccolos, your golden *yurt*-palace, where are gathered all things discussed, your throne, where you became king on the Island of Ködege in the Kerülen, they are here. Your queen, wise Börte Jüsin, met before accomplishing, your great fortunate camping-grounds, Burqatu Qan, your two intimate comrades, Bogharji and Muqali, your realm and administration, established in entirety, they are here. Your wife, Queen Qulan, met by means of magic [lit., transformation], your violins (*qughur*), flutes (*čughur*) and others, your music and song, your two beauteous queens, Yisüi and Yisügen, your golden palace home wherein all is assembled, they are here. Because the Qaraghun Qan [mountain chain] is warm, because the subject Tanguts are many, because Queen Görbeljin is beautiful, have you, in truth, abandoned your old Mongols, my Lord? Although for your warm golden life there be no protection, bringing your illumined origin [i.e., body] like a jade jewel, should we not display [it] to your wife Queen Börte Jüsin, should we not gratify your whole great people?" [2]

At these words the wagon, till now immovable, moves forward, and the funeral cortège takes the road for Upper Mongolia.

The news of Chingis-khan's death was for some time kept a secret: it was important it should not be noised abroad among enemy peoples or ones too recently conquered until appropriate precautions had been taken. The escort accordingly slew as they went any more or less suspect stranger who had the misfortune to cross the path of the bier. This was also an old Altaic custom, thought of as ensuring servitors for the dead man in the hereafter. As they slew the travelers they encountered, so did they their horses and oxen: "Go to serve our master the khan in the hereafter!"

The news was made public that Chingis-khan was dead only when the

[2] [Op. cit., p. 71–72.]

funeral cortège reached the great imperial encampment at the headwaters of the Kerülen. The Conqueror's mortal remains lay in turn in the *ordus*—that is, in the felt palaces—of each of his principal wives, whither, at the invitation of Toluy, princes, princesses of the blood and war chiefs hastened from every quarter of the empire to pay him their last tribute in long lamentation. Those from farthest off were three months on the way.

Up There, Somewhere in the Forest . . .

When the "wailing" was finished, when all the Mongols had filed past the coffin of the man who had given them "empire over the world," Chingis-khan was buried. The site of his grave he had chosen himself, on the flank of one of the heights of the Burqan-qaldun massif, the present-day Kentey. It was the sacred mountain of the ancient Mongols, the same that in the testing days of the hero's youth had saved his life with the shelter it offered him in its impenetrable thickets, and to which at each point of vital decision, at new departures in his life, at the outset of his great campaigns, he had come to invoke the supreme god of the Mongols, the Eternal Blue Heaven, that dwells among the holy springs of its summits. Thence flowed "the Three Rivers"—Onon, Kerülen, and Tula —that watered the ancestral grazing grounds. "Hunting one day in these parts, Chingis-khan had lain down to rest a moment under the leafiness of a great tree standing by itself. He passed some moments in a kind of a dream, and said, as he rose, that at his death this was where he wished to be buried."

The funeral rites over, the place became taboo, and the forest was left to cover it over to hide the spot. The tree at the foot of which he had asked to lie became one among others, and there is nothing today to show where the grave was.

It is under this mantle of cedars, pines, and larch trees that the Conqueror sleeps his last sleep. On the one hand, toward the Far North, stretches the immensity of the Siberian *tayga*, impenetrable forest, for two thirds of the year fast in the grip of snow and ice. On the other, to the south, the Mongol steppe unfurls to the horizon, its expanses studded, in spring, with all the flowers of the meadow, but merging, still further south, into the immense sands of the Gobi. Aloft, a few great wing-beats sending it gliding zone to zone, "the golden-eyed black eagle, prince of the Mongol sky," very symbol of the career of the Hero, ranger from the forest of the Baykal to the Indus, from the Aral steppe to the Great Plain of China.

Other conquerors' slumbers stand to be disturbed forever by the hosts gravitating to their tomb to ponder their destiny. Chingis-khan rests in peace on his mountainside, inaccessible and known to none, protected, hidden, possessed again entirely by the Mongol land with which he is one forever.

Bibliographical note by Denis Sinor
on works dealing with
Mongol history of the 13th-15th centuries

Abbreviations used:

A.K.D.M.—*Abhandlungen für die Kunde des Morgenlandes.* Published by the Deutsche Morgenländische Gesellschaft.
A.M.—*Asia Major.* A pre-war periodical published in Germany.
B.S.O.A.S.—*Bulletin of the School of Oriental and African Studies.* London University.
J.A.—*Journal asiatique.* Published by the Société asiatique in Paris.
J.R.A.S.—*Journal of the Royal Asiatic Society of Great Britain and Ireland.*
H.J.A.S.—*Harvard Journal of Asiatic Studies.*
M.S.O.S.O.S.—*Mitteilungen des Seminars für Orientalische Sprachen.* Ostasiatische Studien. Pre-war periodical published in Berlin.
O.Z.—*Ostasiatische Zeitschrift.* Pre-war periodical published in Germany.
T.P.—*T'oung Pao.* Periodical published in Leiden.

One would like to be able to recommend a really modern and scholarly history of the Mongols. Unfortunately no such work exists and the material has to be collected from a great many books and monographs, not to mention the sources themselves which, very often, are not available in translation. Students of Mongol history should remember that no original contribution to the subject can be made without at least a good reading knowledge of several foreign languages.

It is hoped that the following indications will facilitate further study and may also, perhaps, be of some help to librarians anxious to build up a small nucleus of a library destined to help general historians who, in growing numbers, realise the importance of the Mongol impact on world history.

For further study I can do no better than to recommend *[1]* DENIS SINOR, *Introduction à l'étude de l'Eurasie Centrale,* Wiesbaden, 1963, an annotated bibliography with several hundred entries on the Mongols.

[2] HENRY H. HOWORTH, *History of the Mongols from the 9th to the 19th century, I-IV,* 5 vols., London, 1876-88, with "Supplement and Indices," published in 1927, is a poor compilation, now completely outdated. Infinitely superior to this work, and still useful, is *[3]* C. D'OHSSON, *Histoire des Mongols depuis Tchinguiz khan jusqu'à Timour bey ou Tamerlan, I-IV,* La Haye-Amsterdam, 1834-5. The relevant chapters of *[4]* RENÉ GROUSSET, *L'empire des steppes,* Paris, 1939, constitute perhaps the best concise history available on the Mongols. A useful concise survey, *[5]* BERTOLD SPULER, *The Muslim World; II. The Mongol period,* Leiden, 1960, 125 pp., does not cover Mongol history in the Far East.

Whenever possible the sources should be consulted. Some of them are available in translations.

An excellent guide to the Persian sources is *[6]* EDWARD G. BROWNE, *A literary history of Persia; III. The Tartar dominion (1265-1502),* Cambridge, 1928, 586 pp. We are fortunate in having an excellent translation of Juvaini's work written in 1260: *[7]* JOHN ANDREW BOYLE, *The history of the world-conqueror by 'Ala-ad-Din 'Ata-Malik Juvaini, I-II,* Manchester, 1958, XLV + 763 pp. The passages relating the life of Chingis-khan are translated from Rashid ed-Din's chronicle in *[8]* A. A. SEMENOV—O. I. SMIRNOV—B. I. PANKRATOV, *Rašid-ad-Din. Sbornik letopisej, I.2,* Moskva-Leningrad, 1952, 314 pp.

Only a small fraction of the Chinese sources is available in translation. Directly relevant to the subject of this book is *[9]* PAUL PELLIOT—LOUIS HAMBIS, *Histoire des campagnes de Gengis khan.* Cheng-wou ts'in-tcheng lou, 1, (No Vol. II), Leiden 1951, XXVII + 485 pp. On the same work: *[10]* PAUL PELLIOT, *Sur un passage du Cheng-wou ts'ing-tcheng lou,* Supplementary Vol. I of the Bulletin of the Institute of History and Philology of the Academia Sinica, Peiping, 1934, pp. 907-38. Also *[11]* F. E. A. KRAUSE, *Cingis Han. Geschichte seines Lebens nach den chinesischen Reichsannalen,* Heidelberg, 1922, 111 pp. A very important source, extensively used by Grousset, has been beautifully translated by *[12]* ARTHUR WALEY, *The travels of an Alchemist: The journey of the Taoist Ch'ang-ch'un from China to the Hindukush at the summons of Chingiz khan. Recorded by his disciple Chih-ch'ang,* London, 1931, XI + 166 pp. Much reliable information based directly on the sources can be found in *[13]* E. BRET-SCHNEIDER, *Mediaeval researches from Eastern Asiatic sources: Fragments towards the knowledge of the geography and history of Central and Western Asia from the 13th to the 17th century, I-II,* London 1910, 334 + 352 pp.

The works of the European travellers to the Mongols, and particularly those of the Franciscans Plano Carpini and Rubruck and of Marco Polo, are available in scores of translations. For the former I would recommend that made by an anonymous "Nun of Stanbrook Abbey" and edited by *[14]* CHRISTOPHER DAWSON, *The Mongol Mission: Narratives and letters of the Franciscan missionaries in Mongolia and China in the thirteenth and fourteenth centuries,* London and New York, 1955, 246 pp. The comments are more useful in *[15]* WOODVILLE ROCKHILL, *The Journeys of William of Rubruck and John of Plan de Carpine to Tartary in the 13th century,* London 1900, 304 pp. The original Latin texts are available in *[16]* ANASTASIUS VAN DEN WYNGAERT, *Sinica Franciscana I: Itinera et relationes Fratrum Minorum saeculi XIII et XIV,* Quaracchi-Firenze, 1929, CXVIII + 637 pp.

Many of the translations of Marco Polo's work are carelessly done for commercial purposes. For the purposes of research *[17]* A. C. MOULE— PAUL PELLIOT, *Marco Polo: The Description of the World, I-II,* London 1938, 595 + 131 pp. should be used. The translation is the work of A. C. Moule. Paul Pelliot's contribution appeared posthumously under the title *[18] Notes on Marco Polo, I-II,* Paris, 1959-64, a commentary prepared with unparalleled wealth of knowledge. A critical edition of the original: *[19]* LUIGI FOSCOLO BENEDETTO, *Marco Polo: Il Milione,* Firenze, 1928, 5 + CCXXXI + 281 pp. For general background reading I should like to recommend the entertaining and scholarly work of *[20]* LEONARDO OLSCHKI, *Marco Polo's Asia: An introduction to his "Description of the World" called "Il Milione,"* University of California Press, 1960, 459 pp. The translation and the commentaries by Moule and Pelliot replace those of *[21]* SIR HENRY YULE, *The book of Ser Marco Polo the Venetian concerning the kingdoms and marvels of the East, I-II,* 3rd ed. revised by HENRI CORDIER, London 1903, 462 + 662 pp.—still worth reading.

Armenian and Syriac sources are made available in the following publications: *[22]* ROBERT P. BLAKE—RICHARD N. FRYE, *History of the Nation of the Archers (The Mongols) by Grigor of Akanc', hitherto ascribed to Maγak' the Monk,* H.J.A.S. XII, 1949, pp. 269-399, *[23]* F. E. A. KRAUSE, *Das Mongolenreich nach der Darstellung des Armeniers Haithon,* OZ. VIII, 1919-20, pp. 238-67; *[24]* SIR E. A. WALLIS BUDGE, *The monks of Kûblâi Khan Emperor of China, or the history of the life and travels of Rabban Sâwmâ envoy and plenipotentiary of the Mongol khâns to the kings of Europe, and Markôs who as Mâr Yahballâhâ III became Patriarch of the Nestorian Church in Asia,* London, 1928, 335 pp.

Mongol sources are of capital importance, and Grousset's *The Conqueror of the World* is in no small measure based on the text of a Mongol chronicle entitled *The Secret History of the Mongols.* Written around the middle of the thirteenth century, the work has come down in Chinese transcription. No English translation of this capital work exists. A reasonably reliable German translation was made by the scholar who did most to decipher this document, *[25]* ERICH HAENISCH, *Die Geheime Geschichte der Mongolen. Aus einer mongolischen Niederschrift des Jahres 1240 von der Insel Kode'e in Keluren Fluss, erstmalig übersetzt und erläutert,* 2nd ed., Leipzig, 1948, 196 pp. A posthumously published and incomplete translation into French: *[26]* PAUL PELLIOT, *Histoire secrète des Mongols. Restitution du texte mongol et traduction française des chapitres I à VI,* Paris, 1949, 196 pp. Also: *[27]* S.A. KOZIN, *Sokrovennoe skazanie. Mongol'skaja khronika 1240 g.pod nazvaniem* Mongγol-un niγuča tobčiyan. *Juan' čao bi ši. Mongol'skij obydennyj izbornik, I,* all published Moskva-Leningrad, 1941, 619 pp.

From among the scores of articles written on the *Secret History,* I shall quote *[28]* WILLIAM HUNG, *The transmission of the book known as* The Secret History of the Mongols, H.J.A.S. XIV, 1951, pp. 433-92; *[29]* ANTOINE MOSTAERT, *Sur quelques passages de* l'Histoire secrète des Mongols, *I-III,* published in vols. XIII-XV of the H.J.A.S. and as a separate book, Cambridge, Mass., 1953, 407 pp.; *[30]* ARTHUR WALEY, *Notes on the* Yüanch'ao pi-shih, B.S.O.A.S. XXIII, 1960, pp. 523-29.

Mongol civilization as reflected in the Secret History is the subject of *[31]* PAVEL POUCHA, *Die Geheime Geschichte der Mongolen als Geschichtsquelle und Literaturdenkmal. Ein Beitrag zu ihrer Erklärung,* Prague, 1956, 247 pp.

The seventeenth-century Mongol chronicle written by the Ordos Prince Sagang Sechen is a valuable source for later Mongol history. Grousset made use of it to enliven his presentation of the Chingiskhanid period. The first edition of the text and also its first and hitherto only complete translation were the works of *[32]* I. J. SCHMIDT, *Geschichte der Ost-Mongolen und ihres Fürstenhauses, verfasst von Ssanang Ssetsen Chungtaidschi der Ordus,* St. Petersburg-Leipzig, 1829, XXIV + 509 pp. In recent years several new versions of the original were published. Making use of these variants, JOHN R. KRUEGER published a new translation of the first four chapters, "From the Creation of the World to the Death of Genghis Khan (1227)," under the title *[33]* *Sagang Sechen, Prince of the Ordos Mongols: The Bejewelled Summary of the Origin of Khans,* (Qad-un ündüsün-ü Erdeni-yin Tobči), *A History of the Eastern Mongols to 1662, Pt. I,* Publications of the Mongolia Society, Occasional Papers No. 2, Bloomington, 1964, 72 pp. Care must be taken, as the identity of the translator does not appear on the title-page. Many of the passages translated appear also in the more accessible publication *[34]* JOHN

R. KRUEGER, *Poetical passages in the* Erdeni-yin tobči, 's-Gravenhage, 1961, 231 pp.
There exists no up-to-date, authoritative account of early Mongol history. In the introduction to this volume, I have already pointed out the short-comings of *[35]* RENÉ GROUSSET, *L'empire mongol* (*1re phase*), Paris, 1941, 584 pp. Perhaps the best documented survey of Chingiskhanid history is included in the fourth and fifth volumes of *[37]* OTTO FRANKE, *Geschichte des chinesischen Reiches, I-V,* Berlin, 1930-52. The best biography of Chingis is the one we here present in an English translation. There is also the fine but somewhat out-of-date work of B. JA. VLADIMIRTSOV, originally written in Russian. An English translation *[37] The Life of Chingis-khan,* London, 1930, 169 pp., and a French version *[38] Gengis-khan,* Paris, 1948, 158 pp., made this work more widely known in the west.
The following monographs—most of them highly technical—will provide additional information on some aspects of Chingiskhanid history: *[39]* FRANCIS WOODMAN CLEAVES, *The historicity of the Balǰuna covenant,* H.J.A.S. XVIII, 1955, pp. 357-421; *[40]* PAUL PELLIOT, *Une tribu méconnue des Naiman: les Bätäkin,* TP. XXXVII, 1943, pp. 35-71; *[41]* H. DESMOND MARTIN, *The rise of Chingis khan and his conquest of North China,* Baltimore, 1950, 360 pp.; *[42] The Mongol wars with Hsi Hsia* (*1205-27*), J.R.A.S. 1942, pp. 195-228; *[43]* E. HAENISCH, *Die letzten Feldzüge Cingis Khan's und sein Tod, nach der ostasiatischen Überlieferung,* A.M. IX, 1933, pp. 503-51. These, and all the other publications of Cleaves and Pelliot, are products of scholarship at its best. They should be studied with great care also because they show clearly the research techniques to be employed in the study of Mongol history.
On the social organization of the Mongols, there is the classic *[44]* B. JA. VLADIMIRTSOV, *Le régime social des Mongols: Le féodalisme nomade,* Paris, 1948, XVIII + 291 pp., translation of a Russian original published in 1934. On Mongol law in general: *[45]* VALENTIN A. RIASANOVSKY, *Fundamental principles of Mongol law,* first published in Tientsin 1937, now available as vol. 43 of Indiana University Publications, Uralic and Altaic Series, Bloomington, 1965, 343 pp. On the legal position of hunting: *[46]* ERICH HAENISCH, *Die Jagdgesetze im Mongolischen Ostreich,* Ostasiatische Studien, Berlin, 1959, pp. 85-93. On Mongol administration: *[47]* FRANCIS WOODMAN CLEAVES, *A chancellery practice of the Mongols in the thirteenth and fourteenth century,* H.J.A.S. XIV, 1951, pp. 493-526; *[48]* H. F. SCHURMANN, *Mongolian tributary practices of the 13th century,* H.J.A.S. XIX, 1956, pp. 304-89.
Much valuable information concerning the archaeological remains of the

Mongol Empire in Mongolia can be gleaned from *[49] Drevnemongol' skie goroda,* S. V. KISELEV, ed., Moskva, 1965, 370 pp.

On the Mongols in Iran we are lucky to have fine syntheses. *[50]* BERTOLD SPULER, *Die Mongolen in Iran: Politik, Verwaltung und Kultur der Ilchanzeit 1220-1350,* Leipzig, 1939, 533 pp., with ample and intelligent bibliography, is the best introduction to the subject. On the economic aspects: *[51]* I. P. PETRUŠEVSKIJ, *Zemledelie i agrarnye otnošenija v Irane XIII-XIV vv.,* Moskva-Leningrad, 1960, 492 pp.

On the Mongols in Russia, the so-called Golden Horde, one can consult *[52]* GEORGE VERNADSKY, *The Mongols and Russia,* Yale University Press, 1953, 462 pp., stronger on the Russian than on the Mongol aspect of history; *[53]* B. D. GREKOV—A. JU. JAKUBOVSKIJ, *Zolotaja Orda i ee padenie,* Moskva-Leningrad, 1950, 473 pp.; or—best of all—*[54]* BERTOLD SPULER, *Die Goldene Horde: Die Mongolen in Russland 1223-1502,* Leipzig, 1943, 556 pp., the reading of which should be supplemented by constant recourse to *[55]* PAUL PELLIOT, *Notes sur l'histoire de la Horde d'Or,* Paris, 1950, 292 pp.

There is no up-to-date treatment of the Mongol invasion of Hungary. The most detailed account remains *[56]* G. STRAKOSCH-GRASSMANN, *Der Einfall der Mongolen in Mitteleuropa in den Jahren 1241 und 1242,* Innsbruck, 1893, 227 pp. antiquated and difficult to find. *[57]* EMMA LEDERER, *Tatarskoe našestvie na Vengriju i svjazi s meždunarodnymi sobytijami êpokhy,* Acta Historica Academiae Scientiarium Hungaricae II, 1953, pp. 1-45, contains some useful material but its Stalinist bias makes it almost unpalatable.

A short survey of the relations between the Mongols and Europe by *[58]* DENIS SINOR, *Les relations entre les Mongols et l'Europe jusqu'à la mort d'Arghoun et de Béla IV,* Journal of World History III, 1956, pp. 39-62, may serve as a starting point for further reading. *[59]* GIOVANNI SORANZO, *Il Papato, l'Europa cristiana e i Tartari: Un secolo di penetrazione occidentale in Asia,* Milano, 1930, 624 pp., is a convenient but not always reliable and somewhat unimaginative synthesis. A splendid study by *[60]* PAUL PELLIOT, *Les Mongols et la Papauté,* Revue de l'Orient Chrétien XXIII, 1922, pp. 3-30; XXIV, 1924, pp. 225-335; XXVIII, 1931, pp. 3-84, would tax the intellectual endurance of almost any one. Other studies include: *[61]* ERIC VOEGELIN, *The Mongol orders of submission to European powers, 1245-1253,* Byzantion XV, 1940-1, pp. 378-413; *[62]* E. TISSERANT, *Une lettre de l'ilkhan de Perse Abaga adressée en 1268 au Pape Clément IV,* Mélanges Lefort = Muséon LIX, 1946, pp. 547-56; *[63]* JEAN RICHARD, *Le début des relations entre la Papauté et les Mongols de Perse,* J.A. 1949, pp. 291-97.

The commentaries on some of the basic documents pertaining to Mongolo-

European relations are mostly linguistic. The principal editions are by AN-
TOINE MOSTAERT and FRANCIS WOODMAN CLEAVES, *[64] Les lettres de 1289
et 1305 des ilkhans Arɣun et Öljeitü à Philippe le Bel,* Harvard Yenching
Institute, Scripta Mongolica Monograph Series I, 1962, 104 pp. + 12 plates,
[65] Trois documents mongols des Archives Secrètes Vaticanes, H.J.A.S.
XV, 1952, pp. 419-506.

On the spread of Christianity, and particularly of Nestorianism, in the
Mongol Empire one should consult the fine studies of JEAN DAUVILLIER,
[66] Les provinces chaldéennes "de l'extérieur" au Moyen Âge, Mélanges
Cavallera, Toulouse, 1948, pp. 261-316 and *[67] Byzantins d'Asie Centrale
et d'Extrême Orient au Moyen Âge,* Revue des études byzantines XI, 1953,
pp. 62-87. Also the relevant chapters of *[68]* A. C. MOULE, *Christians in
China before the year 1550,* London, 1930, 293 pp.

Two beautifully produced volumes published in Italy, viz. *[69] Nel VII
Centenario della Nascita de Marco Polo,* Venezia, 1955, 325 pp., and *[70]
Oriente Poliano,* Roma, 1957, 235 pp., contain some fine articles on East-
West relations during the Mongol epoch. A charming and erudite book on
the same topic: *[71]* LEONARDO OLSCHKI, *Guillaume Boucher: A French
artist at the court of the khans,* Baltimore, 1946, 125 pp.

No comprehensive and detailed work exists on the history of the Mongols
in China although, quite obviously, works on Chinese or Far Eastern history
devote some space to the period. The best presentation is that by OTTO
FRANKE referred to above (No. 36). A concise synopsis by *[72]* F. E. A.
KRAUSE, *Die Epoche der Mongolen, ein Kapitel aus der Geschichte und
Kultur Asiens,* M.S.O.S.O.S. XXVI-XXVII, 1924, pp. 1-60, is particularly
useful because it gives the Chinese characters of the proper names used.
HERBERT FRANKE has produced two fine monographs, viz. *[73] Geld und
Wirtschaft in China unter der Mongolenherrschaft: Beiträge zur Wirt-
schaftsgeschichte der Yüan-Zeit,* Leipzig, 1949, 171 pp., and *[74] Beiträge zur
kulturgeschichte Chinas unter der Mongolenherrschaft (Das Shan-kü sin-
hua des Yang Yü),* A.K.D.M. XXXII, 2, 1956, VI + 160 pp. On the famous
postal-system of the Mongols: *[75]* PETER OLBRICHT, *Das Postwesen in
China unter der Mongolenherrschaft im 13. und 14. Jahrhundert,* Wiesbaden,
1954, 111 p.

Also: *[76]* H. F. SCHURMANN, *Economic structure of the Yüan dynasty:
Translation of chapters 93 and 94 of the Yüan-shih,* Harvard Yenching
Institute Studies 16, 1956, 266 pp.; LOUIS HAMBIS, *[77] Le chapitre CVII
du Yuan che: Les généalogies impériales mongoles dans l'histoire officielle
de la dynastie mongole,* with ample notes by Paul Pelliot, T.P. supplement
to vol. XXXVIII, 1945, XII + 184 pp., *[78] Le chapitre CVIII du Yuan*

che: Les fiefs attribués aux membres de la famille impériale et aux ministres de la cour mongole d'après l'histoire chinoise officielle de la dynastie mongole, I, all published Leiden, 1954, XV + 191 pp.; *[79]* PAUL RATCHNEVSKY, *Un code des Yuan,* Paris, 1937, XCIX + 348 pp., translates chapters 102 and 103 of the Yüan-shih dealing with Mongol law.